AFFECT REGULATION TOOLBOX

AFFECT REGULATION TOOLBOX

Practical and Effective
Hypnotic Interventions
for the Over-reactive Client

CAROLYN DAITCH

*Forewords by Daniel Brown, Ph.D.
and Claire Frederick, M.D.*

W. W. Norton & Company

New York • London

For information about permission to reproduce selections from this book, write
to Permissions, W. W. Norton & Company, Inc., 500 Fifth Avenue, New York,
NY 10110

Composition and design by Publication Services
Manufacturing by R.R. Donnelley-Harrisonberg
Production Manger: Leeann Graham

Library of Congress Cataloging-in-Publication Data
Daitch, Carolyn.
    Affect regulation toolbox : practical and effective hypnotic interventions for the
over-reactive client / Carolyn Daitch.
        p. cm. – (A Norton professional book)
    Includes bibliographical references and index.
    ISBN-13: 978-0-393-70495-2
    ISBN-10: 0-393-70495-5
1. Anxiety—Treatment.   2. Hypnotism—Therapeutic use.   I. Title.

RC531.D35 2006
616.85'22326—dc22

                                                                    2006049456

ISBN 13: 978-0-393-70495-2
ISBN 10: 0-393-70495-5

W. W. Norton & Company, Inc., 500 Fifth Avenue, New York, N.Y. 10110
www.wwnorton.com
W. W. Norton & Company Ltd., Castle House, 75/76 Wells St., London
W1T 3QT
3 5 7 9 8 6 4

To Russ and Dan with love.

Contents

═══════

Acknowledgments

===

I am deeply grateful to the many friends and colleagues who have supported me along this journey:

My colleagues Eleanor Payson, Steve Kahn, and Bill O'Hanlon, who believed there was an audience for this book. Jonathan Falk, who provided unflagging encouragement and substantial contributions during our weekly phone meetings in which we reviewed and practiced the scripts. Jeannie Ballew, for her insightful recommendations, coaching, editing, patience, and encouragement. Lissah Lorberbaum, who tirelessly served as a consultant and all-around midwife for this book. David Wark, who brought a professor's critical eye and demand for excellence that I truly appreciated. Claire Frederick, Sheryll Daniel, Steve Lankton, Jeffrey Zeig, Cory Hammond, Helen Adrienne, Marcia Ferstenfeld, Bill DeWitt, Reginald Humphries, and Eric Willmarth, all of whom responded almost immediately to my requests for references and clarification. My colleagues Cheryl Sills, Barb Bokram, Marianne Victor, Eileen Bond, Patricia Knowlton, Susan Dowell, Maya Kollman, Helen Adrienne, and Janice Sherman, who read chapters and buoyed my spirits with their enthusiasm. Cathy Hirsch, my assistant, who offered her unending support.

I was truly fortunate to have Deborah Malmud as my editor at W. W. Norton. Her editing skills, the speed of her responses, and her extensive knowledge of psychology are impressive. I am indebted to the ever-gracious, reassuring, and kind Andrea Costella, for her support and guidance.

I was also blessed with help from my family. Thanks to my brother Richard Daitch and my niece Clare Estelle Daitch for their gentle suggestions, and to my cousin Norman Kolpas for his guidance early in the project. I thank my cousin, Ellen Moore, for her positive support. My son Daniel Rubin along with Lissah Lorberbaum were invaluable neuroscience consultants. Finally, I want to thank my husband Russell Graham who offered loving support and patience throughout the entire process, even as I fell asleep with my laptop, endeavoring to finish the book.

One final acknowledgment and note: This book is meant to be a compilation of useful techniques for the effective practice of hypnosis in therapy. The techniques discussed are ones that I have used and adapted since 1982. Many have been part of hypnosis literature and practice for a very long time, and I have done my utmost to ensure that these contributions are appropriately acknowledged. Others I have developed to deal with specific conditions or circumstances. While I consider some of these techniques to be original contributions, it is possible that I have been influenced "unconsciously" by talented and creative colleagues whose work has shaped my own. I've had the privilege of working with a great many fine practitioners who have had an impact on my practice. Therefore, I make no claims to ownership about any technique, except to say that I have successfully used all the methodologies discussed. Ultimately, the practice of hypnotherapy owes as much to artistry as it does to methodology.

Foreword by Daniel Brown, Ph.D.

═══════════

Ever since the origins of psychotherapy, most clinicians have readily assumed that emotion plays a central role in psychotherapy. Yet, scientific research on emotion is relatively recent in the history of psychotherapy. The earliest modern studies on emotion consisted primarily of the descriptions and functions of specific emotions, such as interest, anger, fear, shame, etc. The main contribution of differential emotions theory was essentially a detailed catalogue of discrete emotions and their functions (Izard, 1977; Socarides, 1977; Tomkins, 1962, 1963).

Systematic child observational studies led to the earliest accounts of affective development. These studies detailed the central role affect played in perceptual maturation, the regulation of internal state (Sroufe, 1979), and the development of the self (Emde, 1983; Lewis & Brooks, 1978). Other important works emphasized the dyadic regulation of affective states through the infant-caregiver attachment bond (Greenspan & Greenspan, 1985; Stern, 1985). Psychoanalytic studies of the same period emphasized the neutralization of intense affective states through cognitive maturation—that is, learning to discharge impulses through fantasy and verbalization rather than through somatic discharge (Krystal, 1974). Most of these studies of the 1970s and early

1980s were primarily restricted to affective development in infancy and early childhood.

Stage models for affective development across the lifespan from infancy through adulthood appeared nearly a decade later (Brown, 1993; Schore, 1994). These works described a normal developmental line for affect and for the sense of self, and depicted psychopathology emerging in later childhood or adulthood as a failure to master normal developmental tasks along the line of affective and/or self development. The resulting affect dysregulation and/or failure of self development eventually led to the psychopathology seen in psychotic and personality disorders, and psychosomatic illness in adults.

The 1990s are best characterized as the age of neuroscience. Affective neuroscience integrates research on affective development with attachment research and research on the developing brain throughout infancy, childhood, and adolescence. As a result of such integration, contemporary stage models for affect include a description of (1) the developing brain; (2) how the infant-caregiver attachment bond fosters brain development; (3) how various neurobiological systems develop in the service of affect regulation and self regulation; and (4) how early infant-caregiver attachment disruption and/or trauma in later childhood leads to significant dysregulation of affective and self development and, eventually, to specific forms of psychopathology in adulthood, like personality and dissociative disorders (Fonagy, Gergely, Jurist, & Target, 2002; Ogawa, Sroufe, Weinfield, Carlson, & Egeland, 1997; Schore, 1994; Sroufe, Egeland, Carlson, & Collins, 2005).

Despite the rapidly proliferating and increasingly sophisticated models of affective development, studies specifically on its clinical implications, or better, its applications, are still relatively rare. Within the psychoanalytic tradition, Krystal's (1988) and McDougall's (1985) pioneering works stand out for their detailed descriptions of the clinical manifestations of affect dysregulation in adult psychotherapy patients. Ablon et al. (1993) present a detailed model of the theory of affect development followed by a discussion of a number of areas of its clinical application, including the differential clinical manifestations of affect in patients across the lifespan, from trauma, addiction, psychosomatics, and in everyday life. Fosha (2000) has directly applied attachment research to sitting with adult psychotherapy patients. As the therapist, she provides her mainly adult personality disordered patients with the full presence and careful moment-by-moment attunement of an attachment bond targeted to the patient's immediate emotional state, through which the patient is able to transform negative affective states into the core, positive affects that become apparent when the attachment bond is properly regulated.

A largely underdeveloped area of clinical application pertains to helping the patient learn specific affect regulatory skills. Some of the early works on hypnotherapy contain descriptions of specific affect skills, such as Watkins's affect bridge technique (1971). Brown and Fromm (1986) describe a number of hypnotherapy techniques to enhance affect experience and its expression, and to attenuate intense affect states. Phillips and Frederick (1995) describe a variety of hypnotherapy techniques for mobilizing inner resources, managing affects, and resolving dissociation in traumatized patients. From a cognitive-behavioral perspective, Linehan (1993) developed a workbook that contains a number of practical skills for managing affects in borderline patients, including the core skill of being mindful of and accurately recognizing emotional states; distress tolerance training; self-soothing skills; and skills for decreasing negative emotions and increasing positive emotions.

Carolyn Daitch's new book, *Affect Regulation Toolbox: Practical and Effective Hypnotic Interventions for the Over-reactive Client*, fills a void by making great advances in the skill-based approach to affect regulation. In a single volume she has amassed the most comprehensive collection of affect regulatory skills now available. She describes over 30 specific skills in her affect "toolbox." She gives rich descriptions of each affect "tool" with a carefully worded and detailed script, followed by case examples to illustrate the use of each affect regulatory skill. Rather than a loose collection of affect skills, the book is tightly organized into four different levels or "tiers" of affect skills.

The focus of the book is on the application of these skills to the emotionally over-reactive patient. Dr. Daitch's expertise as a clinician comes forth in her detailed and very clear illustrations of the application of skills from the affect toolbox to patients with anxiety disorders in individual therapy and also to emotionally over-reactive partners in couples therapy.

In her case illustrations she is careful to match specific affect tools to the given patient's presenting complaints and personality style.

While Dr. Daitch presents these affect skills as part of hypnotherapy, they stand in their own right and could be used readily in nonhypnotic therapies. For hypnotherapists, Dr. Daitch's book is the *only* book on clinical hypnosis specifically devoted to affect regulatory skills. More important, Dr. Daitch makes it clear that these affect tools are not intended for the treatment session alone. Rather, they are designed as practical tools that the patient can take with him or her to utilize as needed in everyday life. There is a great deal in this book that any clinician, and most patients, will find immediately useful.

Daniel Brown, Ph.D., ABPH
Harvard Medical School

References

Ablon, S. L., Brown, D., Khantzian, E. J., & Mack, J. E. (Eds.) (1993). *Human feelings: Explorations in affect development and meaning.* Hillsdale, NJ: Erlbaum.

Brown, D. P. (1993). Affective development, psychopathology, and adaptation. In. S. L. Ablon, D. Brown, E. J. Khantzian, & J. E. Mack (Eds.), *Human feelings: Explorations in affect development and meaning* (pp. 5–66). Hillsdale, NJ: The Analytic Press.

Brown, D. P. & Fromm, E. F. (1986). *Hypnotherapy and hypnoanalysis.* Hillsdale, NJ: Erlbaum.

Emde, R. N. (1983). The prerepresentational self and its affective core. *The Psychoanalytic Study of the Child, 38*: 165–192. New Haven, CT: Yale University Press.

Fonagy, P., Gergely, G., Jurist, E. L., & Target, M. (2002). *Affect regulation, mentalization, and the development of the self.* New York: Other Press.

Fosha, D. (2000). *The transforming power of affect: A model for accelerated change.* New York: Basic Books.

Greenspan, S. & Greenspan, N. T. (1985). *First feelings.* New York: Viking Press.

Izard, C. E. (1977). *Human emotions.* New York: Plenum Press.

Krystal, H. (1974). The genetic development of affects and affect regression. *The Annual of Psychoanalysis, 2*: 98–126.

Krystal, H. (1988). *Integration and self-healing.* Hillsdale, NJ: The Analytic Press.

Lewis, M. & Brooks, J. (1978). Self-knowledge and emotional development. In M. Lewis & L. A. Rosenblum (Eds.), *The development of affect* (pp. 205–226). New York: Plenum Press.

Linehan, M. M. (1993). *Skills training manual for treatment of borderline personality disorder.* New York: Basic Books.

McDougall, J. (1985). *Theatres of the mind: Illusion and truth in the psychoanalytic stage.* New York: Brunner/Mazel.

Ogawa, J. R., Sroufe, L. A., Weinfield, N. S., Carlson, E. A. & Egeland, B. (1997). Development and the fragmented self: Longitudinal study of dissociative symptomatology in a nonclinical sample. *Development and Psychopathology, 9*: 855–879.

Phillips, M. & Frederick, C. (1995). *Healing the divided self: Clinical and Ericksonian hypnotherapy for posttraumatic and dissociative conditions.* New York: W. W. Norton.

Schore, A. N. (1994). *Affect regulation and the origin of self: The neurobiology of emotional development.* Hillsdale, NJ: Erlbaum.

Schore, A.N. (2003). *Affect regulation and the repair of the self.* New York: W. W. Norton.

Socarides, C. W. (1977). *The world of emotions: Clinical studies of affects and their expression.* New York: International Universities Press.

Sroufe, L. A. (1979). The ontogenesis of emotion in infancy. In J. Osofsky (Ed.), *The handbook of infant development* (pp. 491–510). New York: Wiley.

Sroufe, L. A., Egeland, B., Carlson, E. A. & Collins, W. A (2005). *The development of the person: The Minnesota study of risk and adaptation from birth to adulthood.* New York: Guilford Press.

Stern, D. (1985). *The interpersonal world of the infant.* New York: Basic Books.

Tomkins, S. S. (1962). *Affect, imagery, consciousness.* Vol 1. New York: Springer.

Tomkins, S. S. (1963). *Affect, imagery, consciousness.* Vol. 2. New York: Springer.

Watkins, J. G. (1971). The affect bridge: A hypnoanalytic technique. *International Journal of Clinical and Experimental Hypnosis, 19*: 21–27.

Foreword by Claire Frederick, M.D.

Although I have a library of hundreds of books in the fields of psychotherapy, hypnosis, trauma, and dissociation, I could fit on one shelf those 10 or 12 books that are of constant help to me in my clinical practice and to which I always return. These are well-thumbed books to which I always come back for theory, for techniques and scripts, and for greater understanding of how to integrate technique into clinical practice. Fortunately, there is room on that hypothetical shelf of invaluable books for one more: Carolyn Daitch's *Affect Regulation Toolbox: Practical and Effective Hypnotic Interventions for the Over-reactive Client.*

Affect Regulation Toolbox helps us deal with a large population of patients who share the problem of over-reactivity. This is a constellation of characteristics that appears across a number of Axis I and Axis II diagnostic categories and that often presents clinicians with enormous clinical challenges. Most of the patients I see who live on the edge of their anxieties and super-sensitivities are usually able to experience the calmness and soothing of the hypnotic experience in my consultation room. However, they often report that they cannot re-create this experience in their everyday lives. To be sure, they are able to experience the beneficial effects of self-hypnosis when they are not facing immediate stress, but they feel naked, raw, and exposed in ordinary life situations. Many of them become severely stressed by events and interactions that do not even appear to be particularly stressful. They are living illustrations of Carolyn Daitch's insight that ". . . talk therapy alone simply does not provide the immediate relief or the long-term results necessary for these clients."

Affect Regulation Toolbox is a clinical classic. In it we are shown why the man who cannot take an ordinary joke because his feelings are so easily hurt, the woman who carries a chip on her shoulder, and, perhaps someone we know who avoids social situations whenever possible, have something in common. A number of treatment modalities ranging from psychopharmacology to Dialectical Behavioral Therapy have attempted to address the needs of this patient population. What is needed in any therapeutic program with the over-reactive patient is a retraining of the perceptions and reaction patterns that will lead to a restructuralization of these new reactions within the central nervous system, a rewiring into better perceptions and responses, a true developmental repair. With *Affect Regulation Toolbox*, Carolyn Daitch shows us exactly how to go about helping patients do this.

Affect Regulation Toolbox offers a tiered and step-by-step program for achieving the necessary therapeutic goals. Because it is firmly rooted in the utilization principle, psychoeducation, and self-hypnosis, it leads the patient into self-care, mastery, and self-efficacy as no extant self-care program of this type does. With elegant eclecticism it shows us how to teach patients to meet their most distressing feelings and develop new ways of thinking, feeling, and responding, which, when learned and incorporated into daily life, will have profound and permanent effects.

Scientifically based, integrative, and comprehensive, this book fills an aching void in the field of hypnotically facilitated psychotherapy. It is a treasure to which I will return again and again.

Claire Frederick, M.D.
Tufts University School of Medicine

Table of Tools

═══════════

TABLE OF TOOLS

TABLE OF TOOLS

The tool Behavioral and Practice Session Rehearsal (explained on pages 107–115) is applicable to any and all of the common issues or disorders listed above.

The following tools are also applicable to any and all of the common issues or disorders listed:

Note: Although this table provides suggestions for a variety of clinical applications of the tools, the tools can be used to meet many clinical challenges that are not listed.

AFFECT
REGULATION
TOOLBOX

Introduction

═══════════

One of my regular clients, Bill, a 43-year-old psychotherapist, was sharing yet another illustration of his wife Karen's insensitivity. His narrative, punctuated by attempts at wry humor, focused on his perception of Karen shaming him at a dinner party they had recently attended. Apparently, as the meal progressed, the guests were discussing their respective home-improvement projects. According to Bill, Karen seized this moment to share a long and detailed account of his failed attempt to put a wood floor in their kitchen, which resulted in an inordinate amount of wasted time and effort. Karen finally insisted that they hire a professional to complete the job, at which point Bill gave in and abandoned the project. Laughing, she went on to recall other examples of his domestic incompetence. Bill felt that she was having a wonderful time at his expense.

Having been raised by a highly critical, less than nurturing mother, Bill was particularly reactive to criticism from anyone, especially his wife. Karen's behavior at the party had made him feel inadequate and belittled in front of their friends. Initially, he responded by becoming angry on the drive home, yelling and berating her for her insensitivity.

Bill stated that Karen in turn reacted to his initial outburst by attacking him for being overly sensitive and lacking a sense of humor.

When they returned home, it was apparent that they were in serious gridlock. Later, he withdrew emotionally from his wife, barely speaking to her for several days. She responded to his emotional withdrawal by not coming home for dinner for three consecutive days, and when she did come home, she avoided contact.

I liked Bill. He was bright and accomplished yet clearly prone to over-reactivity. Furthermore, as he was a respected colleague, I was honored that he had sought my help. I felt internal pressure to give him good counsel. Giving him my best effort, I offered another way to interpret Karen's behavior by pointing out that she was someone who craved attention and had a strong need to be liked by others, which was in part the motivation for her dramatic storytelling. I offered several strategies to help him communicate his hurt feelings to her directly and to engage her in constructive dialogue without yelling or withdrawing.

Upon hearing my suggestions, he sighed and remarked, "It's so easy to think reasonably in this office, but when I'm on the home front, it sometimes feels impossible. It's as if I'm flooded by my emotions, and I'm unable to implement what I've learned in therapy." Bill was astutely describing a common dilemma that confronts therapist and client alike. In the contained and nurturing structure of the therapeutic setting, it is simple enough to teach rational reactions and rehearse intentional responses, but it becomes extremely difficult for over-reactive clients to apply these strategies in situations where stimuli can overwhelm the best of intentions.

Bill stayed in therapy a few more months but eventually dropped out without resolving his relationship issues. He understood the concepts of relationship repair; indeed, he handled those issues in his own practice. And he was motivated to change. In some ways he was an ideal client. However, without explicit tools that he could use immediately to interrupt his over-reactivity, Bill was unable to implement the learning and consistently transfer the therapy work to his life. I was quite disappointed that Bill left therapy prematurely.

Genesis of the Affect Regulation Toolbox

Working with Bill provided an invaluable opportunity to re-examine my standard therapeutic approach and brought me to the realization that individuals with overly reactive emotional styles require a more advanced, integrative therapeutic method to help them make lasting changes in their behavior. This experience reinforced my conviction that talk therapy alone simply does not provide the immediate relief or the long-term results needed by these clients.

A case from somewhat later in my career provides a poignant example of how conceptual strategies and further integration of practical tools for affect regulation can make a difference. Subsequent to her diagnosis with lung cancer, Lydia came to see me for smoking cessation. Although she was able to quit, unfortunately, her condition did not improve. She stayed in psychotherapy for the year and a half before the end of her life.

Lydia was a self-described over-reactor. She had a history of interpersonal conflicts with her daughter, ex-husband, sister, and co-workers. In her previous therapy, she succeeded in gaining insight into the dynamics of these relationships and how they were rooted in her family of origin. But despite the considerable insight she had gained, the patterns persisted. "I get it, intellectually at least," Lydia stated early in her treatment. "I know that my sister and I were injured in so many ways by our parents. But I *have* to change the way I behave; I want things to be different, especially with my daughter. I can't afford to waste any more time on conflicts. And my body certainly doesn't need any more stress." The ensuing therapy focused initially on two primary goals: first, to help her manage the inevitable range of affective responses that a diagnosis of metastatic cancer elicits, and second, to help her become more intentional in her relationships with those closest to her.

In the course of the treatment, Lydia was taught most of the tools in the Toolbox. At the forefront of the treatment was training in developing relaxation to reduce the inevitable waves of terror as she dealt with the threat of her disease and its treatment. Lydia was also taught the interventions that would enhance impulse control to help her be more deliberate in her communications with her daughter and sister. She was provided with tools to access and sustain positive sentiments toward her loved ones, even when she felt criticized or misunderstood. Lydia also learned to self-soothe by regularly imagining her support figures, particularly the members of her cancer self-help group. Lydia practiced the affect regulation tools with consistency and discipline and reported that they were particularly helpful in dealing with the once-overwhelming waves of fear and distress she experienced daily. In one of our last sessions together, she told me that she viewed the tools as a gift in her final years of life.

Profile of the Over-reactive Client

As a therapist, you know that people who are over-reactive pay dearly for their emotional styles in the untold sacrifice of their peace of mind and the diminished satisfaction in their lives. And you know how discouraging it can be to not be able to provide them with techniques that lead to long-term results. For them, help with the following problems can't come quickly enough. They typically experience a series of conflicted relationships, particularly intimate and/or work relationships, display symptoms of anxiety, and often experience psychosomatic illnesses and over-reactions to bodily symptoms. In addition, they find it difficult to do one or more of the following:

- make decisions using rational judgments
- remain calm and clear in the face of stress
- observe and reflect on their emotions and behavior
- tolerate uncomfortable, "negative" affect or concurrent conflicting emotions
- tolerate criticism without defensiveness
- suspend judgment
- soothe themselves or their partners
- consider positive, objective interpretations of events or communications

When clients like Bill who experience such symptoms on a regular basis fail to apply the psychotherapeutic techniques taught in the therapist's office to their outside life, it can often spiral them down into feelings of despair. Many come in feeling hopeless to begin with and then feel terribly desperate when they seem to be beyond repair, even in the hands of a "professional." Some clients will "act in" and blame themselves or be embarrassed by their perceived failure. These feelings of shame therefore reinforce what is often already an overdeveloped sense of inadequacy. Others will "act out," feeling angry at the therapist because "it's not working." They may claim that therapy is a waste of time and money and quit therapy altogether and/or seek out another therapist who will "get it right."

Since the stress reaction is triggered so quickly and powerfully, it becomes incumbent upon the therapist to teach clients to intervene with rapidly induced calm states. One must offer interventions that are sufficiently powerful to make it possible for them to reinterpret events more reasonably and to elicit greater control of inappropriate or excessively reactive responses. *Simply providing insight or teaching them to reinterpret triggers by altering cognitive schemas alone is often insufficient. In my experience, one must diffuse the stress response first before a change of interpretation of an event or reaction is possible.* This understanding is fundamental to the successful treatment of over-reactive clients.

How Incorporating Hypnosis into Psychotherapy Enhances Treatment Outcome

Clients experience a wide range of short- and long-term benefits when therapists combine hypnotherapeutic techniques with psychotherapy. Therapists can expect to see the following results in a relatively short period of time.

Immediate Benefits to Clients
Clients are better able to:

- stop escalation of conflict with others
- have tolerance when experiencing difficult emotions
- handle a juxtaposition of different emotions
- remain calm and flexible within stressful situations

Long-term Benefits to Clients
In the long run, you can expect clients to experience:

- more resiliency in the face of long-term stress/conflict
- significant reduction in symptoms of anxiety disorders

- increased maturity and spiritual development
- greater receptivity to the wisdom of others
- increased trust and connection with others and self
- a healthier sense of self (self-esteem, productive perspective)
- elevated positive affect

Therapists can find comfort in the fact that they will be in a much better position to bring about the types of deep and lasting changes that have long eluded them in the treatment of the over-reactive client by incorporating these tools into their standard psychotherapeutic practice.

I have been practicing psychotherapy since 1977 and have been studying hypnosis since 1981. I am consistently honored that my clients place their trust in me, and I have always endeavored to be as effective as possible with the people I treat. As a young psychologist, I had the good fortune of learning hypnosis from some excellent teachers, thereby gaining a powerful method of improving therapy outcome. I was pleased to discover that hypnosis shortened the duration of therapy and could incorporate and potentiate other therapeutic approaches. The relaxation component, typically inherent in the trance state, had a dramatic effect in itself—most every clinical complaint improved when the client was able to calm down. And since hypnosis can be a creative process for the therapist, incorporating analytical thinking, intuition, and the poetic use of language to create imagery, it has been a satisfying endeavor, serving to mitigate burnout not only for me but for other overworked clinicians.

Inspiration for This Book

My passion for this work is fueled by the enormous responsibility I share with my colleagues to ensure that clients like Bill, who place their faith in us, are given a solid return for their time, money, and trust. Determined to develop concrete strategies to facilitate transfer and maintenance of therapeutic work, I began drawing on my training in hypnosis to develop a variety of quick, easy-to-learn techniques that would help clients maintain, in their daily lives, the dramatic emotional shifts that they experienced in my office. This work evolved into what I call my Toolbox. After years of refining these tools, using them successfully with clients and teaching them to other clinicians, I bring them to you in this book so that you can experience success with overly reactive clients as well.

Who Are the Intended Readers of This Book?

There are three types of readers for this book. One is psychotherapists with little or no training in hypnosis. These are clinicians with varied backgrounds and theoretical frameworks who wish to expand their skills in order to deliver more efficient and practical solutions to their over-reactive clients. A second group is clinicians who have had some training and/or are in the process of getting trained in hypnosis. A third group consists of experienced hypnotherapists who could benefit from some fresh ideas.

Therapists with Little or No Training in Hypnosis

It is not necessary to have had formal training in hypnosis to master many of the tools in this book. However, as with any psychotherapeutic endeavor, the more training and experience a therapist has, the greater his or her competency and effectiveness will be. Thus this book can serve as a launching pad into the dynamic field of hypnosis. Clinicians who have had minimal training in hypnosis or guided imagery will benefit from this book because it provides a review and summary of standard hypnotic protocol, as well as specific scripts that can be used as templates to address affect dysregulation. Specifically, Chapter 3 addresses preliminary considerations such as combining the tools with other more standard therapeutic approaches, structuring sessions, and designing and delivering customized scripts. Chapter 4 provides the keystone to stopping over-reactivity, including the Time Out tool and how to identify and interrupt the start of an over-reaction. Chapter 5 covers the fundamentals of calming, focusing, and deepening a hypnotic state. Most therapists have had some exposure to these relaxation techniques as part of their training and should be able to easily incorporate them into their practice. Mastery of many of the other tools such as those found in Chapter 6 can be acquired with relative ease. Clinicians who find the tools useful in creating therapeutic change are encouraged to acquire training in clinical hypnosis. Excellent training is available through the American Society of Clinical Hypnosis, the Society for Clinical and Experimental Hypnosis, and the International Society of Hypnosis. (See the Appendix for contact information.)

Intermediate-level Hypnotherapists

For therapists who are in the process of gaining mastery in hypnotherapy, this book offers new tools that can help their development. Chapter 6, which presents the core of the Toolbox, and Chapter 7, which focuses on rehearsal and transfer of tools, should be particularly useful. For those who are refining their skills in hypnosis, this book can resolve the ongoing dilemma that plagues so many beginning- and intermediate-level hypnotherapists. I call it the "What do I do when I get there?" dilemma because many therapists know how to lead a client into trance but don't know how to go further with hypnosis to work specifically with an individual client's needs. Chapters 8 through 11 are intended to help answer that question by providing readers with customized scripts that address a specific constellation of symptoms.

Experienced Hypnotherapists

For experienced hypnotherapists, the book provides applications of theories and hypnotic interventions that they may already know but with a different twist. While Chapters 4 and 5 can certainly serve as an excellent review of the basics for more experienced hypnotherapists, newer, more challenging material may be found in Chapter 6 as well as in the subsequent chapters in which a range of tools are applied to varying case studies. Chapter 7 focuses on rehearsal and transfer of therapeutic learning, a theme that is underemphasized in many books on hypnosis. Material that may be of special interest to experienced hypnotherapists includes:

- a focus on teaching *clients* to master the tools
- application of hypnosis with relationship therapy
- a range of clinical applications, including severe anxiety disorders

The ultimate goal of this approach is to teach clients mastery of the affect regulation tools in order to decrease dependency on the therapist and to increase generalization of the results beyond the office. To this end, the foundational tools are presented that will empower clients to be able to help themselves whenever they sense the onset of an over-reaction outside the therapeutic setting. *The Affect Regulation Toolbox* also provides fresh tools and scripts to help address ongoing clinical challenges that are commonly seen in our practices. There is a distinct emphasis on what I have found to be especially effective hypnotic language and phrasing. Chapters 10 and 11 will also be of interest as they present practical strategies for how to incorporate hypnotic tools into the treatment of relationships.

All Readers

For *all* therapists reading this book, I cannot overemphasize the importance of training clients to *take time out to identify and interrupt the over-reaction,* as covered in Chapter 4. Regardless of what clients are presenting as their therapeutic goals, therapists need to instill in them the importance of taking time out to interrupt habitual response patterns. On this note, even seasoned hypnotherapists would do well to review Chapter 4.

Another part of the process that hypnotherapists at all levels should note is the benefits of rehearsal as outlined in Chapter 7. Behavioral rehearsal requires the client to be proactive and involved. In many books on hypnosis and in training sessions, the need for clients to be proactive in their recovery is missing or at least underemphasized. Specifically, clients need to be trained in taking regular time out and practicing the tools when they are experiencing distressful emotional reactions, and these strategies can only be effective if they repeatedly practice the techniques on their own at home.

Please note that it's not necessary to use the tools in every session or for the entirety of any given session. Often a therapy session that has been spent using hypnosis is followed by a subsequent session in which attention is focused on client stories that need to be told, progress reports, impasses encountered, and other aspects of more traditional therapy. At other times, just a few minutes of internal focus with an abbreviated version of a tool can reinforce its use and emphasize a message to a client.

The Affect Regulation Toolbox

The toolbox is a compendium of resources for busy clinicians who want interventions that are practical and easy to teach. A significant benefit is that the tools are adaptable and can be individualized for each client. They can also be used as an adjunct to any psychotherapy modality.

Tools Are Highly Adaptable

Please note that the same tools can be used with all clients, and each tool can also be altered and individualized to best address a client's specific distress. *How* you use them will vary depending on the client's needs at any given moment in the session. Each client's unique history, expressions, and responses will guide you in adapting the tools for the perfect fit. For example, there is a category of tools that helps clients develop dual perspectives. Using these tools, clients come to recognize that it is possible to access two opposing thoughts and feelings in a situation. This concept could be applicable to someone with anxiety who can experience transient fear, as well as trust that things will work out. A person who experiences excessive irritation with his or her partner can also access feelings of endearment and appreciation.

A particular tool can be altered to meet a client's needs by customizing it using personal information that you know about the client such as previous successes, strengths, interests, or intellectual capacity. If the therapist observes the client reverting to over-reactivity in the middle of marital counseling or when faced with exposure to a feared stimulus in the therapy session, he or she may be advised to take another time out and repeat the process. Further direction for how to select and/or adapt tools to fit the needs of your individual clients can be found in Chapter 3.

The Toolbox Provides an Adjunct to Other Forms of Therapy

In addition, clients can benefit from other therapies such as cognitive-behavioral techniques by using concrete tools to reduce over-reactivity.

Bill O'Hanlon, a noted Ericksonian psychotherapist, compared the process of traditional psychotherapy to that of "attempting to nail jelly to a tree" (personal communication, July 9, 1989). As O'Hanlon aptly described it, working with traditional psychotherapy is challenging in its own right; therefore, one can see why an additional therapeutic tool such as hypnosis might be useful. These tools can also be paired quite effectively with other approaches such as Imago therapy for relationships, desensitization techniques, exposure therapy, and Ego State Therapy, to name a few. See Chapter 3 for further examples of how to combine the tools with other therapeutic approaches.

When a client experiences a resolution of issues, improved relationships, and overall success with the therapy, the therapist benefits, too. There is nothing more satisfying for a therapist than saying he or she can help someone and then being able to do it. This brings the therapist a great sense of relief and enhances both confidence and feelings of competence.

Overview of the Book

Chapter 1 provides an overview of the ways in which over-reactivity impacts the lives of clients and the benefits of using hypnotherapeutic focusing techniques. Since many therapists have not been given adequate training in neuroscience, Chapter 2 offers a brief review of basic biological psychology and how it relates to emotions and over-reactivity. Chapter 3 discusses how the tools complement other therapeutic approaches and offers preliminary guidelines to enhance the therapist's effective delivery of the tools, including psychoeducation, how to structure the sessions to create an optimum environment, how to individualize the scripts with an emphasis on utilization, and how to manage roadblocks such as resistance and poor response. Chapters 4 through 7 present the Toolbox itself, which I have divided into four tiers. In Chapter 4, the reader is introduced to Tier 1, the fundamentals of the Toolbox, including the Time Out tool to interrupt over-reactions. Chapter 5 covers Tier 2, how to establish and deepen a state of calm, focused attention by incorporating several traditional hypnotic inductions. Readers first encounter the majority of the tools in Tier 3 of

Chapter 6. This includes a detailed description of each technique coupled with suggested scripting. Chapter 7 focuses on Tier 4, rehearsal and transfer, and Chapters 8, 9, 10, and 11 apply the tools to case studies in a variety of different therapeutic contexts, such as when working with anxiety disorders, marital and committed relationships, and other relationships (parent/child, co-worker, and friend). (It should be noted that the case studies presented are a combination of real cases, with clients' permission, and composite cases. In all cases, the names and other identifying information have been changed.) Chapter 12 focuses on roadblocks and challenges. Chapter 13 concludes the book, and the Appendix provides readers with a list of recommended reading, videos, and other resources for those who want to go deeper into the study of hypnotherapy.

My goal over the course of this book is to provide you with an array of tools to launch your clients out of the "reactivity rut" and into empowered, successful, joyful lives. I also hope that you will finally feel that deep satisfaction that other therapists have felt using the Toolbox, of providing the best therapy possible—that which comes from doing your heartfelt best using dynamic yet practical tools that will benefit your clients for the rest of their lives. The old aphorism, "Give a man a fish and feed him for a day. Teach him to fish and feed him for a lifetime" couldn't be more true for these clients. Teaching them how to manage their own over-reactivity can bring about true and lasting transformation.

CHAPTER 1

Confronting the Challenges
of Over-reactivity

We've all experienced it—that exhilarating feeling when one of our therapeutic interventions has contributed to a breakthrough in a client's life. My colleague, Natalie Wick, remarked that when people are "singing and dancing and growing in therapy, it is tremendously moving. At those times, I have no doubt about my purpose in our world" (personal communication, November 29, 2005). Yet as a supervisor and consultant to therapists, I frequently witness the frustration and discouragement of dedicated clinicians who fail to meet the expectations of their clients or themselves, despite their best efforts.

Even gifted, highly experienced clinicians come up against this same dilemma. Geri, a clinical psychologist in private practice, requested a private supervision session, asking that it be scheduled sooner than her regular consultation appointment with me. She shared with me a case of a single mother who had adopted two special-needs children ages 11 and 14 who had originally been her foster children. The client was burdened with multiple challenges. She had to cope with her children's special-needs, a limited income, and a low threshold for stress. "The last time I saw her," Geri said, "she looked at me with sullen eyes with barely a glimmer of hope. In the evenings, alone with her children, she would become overwhelmed with the chaos in her house, and frequently lose her temper. My client broke down crying as she admitted that she reacted to her younger son's refusal to eat dinner by slamming his dinner plate into the trash and threatening to send him back to a foster home. Yesterday she cancelled her next appointment. I doubt if she'll reschedule," Geri confided. Geri went on to say how inadequate and helpless she felt as she encountered the horrific pain her client was bearing. Clearly, Geri lacked neither empathy nor motivation to help her client. She did lack, however, the resources and therapeutic skills necessary to help her client control her reactivity and prevent any ensuing damage to her children.

"Ah, what therapist hasn't worn those uncomfortable shoes?" said my writing peer and colleague Patricia Heck, addressing the agonizing dilemma that arises when our traditional methods of talk therapy fail. When I inquired as to the approach that Geri had taken, she informed me that she provided supportive, empathetic therapy, which validated the difficulty of raising special-needs children as a single parent. She also encouraged her client to examine the deficits in effective parenting that she received as a child. Geri needed to add practical, immediate interventions to her treatment that her client could master to increase her stress tolerance and diminish her inappropriate reactions to her children.

The Toolbox was developed with therapists such as Geri in mind, as well as the clinicians who are students of hypnosis. This book is not simply a collection of therapeutic interventions. It establishes a protocol for increasing the likelihood of ensuring transfer of therapeutic learning with the goal of interrupting affect dysregulation. It is divided into four components that I have called tiers, which can be conceptualized as follows: Tier 1, recognition of an over-reaction and initiation of a brief pause to interrupt it; Tier 2, standard hypnotic induction and deepening techniques; Tier 3, tools aimed at shifting unhealthy reactive styles; and Tier 4, tools to address therapeutic transfer of suggestions and practice. The effectiveness of the overall process is facilitated by the sequential implementation. Overall, the Toolbox can be adapted to treat a wide range of individuals and conditions.

Therapists are challenged every day by individuals who struggle with over-reacting in a variety of contexts. Janet was referred to me by her internist to treat her excessive sensitivity to sounds. She is a 47-year-old single woman who is employed as an attorney in a small law firm. During the initial consultation, Janet reported that she was unable to sleep at night because she found the traffic sounds from the main road adjacent to her home to be intolerable. However, when she asked several neighbors if they were also disturbed by the noise, they reported to her that it was barely discernable to them. At the onset of treatment, her reactivity to the auditory stimulation was causing her great distress; the insomnia resulting from the sensitivity to the street noise left her feeling exhausted, irritable, and unable to concentrate at work. Being highly sensitive to any one or a combination of the five senses is just one type of predisposition that might engender over-reactivity.

Physicians and psychotherapists alike also frequently encounter patients who are over-reactive to physical symptoms. Ryan, a 55-year-old electrician, is a "scanner." He obsessively scans his body for somatic symptoms and then worries about whether they portend catastrophic illness. He frequently seeks out medical consultations that consistently reveal that there is no organic basis to his complaints. You may recognize this type of over-reactor as the classic hypochondriac.

Over-reactions are especially damaging for a relationship in which one or both of the individuals in the couple are overly reactive. Consider Meg and Dave, a young, bright, well-educated couple. Meg, a stay-at-home mother, complained that it was nearly impossible to get Dave's attention and cooperation. For example, she said that no matter how often she asked him to call to let her know what time he'd be home for dinner, Dave would seldom comply. When he finally would arrive, usually after the children were in bed, she would typically greet him with a litany of complaints about the children, his neglect, and his inconsideration. He would respond by withdrawing, turning his attention to his computer or the television. Not surprisingly, his isolating behavior triggered more frustration and led to more accusatory and demanding responses from Meg. This in turn elicited further withdrawal from Dave, a common dysfunctional response that impedes intimate connection.

The approach to couples therapy that I employed with Meg and Dave was based on the principles and approaches that I learned in my training as an Imago therapist, emphasizing active listening with validation and empathy. Meg and Dave were quick studies, and after a couple of months of diligent work, they were able to contain over-reactivity and escalation of conflict, thereby enabling them to execute their dialogue with precise mirroring and generous displays of validation and empathy in the therapeutic context. We soon discovered, however, that the transfer of skills fell apart when either Meg or Dave were under stress. Needless to say, they were disappointed in their results and critical of themselves and each other. They also expressed increasing pessimism about the time and expense devoted to therapy. Many clients like those just mentioned are able to find some degree of mastery of their thoughts, feelings, or communication skills while in the therapist's office. It is when they go back to their own environments, however, where the triggers are present that they experience failure and are unable to implement these therapeutic lessons.

Understanding Over-reactivity

Over-reactivity is a term that I have adopted to describe an affective style that can be conceptualized as having three components. One is the distorted and unnecessarily intense qualitative appraisal of routine stimuli and interpersonal contact. The second is the accompanying psychophysiological hyperarousal. It frequently includes the internal experience of being flooded or overwhelmed with emotion and feeling out of control. The third is the emotional, cognitive, and/or behavioral manifestation of affect dysregulation. For example, a person could suffer from extreme anticipatory anxiety, rumination, and avoidance, respectively. As you will learn in Chapter 2, the first and second components are not distinctly separate entities. To an observer, over-reactivity might look like someone is making mountains out of molehills, losing perspective, or worrying excessively. In addition to internal suffering, when the reactivity is externalized, there can be relationship conflicts. Yet over-reactivity doesn't necessarily have to be externally obvious. A person can be in considerable pain due to an excessive, internalized over-reactive response without anyone else ever knowing.

We all experience heightened emotions at various times in our lives. Over-reactivity is certainly a component of many diagnoses such as attention deficit hyperactive disorder (AD/HD), obsessive compulsive disorder (OCD), posttraumatic stress disorder (PTSD), and bipolar disorder, as well as many of the personality disorders. Allan Schore (2006), recognized for his groundbreaking work on affect dysregulation, asserted that problems with affect dysregulation underlie all psychiatric disorders. Regardless of the diagnosis or disorder, the toolbox can be integrated into the treatment plan.

Stress is a part of the normal experience of being human. With sufficient levels of stress, each of us can be flooded with a release of neurochemicals, such as adrenaline, which elicit and maintain a state of hyperarousal and reactivity. (Further discussion of the role of psychophysiological arousal will be presented in Chapter 2.) *The distinction, however, between the normal stress response and pathological over-reactivity is when the reactivity creates chronic discomfort, impedes life functioning, and/or seriously interferes with relationships.* That said, these tools may certainly be used by anyone experiencing painful emotional reactions, even if those reactions do not fit the profile of the classic over-reactor or fall into the category of a clinical diagnosis. In order to better understand this distinction, a deeper dive into the various aspects of over-reactivity may prove useful.

As was mentioned, one of the hallmarks of affect dysregulation is *flooding*. John Gottman, a researcher on marriage stability and divorce prediction, describes flooding as a response to the partner's negativity that is so overwhelming that it can become emotionally incapacitating, making it nearly impossible to reasonably and adequately address a given issue (Gottman & Silver, 1999). Flooding results from a stress response. Gottman refers to this phenomenon as *diffuse physiological arousal* (DPA) (Gottman, 2000). When such a stress reaction is triggered, the cognitive and emotional systems move into hyper drive and cause individuals to perceive danger at every turn, even when there is no substantive cause for alarm (Woolfolk & Lehrer, 1984). It is exactly this flooding response that over-reactive clients experience and feel so unable to control in a given moment.

Although a majority of over-reactors experience flooding, individuals differ in their behavioral expression to the stress response. Harville Hendrix, Ph.D., marital therapist and author of *Getting the Love You Want* and *Keeping the Love You Find*, has identified two primary styles of emotional over-reactors: the *minimizer* and the *maximizer* (Hendrix, 1992). Typically, the minimizer stonewalls others when upset and doesn't always identify his or her feelings, even when flooded. He or she just reacts without knowing why. The maximizer, on the other hand, can usually identify his or her feelings but then takes them to the extreme by blowing up or making mountains out of molehills. It's not long before both types of over-reactors have exhausted friends, family, and those with whom they are in intimate relationships. An example of Hendrix's minimizer and maximizer styles can be found in a case study in Chapter 10 (see page 192).

A sub-category of the minimizer is the *freezer*. I have witnessed this phenomenon in my practice. This person simply shuts down when confronted with an emotional trigger or stressor. He or she becomes immobilized, unable to experience a feeling let alone name it, and unable to participate in productive dialogue about an issue or to take decisive action. The freezer is usually completely disconnected from his or her physiological awareness and may even unconsciously try to "play dead" by taking shallow breaths and making minimal movements, and speaking in hushed tones. The unifying factor in all of these reactions is the over-reactive psychophysiological response.

Insight Is Not Enough

I have found that psychodynamic interventions that encourage insight into the underlying dynamics of dysfunctional emotional patterns and over-reactivity are not powerful enough, in themselves, to break the cycles they address. For example, we all know people who chronically break their diets after a stressful day. An individual who overeats in response to stress may be well aware that he or she is overeating to self-soothe or to numb uncomfortable feelings and emotions. But that insight alone is not enough to alter behavior, thus the disordered eating pattern persists. Likewise, marital problems often arise when partners repeatedly allow work-related stress to impinge upon personal interactions. A husband might return home from a particularly stressful day at work to find that his wife has been delayed at work herself and will not be home for dinner. When she finally arrives, exhausted from an exceptionally long day at the office, he might be excessively critical over the delay in dinner. Although he might be aware that his agitation is a direct result of his own work-related stress as well as his hunger, he may nevertheless be impatient and critical. These clients need more than insight and cognitive awareness to break their cycles.

Perspectives on Hypnosis

The definition of the process and practice of hypnosis has long been debated and remains in flux. Kroger (1977) said that there may be as many definitions of hypnosis as there have been people who have attempted to define it. Two attempts to clarify the definition of hypnosis that appeal to me are the following. Wester (1987) wrote, "[hypnosis is an altered state] characterized by heightened suggestibility as a result of which changes in sensory, motor, and memory functions (cognitive processes) may be readily experienced" (p. 227). Hammond posited that hypnosis "is a phenomenon that is characterized by a state of attentive, receptive concentration containing three concurrent features of varying degrees: dissociation, absorption, and suggestibility, all three of which need to be present" (1998, p. 1). The trance-like state that develops from narrowing attention and eliciting dissociation enhances responsiveness to subsequent suggestion. Green, Barabasz, Barrett, and Montgomery (2005) endeavored to define hypnosis:

> Hypnosis typically involves an introduction to the procedure during which the subject is told that suggestions for imaginative experiences will be presented. The hypnotic induction is an extended initial suggestion for using one's imagination, and may contain further elaborations of the introduction. A hypnotic procedure is used to encourage and evaluate responses to suggestions. When using hypnosis, one person (the subject) is guided by another (the hypnotist) to respond to suggestions for changes in subjective experience, alterations in perception, sensation, emotion, thought, or behavior. Persons can also learn self-hypnosis, which is the act of administering hypnotic procedures on one's own. If the subject responds to hypnotic suggestions,

it is generally inferred that hypnosis has been induced. Many believe that hypnotic responses and experiences are characteristic of a hypnotic state. While some think that it is not necessary to use the word *hypnosis* as part of the hypnotic induction, others view this as essential. (p. 89)

Yapko stresses that the "essence of clinical hypnosis is found in helping people develop sensible skills for the 'real world'" (2005, 2006, p. 107). The emphasis on practical appplication of hypnotic interventions is a unifying theme of this book and certainly echoes Yapko's view. I would also advise the reader to look at the October 2005/January 2006 issue of the *American Journal of Clinical Hypnosis* for thorough, well-informed but varied perspectives on current definitions of hypnosis.

Perspectives on the Relaxation Response

People from a range of disciplines, including clinicians, religious teachers, and researchers, have concluded that deep relaxation is the most effective internal environment in which to facilitate emotional equilibrium. This insight is the basis of the extensive research on the relaxation response by Herbert Benson (1975). In kind, Edmund Jacobson's (1938) early work in neuromuscular tension revealed that deep relaxation attenuated excessive affective responses. Jon Kabat-Zinn (1990) has also introduced many clinicians to the benefits of mindfulness meditation that directs the individual to observe thoughts and sensations with a neutral perspective. Like Kabat-Zinn, Marsha Linehan (1993), developer of dialectical behavior therapy, also incorporates mindfulness with a nonjudgmental attitude as a central aspect of her treatment. These are primarily Western practitioners, but their approaches find their origin in the East.

Many of the Eastern traditions incorporate a quiet state of focused attention or meditation to foster spiritual contact. For example, Buddhism, Hinduism, and Sufism, all Eastern religions with traditions that go back thousands of years, incorporate meditation and prayer as part of their daily practice. Thich Nhat Hahn, the acclaimed Vietnamese Zen Buddhist master, teacher, and author, has inspired many worldwide,

Westerners, in particular, with the values of pausing, attending, and finding peace within. Tibet's Dalai Lama has done the same, as have countless other Eastern spiritual leaders. Virtually every religion uses prayer or meditation to quiet the restless mind and enhance spiritual development. The benefits of meditation and prayer as have been established through practice for countless generations can be found in the hypnotic trance state as well. Hypnosis also takes the individual into a deeply relaxed, safe internal zone from which profound wisdom, peace, and fundamental attitudinal changes can arise.

The tools presented in Chapters 4 through 6 and demonstrated throughout the rest of this book are an outgrowth of my personal experience with meditation and a career that has been heavily influenced by my study of hypnosis. Many of my clients have described their hypnotic experiences as spiritual in nature in that they provide an opportunity to go inside and access that which is wisest and most evolved in themselves.

I have found that training in and knowledge of hypnosis as an adjunct to psychotherapy can potentiate any treatment modality one employs. Hypnotic focus, suggestion, and training in self-hypnosis help to modulate affect by eliciting a calming response, thereby diminishing physiological arousal and reactivity.

Advantages of Hypnosis and Relaxation

An advantage of hypnosis is that it allows people to relax. The relaxation response alone, usually elicited in a hypnotic state, can diminish the physiological arousal and emotional flooding that together often lead to escalation of both internal and external conflict. Hypnosis is an ideal intervention to help clients move from reactive to reflective behavior. Contributions by those such as Hammond (1990) and Fromm and Nash (1992) have established the effectiveness of hypnosis as an adjunct to many therapeutic treatments.

Specifically, hypnosis can help clients diminish over-reactivity in the following ways:

- develop self-soothing
- change cognitions

- develop a dual perspective by working with ego states
- develop positive affect
- rehearse desired behaviors and skills
- focus internally
- control impulses

Develop Self-soothing

Self-soothing can be quickly achieved by teaching an individual how to perform hypnotic interventions independently. The ability to self-soothe is beneficial as it allows an individual to diminish the physiological arousal and emotional flooding that often lead to anxiety attacks, overwhelming feelings of shame, or the escalation of conflict. For these individuals, hypnosis can provide a much needed respite for the overworked, hyper-vigilant psyche, as well as for the exhausted immune system.

Change Cognitions

Hypnosis can also help alter cognitions, thereby increasing the effectiveness of cognitive behavioral treatment (Kirsch, Montgomery, & Saperstein, 1995). Hypnosis can calm individuals enough so that they can absorb rational, nonreactive, cognitive self-statements that will lead to making calm, rational, and healthy decisions.

Develop Dual Perspectives

It is possible to access a wise and rational side even while one is overwhelmed by feelings such as anxiety or anger; this can be described as experiencing a dual perspective. The concept of using dual perspectives was inspired partly through my study of Ego State Therapy but also through my training in gestalt therapy, transactional analysis, voice dialogue therapy, and internal family systems. Of all of these, I have drawn deeply from Ego State Therapy and am particularly indebted to the pioneering work of Helen and John Watkins. The Watkinses are internationally recognized for their contributions in the fields of hypnosis and psychology. Helen Watkins defined ego state therapy as follows: "Ego State Therapy is a psychodynamic approach in which techniques of group and family therapy are employed to resolve conflicts between the various 'ego states' that constitute a 'family of self' within a single individual" (1993, p. 236). Ego state therapists often engage the client's discrete ego states in order to assist them in making decisions and managing stress. The therapist may introduce these ego states to clients through the use of metaphor. For example, they commonly call on the "inner advisor" to counsel the more vulnerable, injured parts of the personality (Lynn, Kirsch, Neufeld, & Rhue, 1996). Claire Frederick has expanded the work of the Watkinses in her teaching and has inspired many to incorporate it into their clinical practices. According to Frederick, ego state therapy "appears to have the capacity to produce deep changes in personality structure" (2005, p. 348). These theories are similar to many other treatment modalities.

The concept of multiple perspectives has been incorporated in a number of other therapeutic models, including that of Richard Schwartz (1995), who views the mind as an inner family consisting of disparate sub-personalities, and Stone and Stone (1989), who developed Voice Dialogue, an approach that focuses on the different sub-personalities within the self. Previously, Eric Berne (1961) presented ego states as part of his transactional analysis treatment model. That multiple perspectives coexist within the same individual is, therefore, a well-established, respected framework that has been used in a variety of therapeutic contexts.

Develop Positive Affect

Those who come into therapy are not usually complaining about an over-reaction of love, serenity, or contentment; in fact, quite often they are unable to easily access these feelings on a regular basis. It is the more painful feelings such as anger, fear, or sadness that are problematic for over-reactors. For many who suffer from chronic anxiety or issues of the wounded self, experiencing warm, safe, loving feelings is more the exception than the rule. Once a positive state is identified or generated, the therapist can lead the client to transfer this state of mind to a context in which such a positive state is lacking (Brown & Fromm, 1986).

Generating and amplifying positive affect not only helps the client face a challenge in the moment but makes deposits into a "bank account" of good feelings that he or she can draw on later as a reminder of hope when things get tough.

Accessing positive affect can also provide tremendous benefits to over-reactivity in a relationship because viewing the relationship positively is an essential ingredient for success. Gottman asserted that the most important finding in his extensive research was as follows: "More positive affect was the only variable that predicted both stability and happiness [in marriages]" (2000, p. 11). In addition to accessing positive affect, hypnosis can also be useful as a preparation for incorporating new skills and/or behaviors.

Rehearse Desired Skills and Behaviors

Hypnosis can provide an opportunity for skill rehearsal. It has been suggested that when we practice hypnosis, we are conditioning response patterns to activate in the future (Humphries & Eagan, 1999). This ability to visualize or perceive oneself doing a proposed action or engaging in a desired response helps to facilitate its integration into daily practice (Fromm & Nash, 1992).

Focus Internally

The internal focus that occurs in trance can also lead to a feeling of safety and comfort that allows the client to turn inward, thus heightening self-awareness. This state of heightened self-awareness can help prevent a client from reacting to a situation impulsively and behaving in a way that may cause embarrassment or regret later on. It can also help in "owning one's piece" in a power struggle, therefore enabling one to act less defensively in an ensuing conflict (Gottman, 1994).

Control Impulses

Hypnosis also mitigates a loss of control and helps manage the pull of impulsive behaviors. It serves to interrupt patterns by offering an alternative way of responding to established response patterns.

Hypnosis offers benefits to a wide variety of clinical concerns. It would be nearly impossible to go in depth into every clinical problem that would benefit from hypnosis as an adjunct to treatment. However, since the following problems are the ones most frequently presented in my clinical practice, I have chosen to focus on them in particular.

Over-reactivity in Individuals with Anxiety Disorders

People with anxiety disorders have a strong tendency to be over-reactors. They often have unyielding fears that are so strong that they interfere with their daily ability to cope and function. Symptoms of anxiety disorders include the following:

- uncontrollable worrying
- panic attacks
- poor concentration
- addictive behaviors
- obsessive thoughts
- phobias

Over-reactivity and Wounded Self Issues

Other types of disorders stemming from a "wounded self" have a different set of symptoms but may also present with some of the above-mentioned anxiety symptoms. Quite often people with "wounded self" issues such as a narcissistic personality disorder or low self-esteem also have a tendency to over-react in the following ways:

- blaming others or taking on a disproportionate amount of blame
- overcompensating
- using anger as a first defense
- judging harshly or being highly critical due to an inability to empathize

These people have particular difficulty with relationships. If they also have symptoms of anxiety, this may make treatment especially challenging. Any one of these constellations of symptoms will inevitably cause distress.

Painful Consequences of Over-reactive Behavior

Such emotional over-reactions can lead to serious ineffectiveness in the daily lives of these individuals. Their pervasive emotionality can be so disruptive that they find themselves unable to accomplish goals or remain focused. Being easily distracted can in turn lead to poor job performance and, in some cases, job loss. Being run by overly strong emotions can also significantly interfere with one's ability to make sound, clear, healthy decisions.

In terms of other people in their lives, this kind of intensity often erodes the best of relationships—over-reactors simply wear others out. This in turn can lead to isolation, which then leaves the individual alone with his or her distorted worldview, thereby often aggravating the situation. This can be especially trying in family situations.

Parents with these issues often experience a loss of closeness with their child/children, be they single parents or those with partners. This can occur as early as infancy or as late as in the teen or adult years. Over-reactors with anxiety disorders or wounded self issues will often find it especially difficult to tolerate the normal challenges of a child without exhibiting behaviors such as losing their tempers, collapsing in a fit of uncontrolled sobbing, stalking off and maintaining an icy silence, or any other number of highly charged scenarios. These intense, uncontrollable emotions can not only wreak havoc on a family but can be a contributing factor to a number of other issues.

Over-reactivity can be at the root of a number of destructive behaviors. For example, individuals who over-react tend to self-soothe with an assortment of addictive behaviors. They also tend to experience an inordinate number of physical complaints ranging from sleep disorders and ensuing exhaustion to eating disorders, stress-related problems like high blood pressure and irritable bowel syndrome, and a general deterioration of the body's immune system. And perhaps most important, living with these types of over-reactions can definitely inhibit the feelings of joy, happiness, or spontaneity that many of us take for granted. Some of the most damaging consequences, however, can often be found within relationships.

Over-reactivity in Relationships

Just like the old saying that says it takes two to tango, it always takes two over-reactors for escalation of conflict to ensue. If one of the parties is able to maintain a relatively objective stance and a sense of inner calm and reasonability, then there is a much higher chance that the two will be able to work through the conflict, regardless of the content. It is when both parties are unable to stop negative behaviors that potentially destructive escalation occurs.

Frequently, overly reactive behaviors tend to be at the core of many troubled relationships. The practice of any of these behaviors within a conflict situation typically causes the following effects:

- escalation of conflict
- disconnection from each other emotionally
- inability to access positive affect
- inability to practice beneficial therapeutic behaviors

When two people experience such negative outcomes every time they enter into a conflict situation, it can be the death knell for the life expectancy of the relationship. These types of chronic exchanges have long-term impact such as the following:

- breakdown of communication
- breakdown of trust
- breakdown of positive expectancy of partner as a resource
- loss of empathy
- loss of willingness to work on issues
- inability to access positive affect (even out of a conflict situation)
- hopelessness

Overall, we can see how difficult and painful being overly emotional can be for an individual, and it is equally clear the devastating role it plays in the destruction of a relationship over time. Many a well-intentioned, highly trained therapist has used every approach he or she has to help these individuals only to have a discouragingly low success rate. With the incorporation of a few simple, easy-to-learn, easy-to-practice hypnotic interventions, however, clients can experience a dramatic turn-around in the effectiveness of cognitive behavioral and psychotherapeutic therapies, which in turn can lead to tremendous benefits for both clients and therapists. This book presents a wide-ranging selection of different hypnotherapeutic tools that can be used to address a number of types of overly reactive clients.

Themes and Objectives of the Toolbox

Specifically, the interventions in the therapist's Toolbox found in Chapters 4 through 6 can help the client diminish over-reactivity by developing the following skills:

- *Identifying the Start of an Over-reaction and Responding Appropriately*: This enables one to take a "time out" to practice self-soothing interventions.
- *Calming and Focusing*: Ability to quickly center one's attention and calm the physiological arousal that accompanies affect dysregulation.
- *Mindfulness*: Development of skills in mindfulness and detached observation of transient affective states allows one to become aware of a feeling as it occurs without judgment.
- *Somatic Awareness and Cues*: Development of awareness of bodily expressions of stress and an ability to regulate and modulate those expressions.
- *Impulse Control*: Ability to quickly establish impulse control.
- *Coexisting Affective States*: Ability to have two conflicting feelings or thoughts at the same time.
- *Resource Utilization*: Ability to access resources that are internal or external in origin such as positive memories, real or imagined support figures, comforting, safe places, and/or parts of the self.
- *Positive Affect Development*: Development and maintenance of positive affective states.

It is the mastery of these skills outside of the therapeutic office setting in the midst of stress, conflict, and/or anxiety-provoking triggers that will truly enable clients to experience freedom from the patterned emotional reactions that have kept them trapped for so long.

CHAPTER 2

The Psychophysiology of Emotional Reactivity

═══════

I have found that knowing my way around the brain has helped me become a better psychotherapist. However, like most psychotherapists, I have not received formal training in the field of neuroscience. Whereas mastering this field is an unrealistic endeavor for most busy clinicians, I have found it helpful to possess an elementary understanding of psychophysiology in relation to stress responses. This chapter examines the most salient aspects of the rapidly evolving interdisciplinary field of neuroscience, highlighting the psychophysiological underpinnings of emotional reactivity and the biological relevance and necessity of hypnotherapeutic tools for affect regulation. It also provides a brief history of the development of the currently held theory of the mind-body connection. In addition, there is an explication as to why alternative approaches to traditional talk therapy, as exemplified by the hypnotic tools, are more effective in targeting the demands of a complex psychophysiological system.

Psychophysiology and the Challenge of Affect Regulation

Regulating affect is an enormous challenge for any of us because we are confronted with the complicated task of overcoming established neural processes of the brain. The most recent estimate is that the brain consists of 100 billion neurons that are connected in extraordinarily complex ways (Howard, 2000). It is not surprising, therefore, that our understanding of the brain's mechanisms is still in its infancy. To make the challenge of taming our brains even greater, current research suggests that we are hardwired to react to many external stimuli with behavioral responses based on fear or anger; therefore, it is easier to release emotions than to manage them with reason. Joseph LeDoux wrote, "While conscious control over emotions is weak, emotion can flood consciousness. This is so because the wiring of the brain at this point in our evolutionary history is such that connections from the emotional systems to the cognitive systems are stronger than the connections from the cognitive to the emotional systems" (1996, p. 19). Even now we do not fully understand the physiological basis of psychology. The brain still has many secrets to reveal.

Conflicting Theories of the Connection Between Mind, Body, and Emotions

In the process of learning about the psychophysiological bases of psychology, I have been excited to discover the contributions of researchers and scholars who have advanced the development of our current understanding of this field. William James, Carl Lange, Walter Cannon, and Phillip Bard, all of whom were prominent theorists in the early 1880s, are four researchers whose academic interests concern the mind-body relationship and the phenomenological experience of emotion. The former two conceptualized the James-Lange Theory of Emotion, and the latter two conceived the Cannon-Bard Theory of Emotion.

Both theories assume a linear cause and effect: a chain reaction sparked by an encounter with a fearful external stimulus. In the James-Lange theory of emotion, an individual perceives a frightening or threatening emotional stimulus and experiences an initial somatic reaction. In response to this somatic reaction, he feels the subjective emotion of fear. James and Lange observed the body's response to stress and how emotionally evocative stimuli influence an individual's affective response and behavior. They proposed that the seat of the emotion is in the body. The limitation of their theory is that it is not sufficient to say that all emotions arise from the body or from the body state. It fails to take into account the intrinsic emotional mechanisms of the brain. It is nevertheless undeniable that the introspective experience of our visceral or somatic response to experience influences the way we think, feel, and react.

The Cannon-Bard theory challenged the James-Lange theory by proposing that emotions could be experienced independently from their somatic expression. Studying animals as well as humans with spinal cord injuries who could not assess the physiological state of the body, they found that the injured could nevertheless experience emotion.

Both theories are overly simplistic and inadequate, as emotions are more complex than they suggest. The James-Lange theory is weak because there are emotional states that are generated internally. Cannon-Bard's theory is weak because there is a connection between body states and emotions. A secondary drawback is that these theories only address fears generated by an external stimulus. In my practice, I encounter many clients who experience physical agitation in the absence of any discernable fear stimulus whatsoever, such as the client who experiences panic reactions upon waking in the morning in the absence of any acknowledged nightmare.

In the late 1980s, Ernest Rossi asserted that the field of mind-body therapy still required more corroboration from the scientific community to substantiate its conceptual framework or *modus operandi* (Rossi & Cheek, 1988). It is exciting to know that mind-body research is currently coming to fruition. As the title of Antonio Damasio's 1994 book, *Descartes' Error: Emotion, Reason, and the Human Brain* suggests, the Cartesian tenet of mind-body dualism that has been embraced by Western society for centuries is fundamentally flawed: the body and mind cannot accurately be conceptualized as distinct, separate entities. Thus scientists such as Candace Pert (1997) have begun to use terms such as *bodymind* to denote the psychosomatic networks that are becoming fundamental to the understanding of physiology, psychology, and neurology.

In other words, the mind is not simply a puppet master that processes cognitive information without being influenced by physiological sensation. Although traditional psychotherapy relies on reason to access a compartmentalized, rational self through which insight rectifies dysfunctional or pathological thought patterns and behaviors, what we are currently learning from our colleagues in neuroscience and psychophysiology suggests that one must address the bodymind in order to provide a comprehensive therapeutic treatment.

Why Over-reactive Clients Need More Than Talk Therapy

When I encountered Professor LeDoux's (1996) explanations of emotional reactivity, which in turn spurred me to investigate similar research, I experienced the epiphany of stumbling upon scientific corroboration for what I had known intuitively to be true. Suddenly, there was a concrete explanation for some of the difficulties that other therapists and I encounter with our clients. I realized that it was truly asking a lot of my clients to spontaneously react in the most appropriate manner when they became emotionally triggered—in fact, it was unrealistic. I realized that we are hardwired to react with behavioral responses based on fear or anger and that some people are hardwired to be even more reactive than others. In view of this, I was affirmed that clients need concrete tools to use when they are excessively emotional, thus the *Affect Regulation Toolbox*.

In order to clearly understand the psychophysiological support behind the affect regulation tools, we will look at different types of over-reactors, as well as the three primary areas of the "emotional" brain. Following this discussion, we will learn about two different components of the autonomic nervous system (ANS) that mitigate states of arousal and relaxation. The fear, stress, and anger responses are activated and deactivated by these two components.

Before I begin these discussions, however, it is important to note that the brain structures we will be discussing are not limited to performing the functions mentioned. Many psychological phenomena are the product of complex, interactive neural structures. There will be an emphasis on the interconnectedness of multiple physiological systems and axes. Researchers such as Candace Pert (1997) stress that neural networks extend far beyond the realm of the brain itself. Especially in light of empirically supported paradigms of mind-body connection, a reductionistic understanding of areas of the brain and the behaviors that correspond to them can be detrimental and misleading. It is also important that the reader approach this information with the knowledge that the roles of these structures are still poorly understood; this is an area that is still aggressively under study. Keeping these caveats in mind, a description of three mechanisms linked to the fear response, chronic stress, and impulse control, as well as their relationship to behavioral maladaption, will be presented next.

Three Most Common Types of Over-reactors

In my time as a clinical practitioner, I have observed that three distinct profiles of client problems dominate my practice, all of which find their origins in the various brain structures and psychophysiological networks. The first recognizable category consists of specific phobias and aversive associations. A second major category that will be addressed consists of various forms of generalized anxiety. Individuals with generalized anxiety experience intrusive, ruminative, anxious thoughts that they cannot readily control. Quite commonly, these individuals also experience chronic physical symptoms due to their anxiety and often speak of feeling their mental distress manifesting as somatic discomfort. They present with a host of somatic complaints that are often a direct result of the chronic stress, both mental and physical, which they experience on a daily basis. The final recognizable group of problems concerns impulsivity, specifically deficits of impulse control.

Three Primary Areas of the "Emotional" Brain: Amygdala, HPA Axis, Prefrontal Cortex

When studying current knowledge of the brain, I soon learned that the three categories of dysfunctions mentioned above stem from three distinct etiological bases. The first concerns fear conditioning, a process in which the amygdala plays a crucial role. The second concerns problems arising from long-term, chronic stress that is intertwined with a hormonal system that allows the brain's emotional apparati to directly influence the body. This mechanism is referred to as the hypothalamic pituitary adrenocortical axis (HPA axis). Lastly, deficits of impulse control are linked to structures in the prefrontal cortex. An understanding of these three brain mechanisms and the manner in which they under-lie neural functions can help the therapist tailor hypnotic and other ther-apeutic interventions to most effectively address and relieve clients' symptoms.

Fear, Fear Conditioning, and the Amygdala

Hypnotherapeutic interventions for clients dealing with phobias or other problems resulting from aversive conditioning are often geared to interrupt the processes by which the body over-reacts to conditioned, yet relatively innocuous, fear-inducing stimuli. A therapist's ability to understand and in turn provide clients with an understanding and explanation of the fear response can be an integral part of a successful treatment.

The Fight/Flight Response

The fight/flight response, coined by Walter Cannon in the 1920s, refers to an immediate fear reaction in which the body readies itself for defen-sive action in response to a real or perceived life-endangering threat. The amygdala, a small, almond-shaped structure located deep within the temporal lobe of the brain, plays a major role in the initiation and exe-cution of this response. The amygdala independently integrates incom-ing information concerning external stimuli and motivates action when fear is experienced or danger is present. This generates a state of mental and physical readiness in which the individual can pursue one of two courses of defensive action: to fight or to flee. It is important to note that this reaction occurs long before a cognitive appraisal is made of the sit-uation: a threatening stimulus presents, and the body reacts in a split second. Thus many people suffering from phobias experience a physical arousal that signals alarm far before they can make a cognitive assess-ment of the stimulus or situation. The body enters this state of height-ened physical and mental readiness before an individual even makes the judgment of whether or not the stimulus to which they are reacting is even presenting a real threat.

An excellent example of this is the spider/speck in the woods phe-nomenon. While sitting around a campfire or walking in the woods, many have experienced intense fear reactions upon sensing a light tickle on a forearm that might denote the presence of a spider. The body is triggered into alarm, and only seconds later, after the individual has glanced at his or her arm, does the "mind" catch up to make the appraisal, "This isn't a spider. It's just a speck of dirt! I have nothing to be afraid of." Consciously then, the individual makes a decision to calm down: the accelerated heartbeat slows, the muscles and mind become more relaxed, and the individual perhaps returns to a daydream or resumes a conversation.

As exemplified in the spider/speck paradigm, the fight/flight response can be lifesaving. Daniel Siegel, M.D. (1999), author of *The Developing Mind*, aptly terms the mechanisms through which the body constantly scans the environment for possible threat an "anticipation machine" (p. 30). However, any anticipation machine can develop mal-adaptions. When this occurs, anxiety disorders result. Individuals suffering from anxiety disorders often experience the inability to calm themselves once a cognitive appraisal of a fearful stimulus or situation has determined there is no need for alarm. Individuals with varying types of anxiety disorders also have anticipation machines that are hyperalert. For example, individuals who have been diagnosed with posttraumatic stress disorder (PTSD) often demonstrate an exaggerated startle response. Nearly everyone has seen or experienced that excitatory startle when someone walks up behind an unsuspecting friend and taps him or her on the shoulder. However, an individual with PTSD might experience this same startle response with less provocation; for example, when someone calls his or her name from the opposite corner of a room. Regardless of the diagnosis, many a frustrated individual has entered my office saying, "I know I shouldn't be afraid of this. I know that this is completely irrational. But before I can even think, my heart starts racing and my palms start sweating. I just can't stop it." The fight or flight responses are classic and certainly the best known, but there is a third response that I have seen in my practice that can also be found in nature.

Just as a rabbit will freeze when it perceives a threat, many people will freeze up when they feel threatened or intimidated. Humans, like other animals, respond to a moderate level of fear by shutting down and failing to connect and respond; yet, as the intensity of the fear increases, the adaptive response shifts and freezing gives way to flight. For example, though a rabbit freezes when it first catches sight of a perceived threat, it flees as soon as the threat comes closer. Likewise, people may freeze first and then flee from stressful environments that are perceived as threatening, whereas other individuals feel trapped, like there is no safe exit, so they stay put.

Fear Conditioning

The brain is also highly adept at storing long-term memory events in which an individual experienced fear or alarm. This, too, can be a highly adaptive survival mechanism. A single encounter with a highly aversive stimulus, such as burning one's finger on a hot stove, is usually highly memorable, even if it occurred when an individual was very young. The brain incorporates past experience to aid in its identification of present danger and classification of environmental stimuli. The amygdala plays a crucial role in this process as well: it makes sure that the brain remembers aversive encounters from the past. Once an extremely aversive event has taken place, neurons in the amygdala can be designated to "remember" the external trigger.

While the brain's amazing ability to incorporate the knowledge of fearful/threatening stimuli from past experiences into memory is very adaptive, it can also become a trap for those suffering from anxiety disorders. In response to a single, highly aversive event, an individual can acquire a profoundly negative, maladaptive association to any situation that resembles the initial aversive experience. This is referred to as stimulus generalization. For example, an individual who has developed a bee phobia after being stung in a garage might develop an intense aversion to being in garages. In extreme cases, this fear might generalize to being in outdoor environments during clement months when there is a possibility, albeit remote, that one could be stung again. When a phobia interferes with daily functioning, generalizes to other fears, and/or hinders an individual's ability to engage in desired activities (e.g., a fear of flying), treatment is indicated.

Physiological Recognition of Stress and the Hypothalamic Pituitary Adrenocortical (HPA) Axis

Neurosurgeon and brain researcher Richard Bergland suggested that "thought is not caged in the brain but is scattered all over the body"

(Restak, 1994, p. 207). Similarly, in Candace Pert's (1997) *Molecules of Emotions*, we learn that our bodies and minds are not only connected but that the body and mind are one. Pert presents a conceptualization of the "mobile brain" wherein there are receptors translating emotional responses in every part of the body. This mobile brain creates a psycho-somatic network through which intelligent information travels from one system to another. Much of the conception of mind-body connection is based on an understanding of the functions of the HPA axis.

Individuals' mental stress finds bodily expression through adrenalin and cortisol release, as well as a vast number of other related endoge-nous chemical messengers. The experience of bodily stress, in turn, often feeds into the feeling of mental distress. To put it simply, people get upset, become reactive, and then become even more stressed in response to their maladaptive reactivity. The physiological impact of chronic stress adds to this downward spiral. Stress results in the pro-duction of cortisol, which mediates the physiological changes associ-ated with stress. When individuals suffer from chronic stress, cortisol release becomes excessive. It maintains, intensifies, and reinforces the initial psychophysiological state of distress. In the absence of a power-ful intervention, this cycle can worsen indefinitely. By facilitating relaxation and modifying the way individuals subjectively experience their own body states, hypnotic interventions can break this cycle of anxiety and prevent it from getting out of control.

Physiological responses to chronic stress are far-reaching and may include chronic headaches, gastrointestinal distress, hypertension, ulcers, asthma, and infertility. Cognitive functioning can also be affected by energy depletion, resulting in a lack of ability to concentrate and poor memory. The immune system is also significantly weakened, resulting in an increased susceptibility to colds, flu, allergies, and migraine or ten-sion headaches. All of these further increase an already stressed individ-ual's perturbation.

Impulsivity

A common feature of problems that arise in relationship and work-place settings stems from the failure to manage impulsive thoughts and contain the expression of impulsive behaviors. Such deficits sometimes manifest as extreme outbursts but more frequently are evidenced as subtle interpersonal conflicts in marriages and other close relationships. Clients who do not necessarily present with diagnosable impulse control disorders may demonstrate subclinical features of lack of control in specific situations that interfere with optimum interpersonal functioning. (Examples of these subclinical disturbances in interpersonal relationships will be examined in Chapters 10 and 11.)

An additional factor to consider when presented with impulsive and/or over-reactive behavior is the possible diagnosis of AD/HD. Many times this is overlooked by clinicians who give a diagnosis of impulsivity without having a client properly assessed for AD/HD. I would suggest that clinicians obtain a basic assessment for AD/HD, and if there is any indication that it might be a problem, refer the client out to an AD/HD specialist. And, of course, there is always the possibility of a dual diagnosis of AD/HD and over-reactivity that can indeed be supported with hypnotherapeutic tools. Indeed, even if the impulsivity is due to pure AD/HD, training clients with this diagnosis to use the affect regulation tools is very helpful.

The Role of the Prefrontal Cortex in Impulsivity

The prefrontal cortex is intimately involved in the inhibition of these impulses. Prefrontal cortical structures subdue intense impulsive thoughts or motives, allowing us to exert control upon our urges. In other words, the prefrontal cortex is what allows us to "put the breaks" on our impulsive behaviors. Individuals with prefrontal deficits thus often behave in an impulsive and imprudent manner. *However, this is not to suggest that everyone who behaves impulsively has damage or a deficit in the prefrontal cortex, as will be discussed later in the chapter. There are a number of other factors that may contribute and/or be the root cause of impulsivity.*

The prefrontal cortex occupies the area around the temples, forebrow, and between the eyes. A striking illustration of the role of the prefrontal cortex was provided in the case of Phineas Gage. Gage was involved in an industrial accident that resulted in severe damage to his prefrontal cortex. After the incident, Gage's personality drastically changed. The description of Gage, published in 1868 by his primary physician, Dr. John Harlow offers one of the first and most extreme examples of impaired impulse control due to a functional impairment of the prefrontal cortex. It is included here because it is a good illustration of problems that manifest, to a much lesser extent, in clients whom I treat for impulse-control problems that present in relationship therapy. Gage's new behavior was described as follows:

> . . . fitful, irreverent, indulging at times in the grossest profanity . . . manifesting but little deference for his fellows, impatient of restraint or advice when it conflicts with his desires, at times pertinaciously obstinate, yet capricious and vacillating. (Bear, Connors, & Paradiso, 2001, pp. 586–587)

The prefrontal cortex allows us to contain our normal impulses and feelings and helps us to become intentional in our responses. An angry, aggressive outburst can be devastating to a relationship. Ardent apologies are often insufficient to heal the damage that results when one partner or both cannot control an aggressive impulse. More subtle yet still injurious expressions that result from poor containment of impulses can include irritability, impatience, obstinacy, and rigidity.

The Amygdala and Its Role in Aggression

Of the many different types of impulsivity, aggression is one of the most challenging. Thus, when addressing impulse control, it is important to focus on calming the aggression that is often inherent in impulsive acts and responses. The amygdala, a structure that we discussed above in its relationship to the fear response, also plays a major role in the mediation and expression of aggression. Two distinct pathways have been identified by which two different types of aggression are triggered. The former is classified as *predatory aggression*. The latter is termed *affective aggression*. Not all aggression is physical. Much of what I deal with in my clinical practice, particularly in relationship therapy, is what I consider affective aggression.

Current studies suggest that the neurotransmitter serotonin has recently been implicated in the expression of aggressive behavior, as well as being a factor in the development of clinical depression. The relaxation response, which is presented in Tier 2 of the Toolbox, is likely, as is medication, to elicit a decrease in the turnover rate of serotonin, thereby increasing the body's effective use of the neurotransmitter.

In the next section of this chapter, we will build upon our understanding of the fight/flight response and the psychophysiological bases and consequences of chronic stress that were examined in the discussion of the HPA axis. We will look at the sympathetic and parasympathetic divisions of the autonomic nervous system as they relate to states of arousal and relaxation. Within the context of this information, we will then discuss the role of the hypnotic tools in eliciting the desired parasympathetic response.

General Adaptation Syndrome (GAS)

In the 1930s, Hans Selye, a Hungarian endocrinologist, conceptualized what he termed the general adaptation syndrome (GAS). Selye describes GAS as the process by which the body reacts to stress. Selye defined stress as a nonspecific response of the body to any demand. This paradigm introduced the concept that the stress response is universal; the same deleterious effects of chronic stress will be observed regardless of its source. What Selye was actually noting was the deleterious effects of what we today call chronic stress, which, explored above in the HPA section, is linked to an excess of cortisol and other related hormones and steroids throughout the body.

The first of these stages was the initial reaction to fear described above as the first component of the fight/flight response. The second stage was resistance, in which the body mobilizes to respond to the immediate stressor, thus coping with or adapting to the stressor. Current research suggests that these first two processes are not distinct enough to warrant separate categorization; thus, they have been combined into what Rossi terms "an initial complex adaptive response of alarm and arousal" (1993, p. 71). Selye's third stage was termed exhaustion. Given the clearly deleterious effects of the stressor, Selye assumed that the body's resources that were once plentiful had been depleted and exhausted by the continuing response to the stressor. While this is a logical conclusion, research has shown that the psychophysiological deple-tion observed in those suffering from chronic stress is not a result of a lack of neurotransmitters but of an abundance of them. Again, this abundance has been outlined in the discussion of the HPA axis above.

The Autonomic Nervous System

The autonomic nervous system consists of three divisions: the sympa-thetic nervous system, the parasympathetic nervous system, and the enteric division. To effectively prevent emotional over-reactivity, there needs to be a well-functioning interplay of parasympathetic/sympathetic autonomic nervous system arousal. Since these systems play a crucial role in mediating the stress response, we will be focusing on them. The sympathetic nervous system is activated in response to stressors and is the component of the nervous system responsible for the mobilization of resources involved in the fight/flight response. When the sympathetic nervous system kicks in, adrenaline is released, eliciting reactions in every organ of the body. A clear explanation of its functioning is pre-sented by Sapolsky: "Originating in the brain, sympathetic projections exit your spine and branch out to nearly every organ, every blood vessel, and every sweat gland in your body . . . It helps mediate vigilance, arousal, activation, mobilization" (1994, p. 23).

If the sympathetic nervous system (SNS) can be thought of as the revving-up system, the parasympathetic nervous system (PNS) is its oppo-site. The parasympathetic division of the autonomic nervous system is associated with sleep and other states of relaxation. Thus, it is activated during meditation, hypnosis, yoga, and other activities associated with relaxation. When the body is not under immediate stress, the PNS focuses on maintaining heart rate, respiratory, metabolic, and digestive functions.

What Role Can Hypnosis Play in Affecting the
Autonomic Nervous System?

In view of the challenge of combating various states of arousal that appear to be a precursor to inappropriate interactions, clients need concrete tools to utilize when they are excessively emotional; hypnosis offers especially effective methods to minimize the effects of stress.

Typically, in hypnosis the intention is to elicit a parasympathetic response and return the system to a state of equilibrium that would interrupt emotional reactivity.

On occasion, however, hypnosis is aimed at stimulating the sympathetic nervous system. Humphreys (2003) has provided a useful model of hypnotic intervention based on the need to stimulate the division of the autonomic nervous system that is underactive. For example, clients who exhibit withdrawal or passive coping styles may require a stimulating approach with the goal of helping the client become more appropriately driven and activated. With the application of the Toolbox, I often direct my clients to revivify emotionally charged memories of interpersonal conflict or anxiety reactions. I do this within the context of my office so that I can then intervene directly by teaching one of the tools to address the overactive response. Regardless of the response that is elicited in treatment, in changing my clients' mentality, I am also inevitably changing their physiology.

Earlier we discussed the necessity of intervening in the negative feedback loops that accompany chronic states of stress, fear reactions, and excessive reactivity. The use of the tools to elicit a parasympathetic response after an initial state of stress has been re-elicited accomplishes just this. In re-eliciting the highly charged emotion and then intervening with tools that elicit a parasympathetic response, we are creating the kind of "loop of healing" that Pert references in her discussion of alternative therapies (1999, p. 274). The loop of healing involves first re-experiencing distressful feelings, then teaching self-soothing tools.

Another way of understanding this arousal/calming response is through what has been termed the reticular activation system (RAS). It has been referred to as a kind of "toggle switch" that flips back and forth in response to emotional arousal or calm. According to Howard, when a person feels threatened, the RAS essentially shuts down the cerebral cortex or what he calls the "learning brain" (2000, p. 39). Conversely, when the system is calm and relaxed, the RAS switches the cortex back on and allows the logical part to be in charge.

Rossi addressed a component of this theme from another perspective. In his groundbreaking book, *The Psychobiology of Mind-Body*

Healing, he discussed the concept of the *ultradian* healing response, the goal of which is simply to align with the naturally recurring rhythms of the body through rest breaks and thereby prevent the toxic effects of accumulated stress and its impact on optimum functioning. When discussing the psychobiological benefits of the hour-long format of a 12-step meeting as might be practiced by such a group as Alcoholics Anonymous, Rossi stated that "It is the 'relaxation opportunity' and occasional emotional catharsis . . . that initiates the real healing factor on the psychobiological level" (1993, p. 118). Although he was referring specifically to the twelve-step programs, he is also alluding to the process that occurs when a client uses a tool to self-soothe subsequent to experiencing and/or expressing emotionally charged themes. In a 12-step group, participants begin with a standard, ritualized beginning that includes a reading of the steps and traditions. This serves to focus attention and create a "time out," in which going inside and attending to the self is encouraged. As Rossi mentioned, there can be an occasional emotional catharsis as people share their experiences. Then the meeting typically ends with a prayer. All of these practices combine to calm the emotional system.

Individual and Situational Factors That Influence a Stress Response

You might ask yourself on any given day when confronted with a stressful situation what will influence your response. Will it be your "emotional brain" or your more evolved "logical brain?" There are a number of concurrently functioning factors that could contribute to the expression of the reaction, including the following.

Hormone Levels

Hormone levels that are out of balance can dramatically affect the intensity of an emotional response. Excessive or insufficient hormone levels due to an endocrine imbalance (e.g., thyroid or estrogen imbalance) can contribute to dysregulation. Hormone imbalance can also be caused by a stress hormone such as coritsol when the system is under fire.

Sleep Cycles

Everyone knows that things feel worse after a night of insufficient sleep. Howard reported on the research of Van Cauter when he said that "the loss of even an hour or so of sleep for two or three nights in a row results in attendant increases in cortisol" (Howard, 2000, p. 141). Prolonged sleep deprivation or any interruption of circadian rhythms (change in work schedules, time zones, jet lag, etc.) can dramatically inhibit resilience to stress.

Genetics

Reactive styles are likely to be heritable, leaving some individuals more vulnerable to stress. Genetics can play a role in the well-functioning interplay of parasympathetic/sympathetic autonomic nervous system arousal (Thomson, 1988).

Trauma

A history of childhood trauma resulting from abuse, neglect, or early-childhood illness or injuries requiring invasive medical interventions can create an established response pattern of moving prematurely into hyperarousal. Referring to the effect of trauma on the developing brain, Schore asserted that "psychological factors 'prune' or 'sculpt' neural networks" (2003, p. 291). In other words, a history of early trauma can affect the development of the brain, thereby shaping future behavior and reactions.

Conclusion

Given the knowledge presented in this chapter concerning the psychophysiology of the stress response, it becomes clear that we need effective tools to interrupt the insidious feedback loops that contribute to over-reactivity. The following chapter provides important preliminary considerations that should be incorporated in the instruction of the tools to the client. Sample scripts will be presented in the remaining chapters of the book.

CHAPTER 3

Preliminary Considerations for Using the Toolbox

═══════════

The Tools as an Adjunct to Psychotherapy

The tools are intended to serve as an adjunct to treatment to enhance and expedite therapeutic progress and are compatible with most any psychotherapeutic modality. In some sessions, I use the tools in combination with other modes of therapy, whereas in other sessions, much of the time is focused specifically on the affect regulation tools themselves. Additionally, the tools can be utilized either in individual therapy or in couples' therapy. And although there are some suggested guidelines as to which tools to use for which conditions, it is best to think of the tools as items on a menu. Although it is quite possible to eat anything on the menu in any order one chooses, there is a generally accepted sequence: appetizer, main course, dessert. Within each of these categories, however, there are a number of choices. Certainly, some days one might choose to order an appetizer as a main course or to eat dessert before dinner. Adaptability and flexibility are the keystones to successful use of these tools.

The underlying themes of the tools are in keeping with an array of psychotherapeutic orientations and can be easily adapted by practitioners with disparate perspectives. For example, tools such as breathing, hand warming, and visualizing the switching of channels or computer screens are directly applicable to behavioral therapy with its emphasis on stress management, relaxation, and desensitization. The tools that challenge erroneous cognitions and provide methods of self-talk are in line with the emphasis on the corrective thinking patterns of cognitive therapy. Tools emphasizing positive expectancy of future outcomes align with the tenets of the humanistic approach in their focus on personal responsibility, action, and growth. Interpersonal therapists can use the tools to help reduce conflict with friends and family and garner support systems. The theme of drawing on a more evolved or higher self, as with the Parts of Self tool, is in keeping with the transpersonal or psychospiritual approach. Therapists who are psychodynamic in orientation or have been influenced by object relations theory, which asserts that human relationships are our primary motivators, may find the Imaginary Support Tool to be useful. The variety of tools that focus on facilitating impulse control and diminishing reactivity are practical and necessary interventions for relationship therapists. Development of the skill of acknowledging coexisting affective states (or two conflicting thoughts or feelings at once) is also congruent with the goals of marital therapists. As can be seen from these examples, the tools make an excellent adjunct to an array of psychotherapeutic approaches. The challenge comes in learning how to integrate them seamlessly into a therapy session. Partially this will come with practice but knowing how to structure your sessions to accommodate the tools can be helpful as well.

Structuring and Planning the Sessions

Conducting effective sessions requires thoughtful planning. Several relevant factors should be considered when devising a treatment plan.

Introducing the Psychotherapeutic Approach

I tend to favor therapy that is both strategic and goal oriented, as do many other therapists. In my sessions, I begin by identifying specific therapeutic goals based on the client's presenting problems and utilize the tools to work explicitly toward a reduction of the problematic symptoms. Further, the client is told that a variety of tools will be used to develop skills to help him or her handle presenting emotions more effectively. Clients are also informed that many of the interventions have their roots in hypnosis. This then leads us to address psychoeducation concerning hypnosis.

Psychoeducation on Hypnosis

Psychoeducation is an important component of all treatment. Clients need to be provided with information regarding their styles of reactivity, symptoms, and the effects on their functioning. Frequently, clients, particularly those with anxious temperaments, catastrophize their symptoms and fear dire outcomes if those symptoms don't diminish. They berate themselves for being weak and capitulating to their problems. These clients need to be assured that their symptoms are not unusual and are common expressions of the interplay of genetics, temperament, and environmental factors. As mentioned earlier, they must be assured that their condition is treatable and that they will learn specific strategies that have been successful with many others.

Since the tools are essentially hypnotic in nature, it is important that clients be educated about the nature of hypnosis and that the myths and misconceptions of hypnosis be thoroughly discussed. All too many clients are familiar with hypnosis through distortions that are presented in movies and the media, as well as by stage hypnotists. Yapko (2003) has provided a thorough listing of the myths and misconceptions of hypnosis in his highly regarded introductory text, *Trancework: An Introduction to the Practice of Clinical Hypnosis*, which I present to my clients. I emphasize particularly that no one can be hypnotized against his or her will and that clients retain control during the session. Further, I inform them that although hypnosis is an altered state of consciousness, it is a kind of mental state that they have almost certainly previously experienced. Clients are told that hypnosis is a normal state of consciousness that we all go in and out of several times a day. I usually give the common example that most people have experienced driving their cars on the expressway and becoming so absorbed in their thoughts that they nearly miss their exit. A similar, naturally occurring experience is becoming nearly oblivious to the audience when we are absorbed in a good movie. In both instances, the attention of the conscious mind is so fully absorbed that our attention withdraws from the external environment and only a vestigial unconscious awareness of the external environment remains. In both examples, the conscious mind can be alerted quickly if needed, for example, if a truck cuts you off in traffic or someone begins to cough excessively in the theater. It is in this dissociated state between conscious and unconscious functioning that one might be open to hypnotic suggestion.

Psychoeducation is also a critical part of establishing a strong, trust-based therapeutic relationship. Communicating openly with the client about which approaches you are using and why will help the client to feel empowered as an active participant in the process, which can only serve to enhance the therapeutic outcome. In addition to psychoeducation, the client is told that although therapy will be heavily weighted with hypnotic interventions, not every session nor the entirety of any given session will be focused on strategic interventions.

Introducing the Tools to New Clients

Generally, I teach my clients a variety of focusing techniques, as it is uncertain which intervention will be most effective for a given individual. I always start, however, with Tiers 1 and 2 of the Toolbox because these are so critical for the client to learn to manage his or her over-reactivity outside the realm of my office. In most cases, if the client is comfortable with hypnosis, the quick interventions are combined with longer, more in-depth hypnotic trances. Deep trance work is used to elicit behavioral shifts, reinforce pattern interruption, or deepen the emotional connection in a relationship. These long trance sessions are typically audiotaped with the recommendation that the client listens to the tape daily. Further, the client is instructed to practice the quick self-hypnotic techniques at least three times a day and each time he or she finds him or herself triggered or anxious. The client is also provided with notes that delineate the steps of the tools. All of these ideas help to introduce a new client to this distinctive approach to therapy. Sometimes, though, you may want to integrate these tools within a well-established case.

Introducing the Tools to Established Clients

Therapists who have been using a more traditional talk therapy approach and who want to start using the tools will facilitate this shift by clearly introducing the tools into their ongoing treatment. In such cases, they might directly state to the clients, "I'd like to try something new today. Would you be open to experiencing a different way of handling your reactions (emotions, fears, impulses, etc.)?" If a good therapeutic relationship has been established, it is unlikely that the client will refuse to experiment with a new approach.

Checking In

As in traditional psychotherapy sessions, a typical session begins with a review of issues discussed in the previous session, as well as a report on what the client has been experiencing outside of therapy. Sometimes beginning the session with the question, "What's better since I've seen you?" helps the client focus positively on that which is going well in his or her life. The next step is to check in on the practice sessions that were previously assigned. The success of treatment is directly related to compliance with practice; therefore, it is vital that the therapist follow up on homework assignments. Once these more routine preliminary checks have been accomplished, you are ready to enter into the deeper, more pressing issues. I frequently begin with a direct question such as, "What do you want to accomplish today?" Once a goal is apparent, then the client is taught appropriate tools.

How to Manage Time When Using the Tools

When integrating the tools into a psychotherapy session, it is important to structure the session thoughtfully and with a mind to time constraints. It is necessary to save enough time for the client to rehearse using the newly learned tool, utilizing visualization techniques through which the client can actually imagine implementing the tool throughout the day as needed. The clinician will be provided with guidelines to promote the integration and transfer of skills in Tier 4 of the Toolbox.

The Art of Hypnotherapy

Becoming a competent hypnotherapist can take considerable time and practice. A practitioner's first step is to become familiar with the language of hypnosis and the artful use of the voice.

Learning Hypnotherapeutic Language and Delivery

Language

Hypnotic language, unlike good prose writing, is often wordy and repetitive. It is the goal of the therapist to establish a rhythmic, slowly paced yet flowing narrative through which the client is easily guided to elicit thoughts, kinesthetic sensations, or images, which facilitate healing and growth. The frequent use of ellipses in the application scripts denotes the numerous pauses taken throughout this calming, rhythmic narrative as the client both listens and responds to the therapist's suggestions. Clients' efforts are continually reinforced by the therapist with comments such as, "That's good" or "That's right." The therapist also uses multiple descriptors and repetitive elaborations of the desired response such as, "And I want you to notice how soothing . . . calming . . . and relaxing this feeling is . . . so very relaxing . . . such a nice feeling, isn't it?" The use of repetition to guide and mold the client's attention, emphasizing and reinforcing key themes that are suitable for hypnotic protocols would, in printed form, sound tedious and tiresomely redundant in normal speech. Just as the wording is distinctive in hypnosis, so is the use of the voice to deliver the message.

Delivery

When leading a client through a hypnotic script, the tone and modulation of the therapist's voice is just as important as the actual words being conveyed. I suggest that the therapist view his or her voice as a musical instrument through which he or she might convey a relaxed ease, comfort, confidence, and reassurance. Thus, the therapist should work on developing and fine-tuning a modulated, soothing voice to express his or her words. Listening to tapes and CDs of skilled practitioners can be helpful, as can seeking professional training with consultants approved by various national and international societies of clinical hypnosis (see the Appendix). Availing yourself of mentoring opportunities with master clinicians who will give you honest feedback on your work can also be enormously helpful. In my training and mentoring groups, I listen to the therapists practice and give detailed critiques on their word choice, as well as the use of their voice. Tape recording yourself reading the scripts of the tools aloud and listening to them repeatedly can also be helpful in providing feedback regarding your performance.

Utilization: Going with the Flow

The *utilization* principle encourages the therapist to view behaviors that seem to interfere with the therapy as qualities or behaviors that can be reframed positively and incorporated into the therapy (Erickson & Rossi, 1979; Gilligan, 1987; Hammond, 1990; Havens, 1989; Lankton, 1985; O'Hanlon, 1987; Rossi, 1980). Although I never had the opportunity to study with Milton Erickson directly, early in my career I had the good fortune of studying with some of his most ardent and gifted followers, including Bill O'Hanlon, Jeff Zeig, Steve and Carol Lankton, Steve Gilligan, Ernie Rossi, and others. I learned different and valuable lessons from each, but all instilled in me the crucial value of utilization to promote the successful outcome of a hypnotherapeutic intervention.

It is always important to honor and work with whatever a client presents and not "paddle against the river" by forcing the client to do something unnatural or uncomfortable for him or her. This is a very important part of the success of this approach. Whatever response the client presents needs to be framed as the right one. This decreases the possibility of engaging in a power struggle. Clients want to make sure that they are responding correctly. It is critical that you never make a client feel inadequate or shamed.

As with any art, some people have more natural talent than others. Many can learn the skills and strategies needed to play a decent game of golf, but not everyone is a Tiger Woods. However, there are personal qualities that can be developed to enhance success. Barber identifies these qualities as follows: ". . . confidence, vitality, enthusiasm, charm, benevolence . . . [and] the ability to induce affective states through the creative use of words" (1999, p. 40). However, even the most innately talented clinician must devote a significant amount of study, preparation, and dedication to become fluent in the execution of the interventions.

Customizing the Toolbox to the Individual Client

Individualizing the Scripts

Although the Toolbox provides specific scripts for therapists, readers are encouraged to use the tools as templates and to develop scripts that are individualized for each client. I have often found that even experienced clinicians falsely assume that a script in a published book is better than something they can develop themselves. In reality, the therapist has access to considerable data about the client that should be utilized in hypnotherapeutic communication such as the client's individual strengths, weaknesses, and emotional triggers. I encourage therapists to plan ahead before sessions and to make brief notes about what they have learned about their clients that can be incorporated into the scripts.

In addition to the planning, it is crucial that you attend to the moment-to-moment and often unexpected responses of the client and redirect the interventions accordingly. Immediate recognition and response to the client's verbal or nonverbal feedback gives the client the assurance that he or she is being listened to and that his or her responses are under-standable, valid, and respected. Challenge yourself to change course during the session. Watch your client with steadfast attention, being ready to move from one direction to another as you apply the tools. A skilled therapist traverses through a session like a river: when water meets resistance, it changes course and continues in one fluid motion toward its goal. As I have learned from Yvonne Dolan (1992), as well as from Steve and Carol Lankton's *The Answer Within* (1983), a clinician should be willing to dis-regard a plan (or tool) if it does not align with what the client is presenting at the moment. Rather, one should incorporate or *utilize* immediate verbal or nonverbal feedback from the client.

Individualization

The *individualization* principle of Ericksonian hypnosis asserts that incor-poration of the client's own language, values, and interests, as well as the observable responses he expresses in the hypnotic session, increase rapport and potentiate the therapy (Hammond, 1990). I encourage the clinicians who I train to attend to the following signs and then to utilize these obser-vations to further the hypnotic goal by adjusting their language accordingly:

Nonverbal Data
- body language such as tears, grimaces, etc.
- tone of voice

Verbal Data
- responses such as "No, not yet," "I can't visualize that," etc.
- unexpected responses

Prior or Inferred Data
- stories or anecdotes that he or she has shared in previous sessions
- personal history
- past successes and challenges
- values, both explicitly and implicitly expressed
- experience of being a parent or pet owner (if applicable)

The simple remembrance and incorporation of the person's unique features and biographical material can do much to create a sense of attunement that enhances the relationship. Utilizing bodily cues as they arise is also important as it communicates to the client that any response can be viewed positively as part of the hypnotic experience.

Incorporating Ericksonian Theme of Learning

Frequently in the scripts, I state that we are creating an opportunity to learn something new that will be helpful in overcoming reactivity. I also refer to past successful acquisition of skills to plant the idea that the person can indeed learn anew. Once again, this theme is inspired by the work of Milton Erickson who viewed therapy as an opportunity for new learning as well as a way of acknowledging the rich learning the individual has already mastered (Erickson, 1980; Havens, 1989; Lankton, 1983; Zeig, 1980).

What If These Skills Don't Come Naturally for the Therapist?

When I am teaching hypnosis, clinicians frequently ask me how they can learn this practice of remembering essential details and/or observing pertinent cues if they do not naturally know how to do this. Don't be afraid to state the obvious to your clients. Clients are often blind to their own pre-vious accomplishments and deaf to the voice of their own inner strength. By this I mean that the therapist, by nature of his or her external position, is better able to identify the client's strengths, bring them to his attention, and help him capitalize upon them. For example, a client was distressed about the recent arrest of her son for driving under the influence. Knowing that five years earlier she had successfully battled breast cancer, I said in one of our sessions, "You have already survived cancer . . . you've survived chemotherapy, you've survived radiation, your mastectomy, your hair loss . . . you know you can survive tremendous life challenges, so you can take a moment and get in touch with that survivor part of yourself that will give you strength to get through your son's arrest. . . ."

Again, I suggest obtaining audio recordings and videos of master hypnotherapists (see Appendix) and seeking individual or small group mentorship with a well-trained, skilled consultant. Finally, using the tools yourself, particularly the rehearsal tool, for just a few minutes prior to the session can help you to encounter the client with the most sensi-tive and intuitive part of yourself.

General Considerations in Teaching the Toolbox

The following section will cover important considerations that the therapist should attend to before introducing a client to the tools such as preparing for the session, structuring the session, and selecting appropriate tools.

Preparation

Klippstein called this phase "warming up" or "the process of getting tuned in ready for a humming start and a good run" (1991, p. 2). To elicit the most positive response to the tools, therapists should attend to the following preliminary considerations:

- positive expectancy (on the phone and in the first session)
- establishing rapport
- creating an optimum environment in the office: music, lighting, seating, etc.

Positive Expectancy

A well-executed initial session that results in positive expectancy on the part of the client is crucial in the treatment of all psychotherapy clients. Gafner and Benson (2003) noted the significance of the first session by aptly suggesting that we cannot help clients if they don't return to treatment. This initial session is particularly important for clients who suffer from anxiety because they tend to be reluctant to seek treatment in the first place. In addition, when they do reach out, they are typically in a hurry to reap quick results from therapy because of the great level of distress they are experiencing.

There are two factors that greatly impact the outcome of the first session: initial phone contact and the therapist's self-assurance. Informing clients in the first telephone contact that they can be optimistic about the outcome of the treatment can set the stage for positive results. All too often clients have suffered for long periods of time before their first contact with a psychotherapist and/or have been discouraged by prior ineffective therapy, so it is especially important that therapists provide encouragement with this initial contact. In addition, Erickson suggested that "a good therapist should be utterly confident" (Zeig, 1980, p. 61). A confident, self-assured manner in the therapist helps the client believe that she is in good, capable hands and therefore can expect that this therapist will indeed help.

Establishing Rapport and a Safe, Healing Atmosphere

Although rapport is essential for effective therapeutic work with any client, when using hypnosis, it becomes especially important. Closing the eyes, which is often suggested, creates vulnerability in and of itself. Simply turning one's attention inward and going "inside" can lower defenses. Anxious clients, in particular, are often vigilant and need to trust the therapist before proceeding. I have found that healing will not take place unless the client experiences a safe environment. This perspective is informed by my training in Imago relationship therapy, which emphasizes the importance of creating a holding environment or "container." Using the components of the Couples Dialogue (Hendrix, 1988), validating feelings and perspectives and providing empathy helps establish a climate of safety. I attempt to provide a safe container for the client from the first contact. In the initial session, I mirror the client's story with active listening. Then I validate her perspective and let her know that it makes sense that she is experiencing the symptoms given her particular temperament and life experiences. In view of the critical need to establish rapport and the necessity of thoroughly understanding the nature of the presenting problem, I usually do not introduce the client to the tools until the second therapy session at the earliest.

Creating an Optimal Office Environment

Ideally, one should provide a quiet environment to teach and practice the tools. My office environment, however, is far from ideal. It's off a busy road with heavy traffic, and my neighbors across the hall frequently make their cell phone calls right outside my window, so I am grateful for the utilization techniques that I have learned from my study of Erickson and from the teachings I have received from his students, including Zeig, Lankton, and O'Hanlon. For example, if someone noisily opens the door into the mortgage company across the hall, I might say to my client, "And you can open a door to the power of your intuitive mind to develop just the right words you will say to your wife. . ." In other words, I have learned to incorporate intrusive noises into the actual hypnotherapy. I also frequently use a conscious/unconscious split when confronted with extraneous sounds: "A part of your mind, your conscious mind, might be aware of the traffic, the voices in the next office, or people coming in and out of the building. But another part of your mind, your unconscious mind, is really not interested in all of that . . . it is much more interested in the words that I say that are most relevant to your needs at this moment in time."

I also play a specially designed musical CD in the background as I teach the tools. This audio CD muffles sounds and serves as a cue to the client that our work is beginning. I had the CD produced in collaboration with a music engineer who interwove alpha and theta waves with soothing music. It is called *Theta Waves II* (see the Appendix). I find that the music also serves as an excellent cue for me to elicit the right mindset to initiate my own focused attention and externally focused trance state.

I have also found that scent can have a powerful emotional impact. The proximity of the olfactory bulb, which mediates our sense of smell, to the amygdala and its intimate connection to other limbic structures lends credence to this view. Thus, the therapeutic experience can be enhanced by modifying the olfactory environment. I've experimented with using lavender in my office, which has been related to relaxation, and clients have responded positively. I encourage practitioners to be open to other environmental cues that can support the creation of an optimum therapeutic environment.

Tools

For home projects, we may need just one tool such as a hammer when hanging a picture. A more ambitious job, like replacing a door, might call for many tools such as a saw, a drill, a screwdriver, as well as a hammer. In the same way, a client may require one or more of the tools in any given session and/or down the road. I frequently employ a combination of tools in the scripts. For example, a practitioner could combine slow, deep breathing, self-soothing imagery, and supportive self-statements followed by a kinesthetic cue to anchor the experience. Even with the most thorough evaluation of the client's reactive style, it is impossible to know exactly which tool will be most effective in the long run for affect regulation. I encourage clients to bring a notebook to each session to record the techniques, and I usually make a statement like, "Long after you've successfully completed your therapy, you'll have a record of the tools that helped you in case you need to intervene in the future." That comment communicates the presupposition that they will indeed get better, that their improvement will be based on specific interventions, and that they will have tools to use later *on their own* if there is a temporary regression.

CHAPTER 4

Tier 1: Identify the Start of an Over-reaction and Respond Appropriately

═══════════

The tools in Tier 1 of the Toolbox are taught to all clients. Since identification and interruption of the over-reactive response is at the core of affect regulation, it is presented first.

Master List of Tools for Tier 1

Tier 1 includes the use of two tools:

- Tool 1: Recognizing Somatic, Cognitive, and Emotional Cues
- Tool 2: Time Out

These two tools are necessary precursors to teaching affect regulation. They are first taught in the office, but the intent is for them to be used consistently outside the office and to be incorporated into the client's daily life. The first tool trains the client to identify and interrupt the imminent eruption of an over-reaction. Pausing on a regular basis to give oneself an opportunity to calm down is of obvious importance. Intrinsic to most any psychotherapy is an opportunity to objectively reflect on one's reactions. Yet there is an implicit expectation for many clients that the psychotherapeutic process in itself will magically alter the immediacy of a reaction in their own lives. Therapists must challenge this erroneous expectation and tirelessly emphasize the importance of at-home practice.

Please note that Recognizing Somatic, Cognitive, and Emotional Cues and Time Out are used in tandem, but these are the only ones that are used in this manner. All of the other tools are typically either used alone or in a variety of combinations depending on the needs of the individual client. These first tools are typically performed outside the office once the client has been trained to interrupt and identify the start of an over-reaction. Both tools, however, may be used in the office if there is a spontaneous eruption of affect dysregulation. For example, an individual may suddenly experience sensations of panic, or a couple might quickly escalate in conflict. At that point, I might call for a time out wherein I direct clients to stop the process and recognize their cues such as tension in the body, catastrophic thoughts, or feelings of hopelessness. The chapter and page numbers following each tool refer to an example or mention of that tool's application later on in the book.

Tool 1: Recognizing Somatic, Cognitive, and Emotional Cues (Ch. 8, p. 130, GAD)

Goals
- Quickly identify and interrupt the somatic, cognitive, or emotional precursors of an inappropriate reaction, such as worry.
- Reframe these cues as opportunities to practice self-regulation and build in a regimented habit of diffusing tension.
- Develop a curious, nonreactive stance when the cues emerge.
- Prevent accumulation of anxiety from day to day.

Script
Somatic Cues
If you become aware of any sensations in your body . . . perhaps tightness, heaviness, or pain . . . just nod your head and say, "I'm aware that I feel . . ." (Wait for a response.) And now please put your hand on that part of your body that feels the sensation. You can just allow yourself to attend to the feelings in your (name body part) . . . allowing yourself the time to just observe, to notice with curiosity

. . . opening yourself up to learning to familiarize yourself with your body's sensations. And perhaps you can wonder what it is telling you . . . And as you feel your hand touching your (name body part), perhaps you might notice some soothing energy being absorbed just by that soft . . . or firm touch of your hand.

Commentary

When a person experiences anxiety, anger, or a negative cognition, there is an accompanying muscular tension in the body, an increase in heart rate and blood pressure, and sometimes, specifically with anger, an increase in body temperature. For this reason, I place special emphasis on the somatic component of the over-reaction. Even when a client identifies emotions or cognitions as his primary warning signs, I still use the time-out period to begin the process of identifying somatic cues to prepare for diminishing physiological arousal.

When trained to regularly scan their bodies for muscular tension, clients can intervene at the first sign of an over-reaction. All too often, people are unaware of their body signals and ignore this valuable resource that reflects their emotional states. In order to help the client to be sensitive to his body signals, I ask him to close his eyes and simply tune into the body. Note that the client is directed to put his or her hand on the part of the body that feels tension. The hand placement serves two functions: first, to heighten somatic awareness and second, to begin the process of self-soothing.

Script
Cognitive Cues

We all say words to ourselves when we find ourselves upset . . . and start to react or perhaps over-react to . . . (state the person or situation that elicits the over-reaction for that client). These familiar words and phrases (name the phrases the client often uses that he or she has previously identified as negative self-talk) can be used as warning signs, like the captions on the TV screen that warn of a snowstorm . . . they can warn you . . . advise you . . . that a time out is indicated. And you can acknowledge these warning phrases with a gentle, nonreactive welcome . . . as if to say, "There you are again. Come on in . . . we'll sit down and rest together."

Commentary

Marsha Linehan, developer of dialectical cognitive-behavioral therapy, which has grown out of the field of cognitive therapy, summarized common distorted or dysfunctional thinking, including such cognitions as "overgeneralizations," "catastrophizing," "magnification and exaggeration of the meaning or significance of events," and "pessimistic predictions" (1993, p. 123). A client can be trained to take a time out as soon as he or she identifies an overly reactive thought such as, "I can't believe this is happening," or "This is disastrous!"

Script
Emotional Cues

The following example comes from a couple's session. The client, Steve, is demonstrating that he has difficulty distinguishing thoughts from feelings:

CD: What do you feel like when Jill (client's wife) complains about your children's visits?

S: I'm feeling like she's making no effort to understand why it's so important for me to stay connected with my children.

CD: That sounds more like a thought. I wonder if the feeling behind the thought might be frustration, or discouragement, or sadness. So Steve, ask yourself, "What specific feeling am I having right now?" Are you scared, are you worried . . . depleted? (Pause.) Keep attending to yourself until you're able to name the feeling. (Pause.)

S: I feel frustrated, I feel disappointed in my wife, and I'm afraid that I might lose my daughter.

CD: That's right. You are frustrated, disappointed, and afraid. And now you can tell your wife directly these feelings (pause) so that she'll better understand them. And when you identify experiencing the feeling that often precedes a state of being out of control . . . not being your best self . . . acknowledge this feeling with appreciation that it is there to serve you . . . to remind you that it is time to take care of yourself again . . . to excuse yourself and take a break . . . recognize the need to take that time out . . . and practice your self-soothing techniques. And you can appreciate that you are learning something important today. You are learning to identify your emotions and how to express them. And how to take care of yourself when and if they are overwhelming.

Commentary

All too often, clients have difficulty discriminating thoughts from emotions and frequently need training in labeling their reactions. Hence it may be necessary to devote some time in the session to help them do this. As clients become aware of feelings such as sadness, anger, or fear, they are directed to excuse themselves and take a time out in order to utilize one of the tools from the Toolbox.

Tool 2: Time Out (Ch. 8, p. 130, GAD)

Goals
- Pause before reactivity escalates.
- Identify and relax muscular tension.
- Establish a habit of taking Time Outs as needed.

Commentary

An underlying theme of this book is that response patterns cannot be spontaneously altered unless individuals are trained to take immediate, interruptive breaks to identify the beginning of an over-reaction. This training allows individuals sufficient time to gain perspective and reevaluate their responses. I have termed this the Time Out tool. We often use this concept when dealing with small children who become overwhelmed by or feel a lack of control over their surroundings and begin to tantrum in response. The time out usually takes place in a small, quiet room or in a chair that is strategically placed away from the over-stimulating environment. When I teach adults to use the Time Out tool, I suggest that they find a quiet place such as their bedroom or a bathroom where they can separate themselves from the triggering stimuli and have the necessary time to interrupt an untoward reaction. It is wise to inform family members of the nature of the intervention so that they do not think it strange when the client takes frequent breaks in order to contain reactions and regain equilibrium. In my experience, once a spouse or partner understands the purpose of these breaks, they are generally supportive of the practice. With the Time Out tool, I am essentially telling the person to initiate a "cease fire" to the inner turmoil that will lead to affect dysregulation and could potentially escalate if not held in check.

It is difficult to know precisely which warning sign is most prominent for a given individual; indeed, the signs can vary under different circumstances. Typically, someone with an anxiety disorder is more likely to present with somatic manifestations, whereas an individual with relationship difficulties may be more likely to become aware of emotional reactions or negative cognitions. Indeed, the experience tends to be a chain reaction wherein agitation in the body leads to emotional dysregulation. This in turn leads to catastrophic thinking or any other variant of this recursive loop. Given the uncertainty of the reaction, it is wise to teach each individual all of the warning signals.

Once clients have successfully recognized the beginning of an over-reaction and taken the appropriate time out, they are ready to enter into Tier 2 of the affect regulation process. Tier 2 involves practicing some quick techniques to soothe the agitated nervous system and calm the mind. This psychophysiological calming is critical to the success of this course of treatment.

CHAPTER 5

Tier 2: Focus Attention, Calm, and Deepen

========

The following tools should be used during the client's time out after having recognized a somatic, cognitive, or emotional cue. Tier 2 is also used in the office to elicit a hypnotic state that will facilitate the learning of the affect regulation tools in Tier 3. These tools quickly focus the person's attention and calm the physiological arousal that accompanies affect dysregulation when triggered; however, benefits result from the practice of Tier 2 tools regardless of the person's immediate affective state. There are two components to Tier 2:

- **Focusing and Calming:** These tools help clients narrow and focus their attention on their internal experience, and when in the office, to the sound of my voice. Eliciting a calm state is the first goal of reversing the stress reaction.
- **Deepen:** This tool provides suggestions for deepening the relaxation experience to the point that the client is at optimal receptivity to the tools in Tier 3.

Master List of Tools for Tier 2

Focusing and Calming

- Tool 3: Breathing—Attending and Deepening Breath
- Tool 4: Eye Roll
- Tool 5: Arm Drop

Deepening

- Tool 6: Arm and Leg Heaviness
- Tool 7: Hand Warming
- Tool 8: Self-soothing Imagery, Safe Place—Nature Scene and Safe Room
- Tool 9: Stairway
- Tool 10: Elevator

The following tools are typically used by the client after he or she has focused attention and has begun to calm the nervous system. They are effective in providing a deeper level of relaxation. We will now examine each of the tools in depth, including goals, commentaries, and scripts. Chapter and page numbers follow each tool's title to refer you to a mention of or an example of that tool's application.

Tool 3: Breathing—Attending and Deepening Breath (Ch. 8, p. 131, GAD)

Goals

- Focus attention on the breath as a means of self-soothing.
- Use deep, calming breaths to elicit relaxation.

Script
Attending to Breath

Take a moment to focus on your breath . . . You don't need to change your breath, simply notice it, and as you do, perhaps you can notice sensations that accompany your breath . . . with a gentle curiosity, you can notice the texture of your breath, the rhythm of your breath, and even the temperature of the breath. And as you now take a deeper breath in and hold it for a moment, can you begin to experience a letting go of tension as you exhale? . . . That's right . . . and it can be such a relief to let go, can it not? . . . letting go, letting go of concerns, letting go of expectations, letting go of judgments . . . that's right.

Script
Deepening the Breath

Now take five deep breaths, imagining with each inhalation that you are breathing in comfort and with each exhalation that you are releasing any remaining tension. (Pause, watching and counting the client's breaths). . . That's right. Each breath leading you into a comfortable and pleasant state of relaxation. Each breath taking you into a deeper and deeper state of calm and comfort.

Commentary

Attention to and slowing down of the respiration rate is a simple but highly effective way to calm the nervous system. Rapid breathing is associated with increased tension and anxiety reactions. As the respiration rate intensifies, the body is less able to take in oxygen. Conversely, slow breathing is associated with emotional equilibrium and parasympathetic dominance. A gentle, nonintrusive tool involves training the client to simply attend to his or her breath without the need to alter it. The attending process in itself typically serves to slow the respiration rate. A variation to simply observing the breath is to slow and deepen the respiration volitionally. Both breathing techniques are very common hypnotic starting points and are drawn from the literature on mindfulness and breathing, as well as from Buddhist teachings.

Tool 4: Eye Roll (Ch. 10, p. 212)

Goals

- Interrupt an unwanted response or pattern quickly.
- Link a quick, self-hypnotic skill to other tools.

Script

Would you be willing to learn a very quick and effective tool that could help you to interrupt your reactions? (Wait for the client to nod or say yes.) Now I'd like you to stare up toward your eyebrows . . . that's right. Now take a deep breath in through your nose . . . hold the breath while holding the extension of your eyeballs. Good. Now see if you can hold your eyes upward while slowly fluttering your eyelids closed. That's right . . . and now relax your eyes and relax your breath . . . and just float inside. Floating . . . floating . . . perhaps to an image of yourself floating on an air mattress in a pool on a warm, summer day . . . or maybe you prefer an image of floating in a boat . . . a canoe . . . or a row boat . . . but then some people prefer imagining floating on a cloud . . . against the backdrop of a clear blue sky . . . I don't know what image is particularly pleasing to you, . . . but I do know that floating can be such a pleasant feeling, can it not?

Commentary

I have found that an adaptation of the eye roll from Spiegel and Spiegel's (1978) *Hypnotic Induction Profile* is a quick, effective tool to help the individual focus his or her attention, as well as to interrupt a negative response. Herbert Spiegel developed an eye-roll test as part of a way of assessing the ability of an individual to be hypnotized. The degree to which subjects can roll their eyes upward as they slowly close their eyes is correlated with their ability to be hypnotized. Specifically, the eye roll is a measure of the distance—amount of visible sclera between the lower border of the iris and the lower eyelid—exhibited when the subject simultaneously gazes upward as high as possible and slowly closes the eyelids (Spiegel & Spiegel, 1978). The eye roll is particularly useful for those individuals who are naturally able to create a strong eye-roll response. I only use this tool when the person is able to gaze upward with ease and does not report physical discomfort with the procedure. I typically combine the Eye Roll tool with images of floating; however, both the Eye Roll tool and the floating imagery can be used separately, as well.

Tool 5: Arm Drop (Ch. 10, p. 207)

Goals

- Master an easy technique to focus attention.
- Use visual and sensory cues to elicit self-hypnosis.

Script

I'd like you to extend your arm away from your body, elevated just about eye level . . . and as I continue to speak, I'd like you to simply stare at the surface of your hand. And now with your permission, I'd like you to pretend something . . . I'd like you to pretend that a bucket is being placed on your wrist . . . And we are going to place a pound of sand in the bucket . . . that's right. And as you imagine the bucket on your wrist, you can begin to pretend something else . . . that your arm is beginning to get heavy . . . Now I'm not sure when you will forget that you are pretending, and your arm will really start to feel heavy . . . but I do know that after a while anyone's arm can get heavy with the force of gravity. And let's help that heaviness along by pretending that we are putting more and more sand in the bucket until your arm becomes so heavy, so heavy, so that you can really feel the arm wanting to come down all by itself . . . and I wonder if you can wait to close your eyes until your arm is all the way down to your side, or if they are already closed . . . that's right. Waiting or not waiting to go all the way into trance until your arm is all the way down. Good . . . and doesn't it feel good to close your eyes now and go all the way down into a comfortable and pleasant state . . . now?

Commentary

The sand bucket image to increase arm heaviness was inspired by a demonstration done by Kay Thompson when she presented at the American Society of Clinical Hypnosis in March of 1995. It also appears in Klippstein's *Ericksonian Hypnotherapeutic Group Inductions* (1991). I have found it to be a focusing technique that virtually anyone can easily adopt. It incorporates an eye-fixation technique in which the individual stares at his or her hand. This leads to eye fatigue and produces natural heaviness that results from maintaining an arm elevation for a period of time. Both the eye fatigue and the arm heaviness together induce a relaxation response. As this process unfolds, the arm eventually lowers and the eyes close.

Tool 6: Arm and Leg Heaviness (Ch. 10, p. 197)

Goals

- Focus attention and deepen relaxation.
- Identify muscular tension.
- Release muscle tension with sensations of limb heaviness.
- Develop a passive acceptance of body responses.

Script

And so with your body and mind more relaxed, I'd like you to focus on your hands. And as you do, can you imagine that there are lead weights on your wrists? Lead weights making your hands so heavy . . . so heavy, and as they become so very heavy, you can feel even more relaxed . . . Nod your head if you can feel the heaviness. (Wait for the client to nod.) Even more relaxed than you were a moment ago . . . Perhaps your arms are getting heavy, as well . . . following that comfortable heaviness in your hands . . . And maybe that heaviness will spread to your legs . . . nice, heavy legs . . . so heavy that it would be difficult to move them . . . You could if you wished, but they can stay so nicely heavy and still.

Commentary

In developing the Arm and Leg Heaviness and Hand Warming protocols, I borrowed from the pioneering work on autogenics by Johannes Schultz, a Berlin psychiatrist and neurologist who investigated the use of auto-hypnosis exercises to promote relaxation. Schultz proposed that teaching an individual to create a feeling of warmth and heaviness throughout the session elicited a deep state of peacefulness that diminished the stress reaction (Luthe, 1969) Since arm and leg heaviness are frequently reported hypnotic sensations, it has proved efficient to elicit this feeling early on in the deepening tier of the Toolbox, Tier 2.

Tool 7: Hand Warming
(Ch. 9, p. 162, panic disorder)

Goals

- Control somatic responses.
- Deepen relaxation response with sensation of warmth.
- Quickly establish a cue for relaxation.

Script

As you sit in the chair enjoying the relaxation that you have achieved so far, perhaps you would enjoy deepening this experience simply by warming your hands. I'd like you to pay attention to your hands, and as you do, imagine that you are holding a cup of coffee or tea or even hot chocolate . . . Or some people prefer to imagine that their hands are submerged in nice, warm water . . . a bath or a shower . . . It really doesn't matter which image you use to create this sensation of warmth; all that matters is that you focus on your hands and simply be curious as to when the warm feelings emerge . . . And perhaps you might notice that one hand is warmer than the other . . . And when you do, you can communicate this awareness by nodding your head. (Wait for client to nod, and when he or she nods, reinforce with the following: "Good. Now see if you can make that hand even warmer . . . even warmer, and as you do, can you feel how relaxed you are becoming?" Long pause and then continue.) So relaxed, so calm . . . And you can look forward to using this tool of hand warming whenever you wish to deepen your relaxation response or even to initiate it.

Commentary

Warm hands are associated with a calming of the sympathetic nervous system. When the sympathetic nervous system is aroused, blood rushes inward from the extremities to vital organs. Warm hands, conversely, are associated with parasympathetic arousal and relaxation states (Moss, McGrady, Davies & Wickramasekera, 2003; Sargent, Green & Walters, 1972).

Tool 8: Self-soothing Imagery,
Safe Place—Nature Scene and Safe Room
(Ch. 8, p. 132, GAD)

Goals

- Gain mastery of anxiety or counterproductive impulses with self-soothing.
- Distract from worry by focusing on visual imagery.

Commentary

Clients are encouraged to develop a safe place to provide comfort and interrupt the reactive mind. See Brown & Fromm for excellent examples of soothing imagery (1986, pp. 96–98). The script that follows is typical of many guided imagery and hypnotic protocols that encourage the individual to access either a memory of a soothing place in nature or to create one in his or her imagination. The Safe Room imagery is another alternative to the Safe Place Nature Scene.

Script
Safe Place—Nature Scene

And so with your body and mind more relaxed, you may be able to focus your entire attention on developing an image of a pleasant and safe place, a warm, welcoming place that represents peace to you, and you can go there now, perhaps to a wonderfully sheltering, soothing place in nature. It could be a place you've been to or someplace you're creating right now.

And as you drift off to a safe place . . . look around. What do you see? What shapes and colors, what lighting? What smells do you notice? What do you hear? And as you experience this place with all your senses, it becomes more real. And as you float there, you can hold onto this feeling of comfort with all your senses, you can feel so good . . . so good, that's right.

Script
Safe Place—Safe Room

And in this comfortable state, this deeply relaxed state, I wonder if you can continue to use the power of your imagination to picture yourself walking down a hallway, and you see a door with a doorknob. And perhaps you can mentally sense touching the doorknob and turning it to open the door. And I wonder if you'd like to open the door and discover that you are entering a special room . . . a safe room, a retreat room. And you can look around this room, and as you do, you can enjoy decorating it so it will be especially pleasing and comforting for you. Take some time to decorate the room just as you'd like. You are the creator, the designer of this image, so perhaps you can take a special enjoyment in selecting the décor. Furnishing it however you like . . . just the right colors, just the right textures, just the right furnishings that are pleasing to you. And can you see the colors, hear the sounds, and feel the feelings you'd like to feel in this room? Look around your room. What captures your attention? And perhaps now you might like to sit down in a comfortable chair . . . or couch . . . or bed. Taking a special enjoyment in discovering how nice it is to sit or lie down and to rest. And as you mentally sense yourself resting . . . in this lovely room, you can experience a feeling of soothing comfort . . . and isn't it a pleasure to have a room of your own, to rest, to dream, to attend to a growing sense of peace . . . far away from your everyday concerns? And this is a room where you can begin a process of self-management that can change your thinking, change your reactions, and, little by little, change your life.

Commentary

At this point in the script, I add an anchoring technique that uses a cue word or symbol. (Anchoring is a component of Tier 3 of the Toolbox and will be described in this section.) See Grinder and Bandler (1976, 1981) for a clear exposition of auditory, visual, and kinesthetic images and anchoring techniques.

Script

And allow the deeper part of your mind to elicit a word or a symbol that will remind you of this place that you can use to revivify this feeling of comfort. And when this word or symbol comes to your consciousness, nod your head and tell me your cue. Find the little muscles around your vocal chords and tell me the word/symbol . . . and now use the cue word to go back to the safe room and really absorb the comfort.

Tool 9: Stairway (Ch. 8, p. 132, GAD)

Goals

- Associate going down a stairway with deepening the relaxation.
- Easily remember a deepening technique that is transferable to situations outside of practice sessions.

Script

And a familiar image to you is a stairway . . . you have gone down many steps in your lifetime . . . have you not? . . . So it might be easy for you to picture a stairway . . . And perhaps you can imagine a particularly beautiful stairway right now . . . I wonder what it looks like . . . if there's a nice, wooden railing . . . or a polished, brass one . . . or any other kind of railing of your own choosing . . . to support you when you descend down the stairway . . . in a moment or two . . . Perhaps there's a plush, lovely looking carpeting that's so soft to step upon . . . so soft and cushy . . . so luxurious . . . And it can be a pleasure to feel the texture of the carpet under your feet . . . And I wonder what design your stairway is . . . Does it go straight down in an orderly fashion . . . or maybe it's a circular stairway winding round and round . . . What pleases you? . . . Take some time to envision that stairway . . . It really doesn't matter what it looks like . . . All that matters is that you create a stairway that's pleasing in your mind's eye . . . and that you are open to allowing yourself to deepen your relaxation . . . as I count downward from 20 to 1 . . . Now imagine yourself at the top of the stairs . . . on the landing . . . and as I count downward . . . you can pretend that you are stepping downward . . . down the stairs . . . And I will count from 20 to 1 . . . and each number can be a cue for you to go even deeper into complete relaxation . . . And you can look forward to feeling even more comfortable . . . even more comfortable . . . beginning now . . . 20 . . . taking the first step down . . . perhaps feeling yourself gently floating down . . . And in an interesting and enjoyable way . . . you can experience a very relaxed feeling . . . floating like an autumn leaf in a gentle breeze . . . floating down into the chair . . . as you descend down the stairway . . . one step at a time . . . 19 . . . letting go . . . Easy relaxation moving into the shoulders and neck . . . 18 . . . 17 . . . 16 . . . allowing the shoulders to just let go . . . Allowing any unnecessary tension to simply melt . . . melt . . . melt away . . . 15 . . . 14 . . . 13 . . . breathing into the neck . . . letting go . . . letting go . . . letting a warm wave of relaxation . . . undulating relaxation . . . through the neck and jaw . . . 12 . . . 11 . . . relaxing . . . relaxing the little muscles at the corner of the eyes . . . allowing the temples to go limp and slack . . . allowing the forehead to just smooth . . . smooth . . . smooth all the way out . . . And 10 . . . halfway down and at least twice as relaxed . . . twice as relaxed . . . 9 . . . 8 . . . 7 . . . and now you can allow the muscles in your abdomen and stomach to relax . . . with the comfort spreading . . . spreading . . . spreading waves of relaxation . . . 6 . . . 5 . . . 4 . . . allowing the chest and upper back to go limp and slack . . . Giving yourself permission to simply let go . . . 3 . . . continuing comfort . . . shoulders relaxing . . . neck relaxing . . . so much of your body deeply . . . deeply comfortable . . . That's right . . . That's good . . . 2 . . . neck . . . gums . . . relax . . . lips . . . cheeks . . . relax . . . and we are almost there . . . almost all the way down . . . to 1 . . . 1 . . . 1 . . . all the way down . . . into that secure state . . . so completely comfortable . . . so at peace . . . so trance . . . formed. (Whispered)

Commentary

The stairway is a traditional deepening technique. Although it is not a particularly unique or creative tool, I continue to use it, as the image of going down a stairway is very easy for the client to replicate during home practice sessions. Note that there is an emphasis on the tactile sensation of the carpet under the person's feet and that muscle relaxation has been incorporated in this version of the stairway tool.

Although most people are comfortable with the image of a stairway, I have had clients who were physically or sexually abused in basements. For some of such clients, a stairway can be a trigger. So once again it is incumbent upon therapists to know their clients and their histories. As a regular practice, it is a good idea to ask if an image is comfortable for him or her before you proceed. Indeed, you needn't hesitate to ask if a particular image is OK, even once the process has begun.

Tool 10: Elevator (Ch. 8, p. 149, social phobias)

Goals

- Relax the sympathetic nervous system response and deepen the relaxation response by associating it with a descending movement.
- Establish an easily remembered deepening technique that is transferable to situations outside of practice sessions.

Script

I wonder if you can visualize yourself preparing to go into an elevator. Can you imagine standing in front of the elevator? The elevator door opens, and you walk into the elevator that you can design any way that you choose. It might have a bench or a brass railing . . . maybe it is paneled. Is there soft music piped in? As you turn to face the front of the elevator, the doors close, and you notice that the number 20 is lit in a strip of numbers for each floor mounted above the doors . . . and so, you prepare to go down ever so gradually . . . and as I count the floors down with you . . . you may feel yourself going down deeper and deeper into trance . . . more relaxed with each descending floor . . . and so I'll count now from 20 to 1, and as I do, you can notice the lights changing . . . 20 . . . 19 . . . 18 . . . feeling the motion . . . so gradual and pleasant . . . just like the pleasant feeling of relaxation you may notice coming over your body . . . 17 . . . 16 . . . 15, down . . . deeper and deeper and more relaxed. 14 . . . 13 . . . 12 . . . more relaxed with each descending floor . . . 11 . . . 10 . . . halfway down and even more than twice as relaxed now (slowing the counting and softening the voice) . . . 9 . . . 8 . . . 7 at ease, relaxed, deeper and deeper into trance. 6 . . . 5 . . . 4 . . . almost down now . . . deeper and deeper relaxed . . . 3 . . . 2 . . . 1 . . . all the way down now . . . deeply in trance.

Commentary

Like the stairway intervention, the elevator tool is a commonly used hypnotic deepening technique. Please note that references to several senses are included, suggesting that one might *see* the golden door, brass railing, paneling, or bench, *feel* oneself pressing the button, or *hear* the "soft music piped in."

Make sure prior to using this technique that the subject is not claustrophobic, acrophobic (fearful of heights), or anxious in any way about elevators. To determine whether or not a client has either of these phobias, ask the client directly if he or she is comfortable with elevators prior to using the elevator deepening tool.

The purpose of Tier 2 is to lead clients into a full, deeply relaxing state so that they are prepared to engage with the tools in Tier 3. The tools presented in Tier 3 meet six primary therapeutic objectives, can be used for a wide range of conditions, and can be combined in endless variations. Examples of these applications will be seen in the following chapters.

CHAPTER 6

Tier 3: **Healing Strategies**

═══════════

The most challenging part of hypnosis is the design and execution of the therapeutic intervention. I find that students usually master the induction and deepening phases of hypnosis with ease, but when they reach the point in the session where a shift to a healing modality is indicated, their fluency diminishes and they can appear awkward and self-conscious. They are often not prepared to introduce a therapeutic intervention that will specifically address the client's problem. In training groups, some students look at me, shrug their shoulders, and whisper plaintively, "What should I do now?" In other words, "What do I do once I get my client into a trance state?"

It is indeed in the middle phase of the trance, using the Healing Strategies affect regulation tools, that demands the most skill and artfulness. When a therapist is faced with a client in a therapy session, he or she needs to make quick decisions. Thinking on one's feet, both creatively and with precision, and coming up with a powerful intervention that specifically hits the target can be particularly daunting. The tools delineated in this tier can help make this challenging therapeutic task less intimidating. Becoming competent in this phase can take considerable time and practice, but there are a number of basic guidelines to help smooth the path. These tools can be taught to a client in the office but are designed so that he or she can do them independently outside the therapeutic setting.

The tools presented in this chapter are applicable to a wide variety of clinical challenges. To help make the applications of these tools clear in terms of how they can be used to treat particular conditions, each tool is followed by a chapter number and diagnosis or issue. Thus, you can easily reference the chapter that provides an application of the tool for a particular diagnosis or issue. For example, when you read about Tool 21 in this chapter, you will see "Tool 21: Dialing Down Reactivity (Ch. 8, p. 133, GAD)" as the title for the tool. This means that you can turn to Chapter 8, page 133 to see an example of how this tool is used for generalized anxiety disorder. In addition to applying these tools to specific diagnoses, the tools have been broken down according to the six primary therapeutic objectives listed below:

1. *Mindfulness:* Development of mindful, detached observation of transient affective states that allows one to become aware of a feeling as it occurs without judgment.
2. *Sensory Awareness and Cues:* Development of awareness of bodily expressions of stress and ability to regulate and modulate those expressions.
3. *Impulse Control:* Ability to quickly establish impulse control.
4. *Coexisting Affective States:* Ability to have two conflicting feelings or thoughts at the same time.
5. *Resource Utilization:* Ability to access resources that are either internal or external in origin such as positive memories, real or imagined support figures, comforting, safe places, and parts of the self.
6. *Positive Affect Development:* Development and maintenance of positive affective states.

All of the tools in Tier 3 fit under one of the six primary therapeutic objectives listed above.

Master List of Tools for Tier 3

A master list of the six objectives and all of the tools under each is listed below.

Therapeutic Objective 1: Mindfulness
Development of skills in mindfulness and detached observation of transient affective states that allows one to become aware of a feeling as it occurs without judgment.

- Tool 11: Mindfulness with Detached Observation
- Tool 12: Mindfulness and Releasing

Therapeutic Objective 2: Sensory Awareness and Cues
Development of awareness of bodily expressions of stress and ability to regulate and modulate those expressions.

- Tool 13: Sensory Alteration—Anesthesia
- Tool 14: Sensory Alteration—Breathing in the Light
- Tool 15: Sensory Cue/Anchor

Therapeutic Objective 3: Impulse Control
Ability to quickly establish impulse control.

- Tool 16: Thought Stopping
- Tool 17: Quick Impulse Control
- Tool 18: Tight Fist
- Tool 19: Self-statements
- Tool 20: Postponement
- Tool 21: Dialing Down Reactivity

Therapeutic Objective 4: Coexisting Affective States
Ability to have two conflicting feelings or thoughts at the same time.

- Tool 22: Juxtaposition of Two Feelings
- Tool 23: Switching Channels

- Tool 24: Sandwich Technique
- Tool 25: Alternating Hands
- Tool 26: Computer Screen

Therapeutic Objective 5: Resource Utilization

Ability to access resources that are either internal or external in origin such as positive memories, real or imagined support figures, comforting, safe places, and parts of the self.

- Tool 27: Imaginary Support Circle
- Tool 28: Parts of Self
- Tool 29: Watchman

Therapeutic Objective 6: Positive Affect Development

Development and maintenance of positive affective states.

- Tool 30: Age Regression
- Tool 31: Age Progression
- Tool 32: Gratitude

The following sections examine more closely the tools in each category with goals, commentaries, and scripts for each tool.

Mindfulness

Tool 11: Mindfulness with Detached Observation (Ch. 9, p. 163, panic disorder)

Goals
- Shift attention from the uncertainty of the future to present awareness.
- Eliminate self-criticism when negative emotions or thoughts emerge.
- Develop curious detachment.

Script
And you and I both know that emotions come and go . . . transient like a change in the weather . . . inevitably shifting . . . never constant. And because they are always changing, it might make some sense to learn a way of becoming less controlled by them . . . less attached to them . . . I wonder if you would like to have

an opportunity now to have a different way of attending to these changing feelings . . . experiencing the inevitable ebb and flow of emotions . . . without being engulfed or overwhelmed? (Wait for a nod; if no nod, ask if that would be OK.) So, in this moment, would you be open to learning a style of peaceful, nonjudgmental detachment that will allow you to respond differently . . . that will train you to experience emotions with less intensity? You can learn a simple intervention called mindfulness in which you'll learn to stand back and watch your feelings.

And . . . now . . . I would like you to remember a time when you were experiencing a feeling that was uncomfortable for you . . . (fear, anger, whatever the client has identified). And when you can identify that feeling, nod again . . . (Wait for nod.) . . . Good . . . and now I want you to amplify the feeling . . . let the feelings become more intense . . . just let those feelings come up . . . remember where you were . . . how you were triggered, what you were feeling and thinking . . . It is perfectly OK to let those feelings come up now in here . . . because they're going to go away in a few moments, and I'm right here with you . . . and so take all the time you need to remember a time when you were triggered . . . and when you reacted too strongly . . . Bring up the details . . . Let yourself experience that time again . . . right now . . . (Look for nonverbal cues.) . . . Good . . . you're doing very well . . . and, (client's name), I want you to step back . . . and simply observe the feeling . . . without judgment . . . without self-criticism or self-contempt for feeling this way . . . with acceptance . . . releasing judgment . . . like a detached observer . . . like a scientist observing an interesting phenomenon . . . just becoming aware and observant . . . being a kind of silent witness to your feelings . . . observing your emotions without reactivity or self-condemnation . . . And take a few deep breaths, that's right.

Now . . . take some time to notice what it feels like to be calm again . . . to be calm and . . . quiet . . . just letting your mind become focused . . . as you watch the developing stillness in your mind . . . and that stillness will come . . . sooner or later . . . if you watch your mind . . . watch your feelings . . . and just attend. You can be assured that these feelings, even those that are most difficult, will soften, become less intense, less significant.

Be patient with this practice . . . and sooner or later . . . you will become more skilled . . . and you can look forward to getting better and better at creating a comfortable shift in your style of reaction . . . to thoughts . . . to feelings . . . as you engage in an ongoing practice that will help you settle down . . . to be more in control and less reactive to the inevitable triggers that come up in all of our lives.

You will typically notice nonverbal cues indicating a relaxation response. If not, talk them through the following script:

Take a deep, calming breath . . . breathe through the uncomfortable emotion . . . and what do you notice now? (Wait for response and make reassuring comments like, "And I'm not sure when you'll notice that shift . . . when you'll be able to detach further . . . but I am sure as you practice . . . the feeling will inevitably soften and become less important . . . and I'm going to be quiet now while we create an opportunity for you to experience this healing on your own . . . And what do you notice now?" If the subject indicates that emotion is softening, reinforce that by saying, "Very good. . . ." If not, continue with breathing through the emotion, planting the suggestion that the subject will be able to detach in time.)

Discuss with the client what is going on in the trance, then reorient and discuss it further with them with their eyes open.

Commentary

The client is guided to observe thoughts and sensations through a neutral, non-judgmental perspective. Remind the client that attending to his or her feeling as it arises inevitably shifts or softens the feeling. Note that the client is encouraged to re-elicit a distressful reaction so that there is an opportunity to practice interrupting an untoward reaction in the session and replacing it with mindful, detached observation. Included is a suggestion that the person can now look forward to experiencing emotions without the fear of being overwhelmed by them. I encourage the reader to study the literature on mindfulness (Davidson & Goleman, 1977; Kabat-Zinn, 1990; Kutz, Borysenko & Benson, 1985; Linehan, 1993; Tolle, 1999).

Tool 12: Mindfulness and Releasing (Ch. 9, p. 164, panic disorder)

Goals

- Identify feelings.
- Reduce intensity of feelings through breathing.
- Release uncomfortable feelings.

Script

And now would you like to learn a simple yet powerful technique to help you diminish any intense feeling to manageable proportions? (Wait for a nod or other sign.) Simply say to yourself . . . "I am aware of my (say the specific feeling)." Now take a couple deep breaths . . . (pause while client is breathing) . . . and with your next exhalation, say to yourself, "I breathe through my (say the specific feeling)." And now say, "I release this (say specific feeling)." What do you notice now? (Continue with the mindfulness and releasing until the undesired emotion has softened.)

Commentary

This simple tool results in a diminishment in the intensity of a feeling very quickly. Ask the client to repeat the phrases after you as she fills in the blank for how she is feeling in the moment. Repeat until there is a softening of the over-reaction.

Sensory Awareness and Cues

Tool 13: Sensory Alteration—Anesthesia (Ch. 8, p. 139, GAD)

Goals

- Soften intensity of emotional reaction.
- Draw on tangible evidence that the mind can alter his or her response.

Script

As you sit in the chair listening to my voice . . . simply allow your arms to hang down beside you on the outside of the chair . . . that's right . . . making the necessary adjustments to promote your comfort . . . And as you sit with your arms hanging there . . . perhaps you can notice . . . the beginning sensation of a pleasant tingling . . . or inertness . . . or warmth . . . and with time, perhaps a comfortable numbness . . . And you might recall different ways you have experienced a pleasant . . . protective numbness in the past . . . and how your body often knows what to do . . . like when you have been out in the snow . . . a numbness might set in to protect you from the cold and discomfort of the winter . . . and many people have experienced that numbness with dental anesthesia . . . a temporary numbing that's OK to experience because it also protects you . . . and you know that the feeling will come back after the procedure . . . and then, of course, . . . everyone has had the experience of a hand or foot falling asleep, . . . and I'm not sure which imagery is more comfortable for you . . . and you can learn to harness your mind's ability to create those sensations . . . now . . . by recalling experiences . . . by focusing on the sensation of numbness . . . and can you feel it now? . . . (Wait for client to nod or say yes.) Good . . . very good . . . and just as you can elicit numbness in your hand . . . you can also numb your reactions . . . and so the next time that you notice (insert client's specific concern or objective such as irritation at spouse's driving habits) you can take a time out and quiet your mind . . . allowing yourself to recreate this experience of sensory alteration . . . simply by putting your arms down by your side . . . and creating just the right imagery that will help you re-elicit this protective anesthesia . . . which in turn . . . can help you be in charge of the intensity of your reaction . . . softening your reaction . . . perhaps not all the way . . . but just enough so that you can be more in charge of how you wish to respond . . . and your response is softer . . . quieter . . . less intense.

Commentary

This tool is most commonly used to diminish the perception of pain (Barber, 1982; Hammond, 1990; Kroger, 1977). It also can be an excellent intervention to help soften the perceived intensity of any emotional over-reaction. The inspiration for this tool can be attributed to the work of John and Janet Edgette (1995). In the script, the client is instructed in the development of sensory anesthesia in the hands. Once the client reports a sensation of numbness or tingling in either hand, then a link is made to psychological numbing in which he or she can numb or diminish the perception of emotional pain. (Note: this is not a good tool for clients with multiple sclerosis or carpal tunnel syndrome because it creates numbness, and numbness is already a primary symptom in these conditions.) In addition, this tool should be used with caution with clients who exhibit dissociative disorders. Since such clients often experience both physical and emotional numbing as a negative coping response, this approach may work against more pressing therapeutic goals. The Quick Impulse Control tool might be more prudent.

Tool 14: Sensory Alteration—Breathing in the Light (Ch. 11, p. 240, underentitled/ codependent issue)

Goals

- Enhance awareness of where the body holds tension when stressed.
- Calm the muscles as well as the nervous system through visualization.
- Deepen relaxed state by accessing a memory of comfort.

Script

Think of a recent upsetting event in your life that triggered a strong emotional over-reaction . . . one that was more than you were comfortable with . . . or was not in your best interest . . . And focus on this emotional reaction, letting those feelings come up . . . and nod your head when you feel that stress in your body. And now . . . scan your body to identify where you are experiencing your stress . . . and put your hand there . . . And now imagine a light in a soothing color emerge in front of you. The color doesn't matter; just allow the intuitive part of your mind to choose the right color for you . . . And now breathe in that colored light . . . and let it spread all around that area of the body where your hand is (pause 60 seconds). You can soothe yourself with this new tool . . . whenever you notice the tension or stress in any part of your body. This simple tool will help you . . . soften your muscular tension . . . and soften your response . . . enabling you to very quickly regain control and balance.

Commentary

This tool helps clients use imagery to diminish the stress response. Using a healing light is a common guided imagery suggestion (Battino, 2000; Gawain, 1978; Naperstek, 1994; Rossman, 2000). As was discussed in Tier 1 of the Toolbox, it is crucial that clients be trained to recognize the particular ways that tension manifests in their bodies. Therefore, this tool begins with a revivification of a recent memory of an over-reaction through visualization to provide an experience through which the client can first identify where he holds tension when stressed. I have found that suggesting that the person place his hands on the body part that feels tension heightens body awareness and increases the benefit of the visualization. Then the client may use visualization to alter his perception and move into a calmer state. This allows clients to self-regulate as they experience changes in somatic sensations.

Tool 15: Sensory Cue/Anchor (Ch. 9, p. 164, panic disorder)

Goals

- Quickly access a calm state.
- Signal to him- or herself that everything is fine or OK in the moment.
- Focus attention on the present moment.

Script

Take your thumb and forefinger of either hand . . . and make an OK sign. Whenever you feel your thumb and forefinger together . . . this can remind you . . . that you really are safe . . . and secure . . . and that everything is OK right now. And it can be comforting to know that you can use the OK signal in the future . . . when you need to remind yourself that you really are OK . . . that you do have the capacity to handle things in the moment . . . you can connect to this particular moment in time . . . enjoying sitting comfortably in the easy chair . . . right here in my office . . . and acknowledge the indisputable fact that you really *are* getting through this moment . . . and, of course, you will make it through the next moment as well. And you can remind yourself that you really are OK right now, aren't you? And each time that you return to this awareness of the present moment . . . even in times of turmoil . . . you will build your self-confidence . . . so that if you experience temporary imbalance . . . all you need to do . . . is to put your thumb and forefinger together . . . and acknowledge that in the moment . . . everything is OK . . . because it truly is.

Commentary

The OK signal is a reminder that in any given moment the client is indeed managing to handle what is confronting him or her. This Sensory Cue/Anchor can be used with mindfulness as a prompt that "anchors" the person back to the here and now (Grinder & Bandler, 1981). In addition, the Sensory Cue/Anchor can anchor a memory of a safe place (see Self-soothing Imagery tool, p. 72).

Impulse Control

Tool 16: Thought Stopping
(Ch. 11, p. 224, parent/adult child conflict)

Goals

- Interrupt intrusive thoughts.
- Utilize previously demonstrated successes in learning new skills.
- Use cognitive, visual, and kinesthetic tools to reinforce thought stopping.

Script

As you sit comfortably in the chair . . . listening to my voice . . . you are learning about how well you can manage your mind . . . You are learning this new skill of managing and controlling your reactions . . . learning this new skill . . . just like you've learned so many things before . . . You learned how to spell your name . . . and how to write it . . . how to ride your bike . . . and many other things (name things your client has learned that come from your knowledge of the client). Recently you learned . . . that there are a variety of strategies that you can apply to help you manage your life . . . but you may not know . . . that you can very quickly become a master of your thoughts . . . learning to stop thoughts that are not in your best interest. When you drove here today . . . you probably passed a stop sign . . . Take a moment right now . . . to visualize that octagonal red stop sign . . . with white lettering . . . and nod your head when you can see it . . . Now put that stop sign down beside you on the chair . . . and direct your mind to a worrisome thought . . . Let a finger come up . . . on your right hand . . . when you have it. Really let yourself feel . . . that tension and anxiety. Now bring your right arm up . . . as if you're stopping traffic . . . as you see that stop sign . . . and say to yourself, "Stop it!" Now take a deep breath . . . return to your safe place . . . and say to yourself, "Everything is OK right now" . . . because it is.

Commentary

Thought stopping has its roots in cognitive behavioral therapy (Beck, Emery, & Greenberg, 1985; Ellis & Harper, 1961; Meichenbaum, 1977). I've adapted this concept and included it in the Toolbox. My adaptation of Thought Stopping utilizes the visual cue of a stop sign, the kinesthetic cue of arm lifting as a signal to stop action, and a vocal cue verbalizing the words, "Stop it." There is a repeated theme that the interruption of intrusive thoughts is attainable. In keeping with this theme, there is a reference to both past learning and the implication that new learning is possible.

If the Thought Stopping tool is not immediately effective while teaching it in the office, suggest that your client repeat it in a waking state several times. Further, advise the client that he or she may need to practice several repetitions of the tool at home to successfully interrupt undesirable thoughts.

Tool 17: Quick Impulse Control (Ch. 10, p. 212, marital conflict)

Goals
- Quickly and easily interrupt a potentially destructive impulse.
- Master a combination of regulatory tools such as Focusing, Self-statements with Deep Breathing, and the Sensory Cue/Anchor.

Script
Try to imagine a specific time when you experienced that irritated feeling that comes when your (insert typical trigger that is problematic for the client, e.g., a response or behavior from the spouse, child, boss, etc.) does something to upset you . . . And can you let me know the person you've selected? Find your voice. OK . . . now allow that memory and that uncomfortable feeling to come . . . and when you're aware of this feeling . . . nod your head . . . and let yourself really feel the annoyance . . . the irritation . . . the tightening of your muscles . . . Good . . . that's right . . . and now Allow yourself to feel that impulse to react . . . to yell . . . to criticize . . . to lash out defensively to him or her (name partner or other person who is the object of scorn) Allow this feeling to come . . . without judgment or criticism of yourself for feeling this way . . . and let a finger come up when you can re-experience the feeling. (When client raises a finger, state the following.) Good . . . now take five deep breaths . . . and as you do, say to yourself, "With each breath in, I breathe in soothing comfort . . . with each breath out, I release frustration and expectations" (Repeat two to three times.) OK . . . good . . . now make an OK symbol with two fingers of one hand . . . and say to yourself, subvocally, "I am in control" . . . and "I choose to express myself in a soft and controlled way" (Repeat two to three times.) Now open your eyes and tell me what you notice.

Commentary
This tool is structured so that it can be used quickly to enhance impulse control and thereby interrupt a potentially destructive reaction. Clients are advised to

excuse themselves and go to a quiet place where they won't be disturbed. Sometimes just an abbreviated version of the hypnotic tools can quickly enhance self-regulation and the elicitation of intentional responses. At times just a moment or two of slow breathing or an eye roll can provide enough of a pause for effective pattern interruption. This tool was designed to interrupt a reactive impulse quickly. It is particularly useful for people who tend to respond defensively, critically, or contemptuously. Typically, I have clients practice the tool three times in a given session with instructions to practice out of the office any time they feel triggered. They may need to repeat the protocol three times or more until the impulse to react inappropriately is gone. As a post-hypnotic suggestion, offer that they use the OK symbol and state, "I am in control" when feeling out of control.

Tool 18: Tight Fist (See Ch. 9, p. 160, PTSD)

Goals
- Quickly discharge anxiety, fear, or worry.
- Quickly release muscular tension.
- Establish a sense of self-efficacy to manage over-reactions.

Script
Now imagine that all that uncomfortable emotion is going into one of your hands. Make a fist with that hand . . . squeeze it tightly . . . feel the tension . . . magnify it . . . tightening that fist even more. Tighter . . . tighter . . . good. Now allow that tension to become a liquid in a color of your own choosing that represents the distress . . . worry . . . anger . . . or whatever the uncomfortable feeling is that you experience in your body. Imagine that your fist is absorbing all of the colored liquid, all the fear, all the discomfort, that's right . . . (long pause). And then slowly . . . gradually . . . release the fist and allow the colored liquid to flow to the floor . . . to be absorbed under the floor . . . and further absorbed deep into the soil beneath the building . . . where it will be cleansed and released far away from you . . . Good . . . That's right . . . far away from you. And do you notice the difference between tension and relaxation? If you like, you can repeat squeezing the fist and opening it again . . . noticing the difference between tension and relaxation once again. Perhaps you may be pleased to notice as well that the discomfort is diminished or completely gone and how good you feel.

Commentary
I have found this tool particularly applicable to people who carry a lot of muscular tension, as well as to people who are too agitated to respond to some of the other tools. This tool employs the use of visualization to elicit the release of muscular tension. This tool is a variation of Calvert Stein's clenched fist technique

(1963) and bears some relation to Edmund Jacobson's (1938) progressive relaxation that suggests that one achieve relaxation by identifying tension in a part of the body, tensing it further, and then relaxing it. I apply the metaphor of releasing toxins and have found it is helpful to guide the client to visualize the earth as capable of absorbing the toxins and cleansing them.

Tool 19: Self-statements (Ch. 10, p. 207, marital conflict)

Goals
- Develop an assertive response to stressful situations.
- Develop appropriate supportive and positive self-statements.
- Recognize innate coping abilities.
- Enhance self-efficacy.
- Enhance self-regulation.

Script
In this relaxed, balanced, calm state of mind, you can hear and internalize a statement to remind yourself that you really are in control . . . it will give you a more reasonable view of the situation, the necessary perspective, to help you handle this situation in a way that puts you more in control. And as I state these words, I'd like you to repeat them subvocally, quietly repeating them to yourself after you hear me state them. (Vocalize the self-statement that fits best with the client's concern.)
- I am fully present in this moment.
- I can cope with this moment.
- I am safe.
- I choose to stay calm.
- I breathe through my fear (anger, irritation, impulse, etc.).
- I can handle it.
- I release judgment of myself.
- I release judgment of him/her.
- This is not an emergency; it is only anxiety.
- I can be uncomfortable and survive; I've been uncomfortable before and survived.

So now . . . say that phrase to yourself three times . . . (insert phrase), and as you do . . . integrate it . . . store it . . . put it in a mental file . . . for any time that this is exactly what you need to hear from yourself . . . (insert phrase) . . . and repeating such a phrase helps to reinforce it . . . to embed it . . . And now I am going to be quiet for a few moments . . . while you see yourself practicing the calming breath . . . repeating (insert phrase) and doing what you need to in order to embed it . . . to integrate it into your very being . . . You can continue to practice this self-statement whenever you feel triggered or whenever you're tempted to react impulsively. And isn't it nice to know that you can draw upon this simple statement and have it available whenever you need it?

Commentary

Positive self-talk is at the core of cognitive therapy. This tool was inspired by the seminal work of Barlow (1988), Beck, Emery, and Greenberg (1985), Burns (1981), Davis, Eschelman, and McKay (1992), and Meichenbaum (1977). In cognitive therapy, clients are taught to develop supportive self-statements that serve as alternatives to self-critical or destructive thoughts. Self-statements that reinforce a client's self-efficacy and self-regulatory skills can help enhance impulse control. Having already achieved a level of calm and focus, the statements are typically received with less resistance than they would be if they were spoken in an agitated state. I generally repeat aloud a given self-statement three times as repetition reinforces it and increases the likelihood that it will be absorbed. As I articulate the self-statement, I direct the client to repeat it subvocally as they hear my words. The list above includes examples of self-statements, but I encourage you to develop your own that fit the needs of your client. If you discover that your clients encounter road blocks in mastering positive self-statements, make certain that the statements selected are sufficiently credible to the client and are realistically attainable.

Tool 20: Postponement (Ch. 9, p. 179, OCD)

Goals

- Delay impulse to ruminate or react.
- Redirect obsessive thoughts.
- Create a time-limited window for engaging in obsessive thinking or compulsive behavior.
- Compartmentalize reactions such as worries, obsessions, anxiety, or grief.

Script

In this relaxed state . . . you have the mental elasticity to interrupt rigid patterns of behavior . . . and part of such rigidity is going over and over the same thoughts . . . which then blocks your ability to focus on the things you need to at that time. It is important for you . . . to connect to the part of your mind . . . that can choose what you wish to focus on . . . at any given time . . . just like you already have prescribed times to do other things . . . such as wake up . . . go to work . . . eat lunch . . . though it may vary from day to day. In the same way that you've developed the habit of doing those things at those times . . . you can create a prescribed time . . . to worry or obsess. Then you can have the freedom . . . to enjoy your day . . . knowing that at the end of the day . . . you have created a space in time . . . to focus . . . on the accumulated (insert what applies to client such as worries, fears, resentment, grief, or obsessive thoughts). You can even make notes for that later time . . . so that you can let go of the thoughts . . . and worries . . . now secure in the fact . . . that you can get back to them later (long pause).

Commentary
The ability to postpone a reaction or a behavior is a crucial life skill. In order to fully function in our lives, we need to compartmentalize our worries, our obsessions, or our grief over inevitable losses. Individuals with affect dysregulation and impulse-control impairments especially need to learn the practice of postponement. This tool was inspired by the work of Edna Foa and Reid Wilson (2001) who utilize postponement in the treatment of obsessions. The suggestion of mental flexibility is inspired by the writings of Michael Yapko (1990).

Obsessive thoughts function like the snooze alarm button on your clock radio. They often recur after you initially shut them off. Clients who are initially unsuccessful with this tool should be advised to practice the tool repeatedly in daily life each time the unwanted impulse or thought arises. As indicated in the script, the client can make written notes for a later time when he or she can allow themselves to focus on their worries, fears, or obsessive thoughts.

Tool 21: Dialing Down Reactivity (Ch. 8, p. 133, GAD)

Goals
- Calibrate appropriate level of reaction to life event.
- Visualize an image that will help "dial down" a reaction.
- Reinforce ability to diminish anxiety with self-statements.

Script
In your safe room . . . there is a desk with a large dial on it . . . a dial with a needle that points to your current level of tension [or reactivity] on a scale of 0–11 . . . and when you can see the needle registering on the dial, please nod . . . (client nods). OK . . . Good . . . And now . . . I want you to superimpose a shaded area . . . a zone of comfort . . . and also a red zone signifying excessive anxiety or tension . . . intense reactivity . . . Perhaps the optimal shaded range goes from 0 or no reactivity to 2 or 3 . . . just a little bit of tension needed to handle situations that arise . . . and the red zone is from 8 to 11 . . . and, once again, nod when you are able to visualize the dial with the two zones . . . (nods). OK . . . and, if the needle is not in that optimal range . . . if it's on a middle range number . . . or if it's in the red zone . . . can you utilize your power of imagination to dial the number down . . . to move the needle into that optimal

range? . . . Again, nod when you have been able to move the needle into that range . . . focus on your breathing . . . deep, relaxed breaths . . . waves of relaxation . . . slowing your pulse . . . lowering your blood pressure . . . moving that needle down into the optimal range . . . nod when you are there . . . (nods). Very good.

Now think of some event or situation that you are worried about or perhaps simply a stressor that is actually . . . in reality . . . just an inconvenience or an aggravation . . . yet you experience it as much more . . . with too much intensity. And now concentrating on the dial, notice what number the needle on the dial is registering. You can use the power of your mind to dial the number down to be in alignment with the right level of tension that this concern merits. You might even imagine also using your fingers to turn a knob to move the needle down to that desired level.

Your unconscious mind will advise you as to just the right level . . . of reaction this concern merits so that you can be effective, focused, yet relaxed . . . in control . . . It may be that no reactivity is in your best interest, or maybe you just need some emotional energy . . . to handle the situation with measured reactivity. Now slowly take three deep breaths. In and out . . . in and out . . . in and out, relaxing a little bit more . . . you become more, more, and more deeply relaxed and see the situation that was upsetting or worrying you, and you see the needle moving down now to where it should be. Can you notice how much more in control you feel?

Isn't it nice to know that you are in charge and that you can dial down your reactivity with the power of your mind? Sometimes the stress of an event or a relationship or some unavoidable challenge will come into your life, and you can be reassured to know that you can determine how much you'll react or even if you react at all . . . Now I am going to be quiet for a moment or two . . . while you see yourself practicing the calming breath . . . visualizing your quiet room with its desk and its dial . . . and seeing yourself intentionally dialing down as you continue to relax . . . and enjoy this experience . . .

Each time you dial down, it will become easier and easier to feel in charge. You can make a daily commitment to dial down your reactions, and as you do . . . you may say a supportive statement . . . You might say the phrase, "I am in charge of my response." Say that phrase to yourself now three times, and as you do, store it . . . integrate it . . . put it in a mental file . . . holding on to it . . . reinforcing it.

Commentary

This tool allows clients to calibrate the appropriate level of reaction to a triggering event. Brown and Fromm (1986, pp. 175–176) demonstrated the use of an "affect dial" to modulate the intensity of affect. Some life events call for an elevated response, such as preparing for an athletic event or a board exam, but we often react with far more emotionality than a given situation merits. The Dialing Down Reactivity tool helps the client determine just the right level of reaction. I employ this tool specifically for the many over-reactors I see in my office. Notice the use of the kinesthetic "using your fingers" and the use of color to calibrate the range of distress. (The complete version of "Dialing Down Anxiety" is available on audio CD. See Appendix.)

Coexisting Affective States

Tool 22: Juxtaposition of Two Feelings (Ch. 10, p. 209, marital conflict)

Goals

- Recognize that we all have available an alternative affective state.
- Elicit a feeling of "amusement" to help soften reaction to a stressor or trigger.

Script

You already know what it's like to live with extreme thoughts . . . and feelings . . . but when you pause . . . become still . . . as you are now . . . you have an opportunity to experience two feelings at once . . . and to acknowledge the inevitable truth that at any given time you actually have more than that one feeling . . . you can be afraid and trusting . . . you can be angry and forgiving . . . you can be irritated and amused . . . Take a moment now and simply be curious . . . as to whatever contrasting feeling emerges . . . right beside that upsetting feeling . . . that was so present for you just a few moments ago . . . and as you have an opportunity to access that second feeling . . . to allow yourself to experience the contrasting emotion that feels qualitatively different . . . and perhaps you can even enjoy this discovery . . . with a kind of gentle amusement . . . noticing how just considering the contrast can lighten or soften that first feeling.

Commentary

I have found that it is easier for a client who is in the throes of an intense reaction to access another feeling that serves to soften the reaction rather than to try to eliminate the troublesome reaction entirely. Yet when one is upset, it is easy to forget that there are other coexisting affective states. This tool is appropriate to use subsequent to the emergence of an over-reactive response that occurs in the therapeutic session or outside of the office. (This particular tool was developed initially as part of my work with Don, a client who will be introduced in Chapter 10.)

Tool 23: Switching Channels
(Ch. 8, p. 151, social phobia/social anxiety disorder)

Goals

- Develop an ability to have two disparate emotional states at once.
- Access alternative responses to a trigger.
- Use imagery to enhance positive self-perception and visualize an ideal response.
- Use imagery to soften and diminish negative self-perception.
- Enhance ability to be in control of affect.
- Increase flexibility of thinking.
- Develop an ability to reduce the impact of a feared emotional reaction.

Script

As you know . . . when you're feeling reactive . . . for example, frightened . . . worried . . . abandoned . . . irritated . . . or offended . . . these feelings can be so totally consuming. Some people say they see red . . . Others describe feeling the blood rushing to their head. It is very difficult to experience any other feeling when those reactions run high. Wouldn't it be nice to have a tool . . . to be able to soften . . . diminish . . . or even eliminate those reactions? It is . . . quite . . . possible to have a contrasting thought . . . feeling . . . or image of yourself emerge . . . right next to the excessive reactive feelings that don't serve you well.

I wonder if you would be open . . . to learning how to develop your capacity to experience two opposing thoughts or feelings at once . . . Let me show you how . . . Imagine that you're sitting in front of a large screen TV . . . imagine further that you have a remote control in your hand . . . that you can use to change the channels on the screen . . . Now, push "power" on the remote control . . . feel the tip of your index finger as is presses down on the power button . . . hear the click . . . and see the screen illuminate as the power comes on . . . Now, press the number one . . . and let yourself become more and more aware of a mental image . . . or even a partial outline of an image . . . that represents yourself when you feel out of control . . . Now push the number two . . . switching the channel . . . and a picture of your ideal self . . . retaining complete self-control . . . control of your reactions (insert details that apply to client's situation) . . . and hold that image. Let yourself experience how positive it is . . . to see yourself in this ideal way. (Pause for approximately thirty seconds.)

Now push the number once again and switch channels . . . to the image of your reactive self . . . This time the picture is blurrier . . . (do not pause long). Now, immediately push the number two and switch to the ideal scene . . . Enjoy zooming in on this image of your ideal self . . . while you let it become crisper . . . bolder . . . brighter (pause for one minute).

Now push number one again and see the image of the reactive response becoming smaller and blurrier . . . the color has faded . . . perhaps you see it in black and white now . . . Then, quickly, press number two . . . and once again . . . view yourself . . . your ideal self . . . interacting or responding the way you would most like to . . . hold that image . . . resonate with it.

And I'm going to be silent for a few moments . . . while you firmly connect to that ideal image of yourself . . . responding with containment . . . maturity . . . equanimity . . . (long pause), and I encourage you to practice this channel switching daily . . . so that you can look forward to using this Switching Channels tool automatically . . . reflexively . . . whenever you find yourself emotionally triggered . . . responding with excessive reactivity . . . that is not in your best interest.

Commentary

As in the previous tool, the goal of this tool is for clients to develop an ability to experience two disparate emotional states at once. Therefore, this tool begins with the dysfunctional response and gradually diminishes its intensity by pairing it with a more ideal, functional behavior. This tool is similar to the "Split Screen" intervention that has been used by Spiegel in the treatment of the sexually abused client (Lynn, Kirsch, & Rhue, 1996). Also see Brown and Fromm's Television Technique (1986, pp. 159–160). I have found, however, that it is easier for my clients to visualize a channel switch than a divided screen. This tool is especially good for highly visual clients.

Tool 24: Sandwich Technique (Ch. 8, p. 146, specific phobias)

Goals

- Diminish intensity of fearful or avoidant response.
- Increase tolerance of uncomfortable affective states.

Script

Now (client's name), re-elicit your safe place . . . that place you've experienced with me . . . in this relaxed state before. (Mention and repeat sensory details that he or she had delineated in Tier 2.) And, I'm going to be silent now . . . for a minute of clock time . . . while you enjoy this feeling of comfort. (Pause for one minute of clock time.)

OK . . . and now . . . remaining in this relaxed state . . . you can tolerate a whole range of other feelings . . . additional feelings . . . visualize an image of that scene that has been so troubling for you . . . and let those uncomfortable feelings bubble up . . . (Mention feared situation, object, or troubling relationship issue.) . . . rising to your awareness . . . like the bubbles in a bottle of ginger ale . . .

And raise a finger when you have that image . . . when those feelings enter your awareness . . . Good . . . Now . . . return to your soothing imagery . . . and layer it on top of your fear . . . anger . . . or whatever feeling you have . . . and let's see what happens . . . just notice what begins to change for you.

Now . . . hold these soothing . . . these comfortable feelings . . . and once again, we'll both be silent . . . and you can connect to a still, tranquil place inside of you . . . your safe, secure place you carry around with you all the time . . . to provide for softening . . . for healing . . . for the realization of the inevitable truth that we can have very different feelings . . . layer upon layer . . . like a sandwich . . . and just as the bread, cheese, or lettuce . . . tastes different by itself . . . there is also a different taste when they are assembled together . . . layer upon layer . . . blending into a taste that provides a more satisfying . . . and filling meal . . . and . . . similarly . . . at any time that you feel emotionally hungry . . . overwhelmed by strong emotional reactions . . . you can go fix yourself a Feeling Sandwich . . . more satisfying . . . more nourishing . . . more the way you would like to fix your life.

Commentary

Building an affect "sandwich" that alternately layers soothing affective states with uncomfortable affective states can effectively provide an experience for the client that softens an emotional reaction without entirely dismissing it. I developed the previous tool that guides the client to develop soothing imagery and then follows it by eliciting a feared situation or troubling interaction. (The metaphor of the sandwich may be troublesome for clients with disordered eating patterns and can be replaced with a different metaphor.) Daniel Brown uses an intervention in the treatment of trauma he also calls the Sandwich Technique, which has a similar conceptual focus (personal communication, October 31, 2006).

Tool 25: Alternating Hands
(Ch. 11, p. 230, adult child/parent conflict)

Goals

- Tolerate the juxtaposition of two opposing feelings.
- Know that there is always more than one feeling available.
- Experience the merging of negative and positive feelings.

Script

In your relaxed state, picture an image of that scene that has been so troubling for you and let those uncomfortable feelings come up. (Mention feared situation, object, or troubling relationship issue.) Raise a finger when you have that image and those feelings. (Wait for client to raise a finger.) . . . Good. Extend both of your arms out in front of you, bending slightly at the elbows with your palms turned upward, gently cupping the air . . . (Wait for client to do so.) Focus your attention on one of your hands, and as you do, place all of that uncomfortable feeling (mention anger, irritation, fear, avoidance, etc., as it applies to the client's troubling reaction) in one hand, wrap your fingers around it, and hold it (Wait for client to make a fist.) . . . Now focus on your other hand and place a positive feeling there and wrap your fingers around it (Wait for client to make another fist.) . . . maybe even the opposite of your negative feeling (propose a sample feeling such as forgiveness, tolerance, trust, courage, etc.) Now go back to the negative feeling in the other hand and once again return to the hand holding the positive feeling . . . Isn't it nice to know that at any time there is always another feeling and that you are always more than the negative feeling—always? . . . Now take the hand that is holding the negative feeling and release it along with that painful feeling.

Commentary

With the same objective in mind, I used the Alternating Hands tool to teach the client to tolerate the juxtaposition of two opposing feelings. The therapist can teach him or her to imagine holding the negative and overcharged reaction in one hand and the more contained and modulated response in the other hand. This kinesthetic tool is good for clients who have difficulty visualizing.

Tool 26: Computer Screen (Ch. 8, p. 150, SAD)

Goals

- Strengthen the ego.
- Replace negative cognitions with positive self-statements.
- Enhance relaxation response.
- Revivify a calm state quickly.

Script

In your relaxed state, picture an image of that scene that has been so troubling for you . . . and let those uncomfortable feelings come up. (Mention feared situation, object, or troubling relationship issue.) Raise a finger when you have that image and those feelings (Pause until the finger is lifted.) . . . Good. Use the power of your imagination to envision a computer in front of you . . . let me know when you see the computer by allowing a finger on either of your hands to lift. (Pause until the finger is lifted.) Imagine a statement typed on the screen that reflects your feelings. (Have client insert current feeling such as fear, resentment, irritation, etc.) Your conscious mind can be curious as to which negative self-statement will appear on the screen, while your unconscious mind will know just which self-statment is the most problematic for you . . . that needs some correction. The only requirement is that it be a thought that does not serve you. Let that finger come up when you see your problematic statement on the screen. (Pause until the finger is lifted.) What do you see? (Wait for client response.)

Now lift your right hand and pretend that you are pushing the delete button on your computer . . . let your finger come up when the statement is deleted. (Pause until the finger is lifted.) Good. In its place appears a beautiful image on the screen saver. What is that image? (Wait for client response.)

Commentary

The above tool is another example of how to teach an individual to replace negative self-statements with positive ones. Clients who are comfortable with computers have particularly enjoyed this tool. Note that it incorporates the visual image of a soothing scene as well as a kinesthetic cue of "pushing the delete button."

Resource Utilization

Tool 27: Imaginary Support Circle (Ch. 9, p. 171, PTSD)

Goals

- Develop a sense of not being alone when facing feared objects or situations.
- Recognize a network of real or imagined people or entities who care for one's personal safety.

Script

Sometimes we encounter a particular situation that is unsettling . . . or overwhelming (insert specific concern of the client) that makes us feel stressed, overly emotional . . . or alone. At these times, we sometimes forget that we can call upon resources to support us. Psychologists have now recognized that isolation can cause great suffering . . . and can worsen our emotional or even our physical problems. Everyone *needs* to call upon others for support. We can do that in a variety of ways . . . by connecting or reconnecting with our friends and family. Or by remembering people who have been important to us . . . or even imagining spiritual guides . . . or historical figures with whom we can connect.

Everyone has had people in their lives such as teachers, mentors, or supporters . . . who have been fundamental to their sense of well-being. You can draw upon those resources . . . even if they are not physically present . . . or even still alive to support you . . . Now return to your safe place, (client has already established a safe place) . . . Let me know when you are there. (Wait for a signal that he or she has re-elicited the safe place.) And as you sit there, notice someone of your choice who is very wise and kind walking slowly toward you . . . Let a finger come up when that first person is there (wait for finger signal). Good. And now bring someone else in the circle whom you associate with strength and courage . . . and let a finger come up when that person comes into your mind . . . Now I'm going to be quiet while you complete the group. It isn't necessary to think too hard about whom you wish to bring into your support circle. Just allow the intuitive part of your mind . . . that can emerge more easily as you continue to be still . . . and relaxed. You are also welcome to bring me into the circle if you wish . . . But you needn't do so unless it feels right to you . . . All that matters is that you listen to the intuitive voice inside you . . . to guide your selection of just the right people to be in your support circle. When you are finished assembling your circle . . . and have absorbed their support and guidance . . . raise a finger (long pause). Good. Now look around your circle and feel the support, wisdom, strength, genuine caring, and peaceful energy that each special person brings to your circle. And isn't it nice to know that you can return to your safe place and imagine your support circle anytime you need to?

Commentary

I am indebted to the work of Elgan Baker (1981) and Daniel Brown (1986) for their excellent self-object protocols. The Imaginary Support Circle tool could be viewed as a hypnotherapeutic approach to enhance object relatedness and object constancy. With this tool, the client develops an imaginary representation of supportive self-objects. Further, the client can retain the feeling of support that she or he experienced in the imagery when feeling distress.

There is one part of the protocol that should be done with careful consideration. It is important for the therapist to ask the client for permission to enter the safe place in which the imaginary support circle resides. It is not unusual that the client prefer that you remain on the periphery of the image. Indeed, the therapist's placement in the imagery or even exclusion can be important information regarding the development of the therapeutic relationship, as well as possible diagnostic information regarding the personality development of the client (Baker, personal communication, 1999). Typically, an ideomotor signal is used to indicate that it is safe for the therapist to join in.

Tool 28: Parts of Self
(Ch. 10, p. 198, marital conflict)

Goals
- Recognize innate ability to comfort more vulnerable parts of self.
- Identify a more mature developmental state with adult nurturing abilities.
- Increase access to adult parts of self.

Script

When you stop to think of it . . . we are all made up of many different parts, including those parts of us that are very young, adolescent, or adult, or parts that are mature, scared, or vulnerable. There are many different parts that reflect our developmental shifts . . . as well as our experiences. It certainly makes sense that when you are experiencing an uncomfortable emotion, you can access a mature, strong part of yourself . . . that can not only comfort the younger self but can take charge of situations in a reasonable, nonreactive, courageous way. There is always a part of you that is strong, balanced, and mature . . . even if you temporarily overlook it.

Perhaps it would be helpful to remember a situation that you were able to handle with equanimity and balance . . . when that part of you took center stage. So take a minute to get in touch with that part now . . . and let a finger come up when you can feel it coming to the surface. (Pause.)

Now wait for words to come from the wisest, most evolved, strongest, most enlightened part of your being. Maybe images . . . rather than words . . . will come to mind, but really feeling your strength, maturity, and compassion . . . look into the eyes of a younger, more helpless part of yourself . . . touch (his or her) hand and reassure (him or her) that (he or she) is OK and that you . . . the adult part of yourself will handle whatever needs to be handled.

Commentary

The Parts of Self tool is based on Ego State Therapy, which refers to a family of selves within a single individual. Typically, these parts represent varying developmental levels within the person. As was introduced in Chapter 1, Watkins appropriately termed these distinct parts of self "part-persons" (1992, p. 201). In discussing ego state therapy, Hammond wrote that one can "selectively amplify or diminish parts of his or her experience in order to achieve a higher purpose" (1990, p. 322). Frederick and McNeal (1993) also made reference to this higher, stronger, more developed part of the self. When a client is in trance, Ego State Therapy can be utilized to access the part of the self that possesses sufficient wisdom and maturity. This *part-person* can soothe and advise a more child-like part. Using the Parts of Self tool, the therapist can suggest to the client that it is indeed possible to mitigate emotional reactivity and regulate affect by accessing and empowering the most mature parts of the self.

Tool 29: Watchman (Ch. 9, p. 177, OCD)

Goals

- Acknowledge being in control of the hypnotic process.
- Honor the watchful, hesitant side of the self as an internal resource.
- Know that the observing, protective part of the self is accessible in the hypnotic state.

Script

I wouldn't expect someone with your kind of intelligence to immediately jump in with both feet until you are ready . . . until you are more certain of the process . . . and fortunately you have at hand a watchful, careful part of you . . . a kind of watchman . . . that you can always count on . . . that remains in the corner of this experience . . . watching . . . monitoring whatever happens . . . making certain that this hypnotic experience is in alignment with your needs and values . . . and that observing self . . . the conscious mind . . . can change my words or images seamlessly while the unconscious mind can notify the conscious mind if this transformation is relevant . . . and the conscious mind can give permission to your unconscious mind to change my words to your words . . . my images to your images . . . so you can really let go . . . trusting your ability to achieve this wonderful state of relaxation . . . allowing your conscious mind to drift . . . yet assured that you are in control . . . And it can be very reassuring, can it not . . . that this wise and adept observer of the process is there as a guide . . . as a resource when you need (him or her) . . . and as you become more comfortable . . . feeling more competent . . . trusting more and more . . . this observer can rest . . . and yet be on call if needed.

Commentary

Many clients have reservations regarding the hypnotic process. This is particularly true of those individuals suffering from anxiety disorders. Helping them to identify a "watchman" who waits on the sidelines making certain that the suggestions given are in keeping with their own imagery, themes, and values can be highly productive.

Positive Affect Development

Tool 30: Age Regression (Ch. 10, p. 201, marital conflict)

Goals

- Access past memories of self-assurance.
- Use sensory details to revivify memory.

Script

Go back in time (with children or science fiction enthusiasts, a time-travel machine is often effective) to when you felt particularly comfortable with yourself. Go to a time when you felt competent . . . and self-assured . . . and nod when you have an image in mind . . . of a specific scene . . . or a sense of yourself in a specific situation (wait for nod). Good. (Help the client elaborate and mirror back what you hear the client say, perhaps with some change in words and/or emphasis.) Use all of your senses as you relive this scene . . . in great detail. Feel yourself in that scene . . . and experience yourself as though you are right there . . . What do you see? Colors? Shapes? Furniture? Vegetation? Do you hear any sounds . . . or is it quiet? Are other people with you . . . or are you alone? If you bring others in, do they say something? Do you say something? (Long pause.) And what do you smell? Smells are a very powerful connection to memories. Is there a taste in your mouth? Sweet? Salty? Sour? (Again, use any details you've gotten from the client such as cookies baking, flowers, perfume, etc.) Do you feel anything with texture? Is it soft? Smooth? Rough?

Commentary

Age regression can be used to access forgotten memories and experiences. It is a commonly employed hypnotic intervention (Erickson, 1979; Hammond, 1990; Watkins, 1987; Weitzenhoffer, 2000). Age regression provides clients with an opportunity to imagine that they go back in time and enhance their awareness of unfinished business from childhood. This intervention also can help them to reclaim lost resources and memories in a current relationship. To revivify positive affective states with age regression, the therapist should direct the clients to remember a more positive time in his or her life (Edgette & Edgette, 1995); in a relationship, this would typically be early on before power struggles and conflict developed. They are encouraged to access a specific event that was particularly significant in its representation of their ability to experience joy and/or connection with another person. Both Phillips (2000) and Yapko (2003) contend that with visualization it is always advisable to use the senses to revivify the memory more compellingly.

For couples, age regression is particularly helpful when used with Harville Hendrix's (2005) Parent-Child Dialogue, which is an exercise to help couples understand and empathize with their partner's developmental wounding. Couples in difficulty can often have amnesia for their earlier sense of connection and joy with each other.

Tool 31: Age Progression
(Ch. 9, p. 165, panic disorder)

Goals

- Build positive expectancy regarding changes resulting from therapy.
- Experience the satisfaction of positive feelings elicited by imagining symptom relief.
- Incorporate the positive feelings into the present affective state.

Script

Drift ahead to a future time when many or all of the changes that you have worked on in therapy have come to fruition. Picture a screen . . . perhaps a TV or movie screen . . . and nod when you see the screen. (Pause for nod. If no nod occurs, tell client to take his/her time and alternatively suggest that he/she imagine writing in a diary, recording the progress that has been made.) Visualize some of the therapeutic changes you've been working on . . . see them in detail . . . I suggest that you use different senses to make the images come more alive . . . I can't know for certain . . . what you are seeing, but I do know that you have been working very hard in therapy and that change is possible . . . indeed almost inevitable . . . You need to trust that you are truly capable of great changes . . . So take some time to honor yourself for having the courage . . . flexibility . . . and persistence to do the necessary work . . . repeatedly and consistently using all the tools that have helped to bring about these changes. Now watch yourself on the screen . . . and allow positive feelings of satisfaction to emerge as you see yourself with new qualities, new behaviors or letting go of your behaviors that no longer work for you, new ways of reacting (mention current therapeutic goals). (Long pause.) I don't know if you're feeling pride . . . satisfaction, hope . . . or celebratory rejoicing, but you have every right to feel pride (if client has difficulty accepting compliments or allowing good feelings in other ways, consider using a metaphor here of a client who had this difficulty and was able to shed it, and for the first time in his/her life feel true pride and joy.) Record now what you have seen on the screen onto a video or DVD. (For clients who have trouble with the mechanics of recording, you might say, "The image will automatically be recorded; you don't need to be concerned about the mechanics of the process.")

Commentary

The hypnotic phenomena of age progression can be effectively used to assist clients in identifying their hopes for the future. The technique of age progression is attributable to Milton H. Erickson's pseudo-orientation in time (1954/1980). In a relationship, age progression can also help clients to experience the satisfaction that accompanies healthier interactions with their partners. It serves as a template for the couple; when one visualizes new behaviors, it is more likely that they will become manifest (Frederick & Phillips, 1992; Hammond, 1998; Torem, 1992; Yapko, 2003).

Tool 32: Gratitude (Ch. 8, p. 136, GAD)

Goals
- Shift focus from negative events, thoughts, or fears to the multitude of positive things present in the client's life.
- Diminish focusing on the future.
- Elicit positive affect.

Script
In a moment, you can give yourself an opportunity to feel better . . . right now and later on . . . because we're going to focus on gratitude. Many wise people have emphasized the importance of gratitude. In fact, Buddha is reported to have said, "Let us rise up and be thankful, for if we didn't learn a lot today, at least we learned a little, and if we didn't learn a little, at least we didn't get sick, and if we got sick, at least we didn't die; so let us all be thankful."

So you can use your imagination to shift your thinking in such a way that will surely, inevitably soften your fears . . . and increase your satisfaction with your life. Imagine a glass . . . Nod your head when you see that glass appear before you. (Wait for client to nod.) What does your glass look like? (Wait for response and mirror back what you hear to affirm the choice.) Good . . . What a good choice . . . a glass big enough to hold so many things to be grateful for . . . And out of all the things in your life that you are blessed with . . . I wonder which will come to mind first. When it does . . . just nod your head again. (Pause and wait for client to nod.) Now transform that thing for which you are grateful into a concrete representation that you can place in the glass. Perhaps you might write it down on a piece of paper . . . or select a symbol to represent the good thing . . . the good fortune . . . the resource . . . or the loved one. And I'm going to be silent while you enjoy the ability of the deeper part of your mind . . . to fill the glass . . . and enjoy those many things in life for which you are grateful.

Commentary
When a client enters therapy, we first address the immediate problem, the precipitating event or issue. It is important, however, to call attention to the aspects of a client's life that are going well, running smoothly, for which she can currently be grateful. By using the Gratitude tool, we provide an opportunity for the emergence of positive feelings that are brought forth when one focuses on appreciation.

CHAPTER 7

Tier 4: Behavioral and Practice Session Rehearsal

════════

Referring to yoga wisdom, internationally recognized yoga teacher Shakta Kaur Khalsa (2001) stated that it takes 40 days to change a habit, 120 days for the new habit to become who you are, and a thousand days to master the habit. My experience aligns with this reflection in that I have found that for most people it takes many practice sessions for habituated responses to change and for brain patterns to rewire. There is ample documentation to attest to the fact that a client's willingness to engage in therapeutic "homework" is directly related to the success of the therapy (Burns & Spangler, 2000; Coon & Thompson, 2003; Kazantzis & Lampropoulos, 2002). Yet many therapists have an ongoing, pervasive clinical challenge in trying to get clients to comply with directives to practice skills learned in therapy. To address this problem, the final tier of the Toolbox focuses on behavioral and practice session rehearsal. These are critical for the *transfer* of therapeutic learning, because without transfer, neither the client nor the therapist will achieve any measure of lasting success.

I have found that it is extremely important to direct clients to rehearse both their newly acquired behaviors and their practice sessions *while still in a hypnotic state in my office*. First, they visualize the behaviors and altered reaction styles they've learned in therapy, and second, they see themselves engaging in the practice sessions that they will do on their own at home. For example, one might recommend rehearsing the use of the Self-statements tool paired with deep breathing to help a client remain calm and centered in the presence of his or her intrusive mother-in-law over Christmas. Following the behavioral rehearsal, we would then rehearse the client's practice sessions that he or she will do at home. In other words, the client needs to practice practicing!

This rehearsal of the practice sessions is an essential part of Tier 4 and is a ritualized component of the session. In Tier 4, clients visualize an extended daily practice, mini practice sessions, and a number of scenarios in which he or she would be triggered and then successfully use the tools. For example, you might rehearse the use of the Imaginary Support Circle tool with the client if he or she is feeling stressed at work, dealing with a difficult child, or coping with a chronic illness. Another benefit of rehearsing the at-home practice sessions is that it initiates a commitment to using the tools as part of a life-long discipline. The positive effects of using skill rehearsal in therapy are known to many in the therapeutic community.

The concept of coaching a client through the rehearsal of new skills to facilitate transfer can be found in the work of several leading hypnosis experts, though they use different terms and different approaches. For example, Steve and Carol Lankton delineated the concepts of Future-pacing and Self-image Thinking Metaphors. These entail guiding the client to imagine interacting in a variety of contexts with the new behaviors associated with an altered self-image and "assisting clients in the process of rehearsing positive interactions and outcomes in feared situations" (1989, p. 212).

Klippstein referred to this part of the hypnotic protocol as "Future-Pace and Consolidation of Learning" when she said that "Direct or indirect post-hypnotic suggestions and process instructions may point to how transfer from the present work to future everyday reality may be achieved" (1991, p. 296). Again, just like with any of the tools, the actual hypnotic language used to take a client through such rehearsal is critical; therefore, a script guiding a client through rehearsal of the desired behavior is provided below.

Behavioral Rehearsal

Goals

- Visualize ideal behavior.
- Experience desired affective states.
- Rehearse self-talk that supports the desired response.
- Anticipate situations that will require use of the tools.

Script

And as you sit here in this chair, you can transport yourself over there . . . (have client state appropriate location where the desired behaviors will be expressed such as at home, in the office, or at a meeting.) . . . See yourself there now . . . and it can be interesting, can it not, to picture yourself there . . . and let a finger come up when you're there. . . . Good . . . And you can have a pleasant experience of seeing yourself in that situation responding in an ideal way . . . See yourself . . . responding . . . or perhaps not responding . . . just letting things slide off your back . . . seeing yourself as you would like to be . . . And hold that image for a moment. (Pause.) Good . . . And now I'd like you to have a pleasant experience . . . the experience of holding that wonderful feeling of being in control, of feeling calm, composed . . . forgiving . . . (elaborate, mentioning affective states, attitudes, or behaviors that are desired). Now let these feelings intensify . . . and really hold onto them . . . And I'm going to be quiet while you have the pleasure of holding these feelings . . . (Pause for one to two minutes.) That's good . . . And you know, what we tell ourselves is very important. We give ourselves thousands of messages each day. Wouldn't it be nice to give yourself a message to support this new behavior, this new response, this comfortable feeling? So right now, I'd like you to develop a phrase that you will say to yourself that will be supportive. (Give possible self-statements such as "I can handle it," or "I am tolerant and loving," etc.) Let me know when you have that statement. (Pause.) Good . . . Now once again I'd like you to see yourself in that situation(s) with (name circumstances) feeling those relaxed feelings while quietly repeating to yourself . . . words of support . . . messages of confidence . . . and let yourself enjoy saying these positive statements . . . that reinforce that you really can experience changes and appreciate those changes in the way that you interact with yourself and with others.

Once the rehearsal of behaviors has been conducted in the session, the next step is to rehearse practice sessions with the client while the client is still in trance.

Commentary

Behavior rehearsal is included at the close of every session. In the behavioral rehearsal, an essential component of Tier 4, the client imagines him- or herself facing the feared situation, the stressful circumstance, or difficult person with the appropriate affect, behavior, and thoughts. I typically include a multisensory approach that has been strongly influenced by the Lanktons' Self-image Thinking approach. To facilitate transfer, Steve Lankton suggests employing three sensory systems, visual, affective, and self-talk delineated in the four steps below (Lankton, personal communication, February 15, 2005):

1. Get the desired feelings.
2. See the self-image reflecting those feelings.
3. Hold on to those feelings while doing the fantasy rehearsal.
4. Add the sound track [self-talk].

My approach is similar in that I also use a multi-sensory system method. I first guide clients into a calm state and then link the feeling of comfort to the desired behavior enacted in their visualization. I then have clients see themselves interacting or reacting in an ideal way, holding on to the feeling of comfort. In addition, they are encouraged to evoke positive self-statements to reinforce the new behavior. Although it will be different for each client, there is a generic protocol to follow to lead them through behavioral rehearsal. The above script demonstrates how to walk the client through rehearsing the desired changes in the office. Each of the components listed above can be accomplished quickly while the client is in a light trance state but can also be completed after using a tool from Tier 3. It is most important, however, that the client be in a calm state in order to link that feeling of comfort to the desired behavior.

The Four Components of Practice Session Rehearsing

While the preceding section focused on the rehearsal of desired behaviors and cognition, this section will focus on integrating the tools into people's daily lives. We cannot expect that clients will automatically remember and incorporate the tools as they are needed. They must anticipate using them and visualize integrating them in their lives as part of their therapy sessions. There are four discrete circumstances for which I prepare the client to intervene with the tools. All four applications should be practiced by the client at both regular intervals or as needed.

1. **Extended Time Out** (20 minutes a day)
   During the daily time out, the client practices the tools from Tiers 1, 2, and 3.

2. **Mini Sessions** (1–3 minutes, 3–5 times throughout the day)
   These sessions incorporate the tools from Tiers 1 and 2 and do not require a formal time out. These sessions can be used to avert the immediate onslaught of a reaction that has been triggered, as well as simply to help establish a new preventative behavioral habit.

3. **When Triggered or Anxious** (length to be determined)
   These sessions incorporate tools from Tiers 2 and 3 when client is triggered or anxious and are used with a time out period. The duration of the time out will depend on how much time a particular individual needs to regain control, as well as the intensity of his or her reaction.

4. **When Triggered or Anxious but Unable to Take a Time Out** (length to be determined)
   These sessions incorporate tools from Tiers 2 and 3 when client is triggered or anxious and are used when the individual has neither the time nor the privacy that would allow for a time out period. The duration of the tool will typically be brief and will depend upon the person's circumstances when experiencing an over-reaction.

The following section outlines the goals for each of these four components and provides a commentary for each, as well as a sample script.

1. Extended Time Out

Goals
- Establish a time and location for practice sessions.
- Be more compliant with the notion of practice sessions.
- Anticipate and circumvent resistance.

Script
You and I both know that no matter how talented you are that you cannot become truly accomplished at a skill without practicing repeatedly. Every athlete or musician knows this to be true. (Utilize client's interests to support this theme and elaborate.)

I'd like you to take a moment to envision a time of day when you will commit to regularly practicing the skills you learned . . . here today . . . in our session. You can take a few minutes to connect with a part of you that really knows yourself . . . knows your schedule . . . your daily habits when you are engaged in your work . . . and with your family . . . when you are really too busy to practice . . . or when you just think that you are too busy. Yet, I suggest that you discover for yourself a space in your schedule for your practice sessions . . . And select a time when you will adhere to your practice sessions. And when the best time becomes apparent to you, allow a finger to come up . . . so I'll know you have selected the right time in your day for you. (Wait for client's response.)

And now you can select just the right physical space for your practice sessions. You can be curious as to just the right location in your home or office where you'll be undisturbed . . . where you find it soothing.

And once again, you can trust the intuitive part of you . . . to select just the right location for your practice sessions . . . And I wonder where you'll select . . . And again, allow a finger to come up when you've selected just the right setting for you . . . (Wait for a response.) And where is that? Find the little muscles around your vocal chords . . . find your voice, and tell me where that place is . . . and what it's like there. (Once the client describes the location, reinforce and mirror back the features of the place. For example, "That's right, see yourself sitting on that blue leather chair in your den with the cocoa colored walls and the plush carpeting on the floor . . . in those soft beige tones . . . feeling the chair supporting your body, embracing the quiet in the room.") And this will be your practice space.

Now most of us experience some resistance to starting a new habit. Sometimes this resistance is mild . . . easily overcome . . . sometimes it is strong . . . rigid . . . and requires some firmness and direction from a part of the self . . . that is more disciplined . . . just like a parent . . . or a teacher would use with a child . . . a student. A kind of gentle . . . moderate, yet firm guidance to help the more resistant part of you do what you know is in your best interest.

Now I am going to be quiet while you imagine placing yourself in the room you've selected to practice . . . at your scheduled time . . . with a gentle . . . loving . . . pressure that may be needed at first . . . but perhaps not later . . . once the habit of taking regular Time Outs . . . for the self-soothing you deserve . . . has been established . . . (pause). And visualize that satisfying practice session . . . now (long pause).

Commentary

I have found that the combination of at least one extended session daily along with the more quickly applied affect regulation tools, such as Quick Impulse Control or Mindfulness, is the ideal protocol to maintain emotional equilibrium. If a client is particularly agitated, two daily extended sessions are suggested. I advise the client to practice one extended session daily that is at least 20 minutes long (individualized audio tapes are provided to assist in this process).

The length of 20 minutes for a practice session is supported by a number of researchers and traditions. For example, Ernest Rossi (1991) emphasized the need for intermittent 20-minute breaks or rest periods to align the body and mind to what he calls our natural ultradian rhythms; he claims that if we attend to these natural rhythms and take at least 20 minutes to rest on a regular basis, this will restore us to optimal functioning and diminish the stress response. Twenty minutes a day is also the standard amount of time suggested by many different traditions to spend in meditation and other practices that bring about deep relaxation. For some, however, committing to 5 minutes a day, let alone 20 minutes, can bring up feelings of resistance.

Anticipation of the natural resistance to any new discipline must be considered and should be accompanied by guidance that is gentle and moderate yet firm from a parent ego state to help the person overcome the resistance to practice. One strategy to address this is to relate the learning of these skills to other life skills that mandate repeated practice such as playing piano or golf. For clients who remain resistant to incorporating practice, I have found that persistence and patience on my part has helped. When necessary, I have phoned clients in between sessions to encourage them to use their tools and to let them know that I am invested in their success. If non-compliance is a repeated pattern, one might consider referring the client to a life coach to work in tandem with the therapist. Even if the client appears to be resistant at first, the above script, presented to the client after a hypnotic state has been achieved, can often help to soften this initial response.

2. Mini Sessions

Goals

- Increase resiliency to stress.
- Counter the accumulation of stress from day to day.
- Habituate to calming responses in order to be less reactive when emotionally triggered.

Script

Each day you can create many opportunities to take short breaks to rest and to nourish yourself . . . And you and I both know that you work hard in your life . . . and that you really do deserve a break . . . several breaks indeed . . . each day . . . short breaks . . . that calm you . . . that quiet your mind . . . relax your body . . . soothe you . . . soften your senses . . . breaks that create stress resilience . . . to prepare you for the inevitable nervous tension that we all experience in our lives . . . And from my experience, it is more likely that you will adhere to the practice of incorporating these breaks if you link them to activities you already partake in . . . For example, (use an example drawn from something that you know about in the client's personal life). I know that you push a button to open your garage door when you leave for work each morning . . . and you push it again to reopen it when you return home at night . . . The time when you push the button to open that door might be a perfectly good time to open a door to yourself, as well, and to open up a moment . . . just a moment, for a few, slow, deep breaths . . . followed by a supportive self-statement . . . like, "Today I am in control of my reactions." . . . Now take a moment to visualize using one or two of the tools you have learned and applying them at regular intervals throughout the day. And you can be curious as to the activities that inevitably occur throughout the day that you can link with your mini breaks (pause). And what do you notice now? (Wait for client's response and reinforce.) That's right. You can practice your break each time you . . . (insert paired activity he or she has selected).

And now make a promise to yourself that you will stick to this practice of taking regular . . . soothing breaks every day . . . It has been said that life is practice, and so it makes sense that our lives become an accumulation of our practice. And you can look forward with pleasant anticipation to the rewards that will come to you as you incorporate this simple practice of taking short, regular time-out periods . . . for your benefit . . . your growth . . . your mastery of your body, your thoughts, and your feelings.

Commentary

In addition to the full, daily 20-minute practice, clients are encouraged to use a couple of the tools five or six times a day, spending as little as one to three minutes at a time. These mini breaks serve a prophylactic purpose, aiming to develop resiliency to stress, and are to be implemented whether or not the individual is agitated. I typically suggest that clients pair these mini practice sessions with a predictable, routinely occurring cue. For example, they might visualize their safe place along with a sensory cue before they eat any meal or snack. I frequently suggest that clients turn off their radios and cell phones in the car and practice slow, deep breathing and positive self-talk on their way to and from work. (They are discouraged from listening to hypnosis tapes or going deeply into trance while in the car in order to remain safely attentive on the road.)

3. When Triggered or Anxious

Goals
- Interrupt an inappropriate response within the context of a relationship.
- Interrupt a self-destructive behavior or impulse.

- Diminish anxiety such as worry, fears, panic, or obsessions.
- Cope with anger effectively.

Script

And sooner or later . . . you and I don't know just when . . . your emotional reactions will inevitably be triggered . . . and you can view these occasions . . . positively . . . as they are really opportunities for you . . . to become . . . a master of your own reactivity style . . . and what this means, very simply . . . is that each time you experience (insert typical problem, e.g., the body beginning to tense, becoming aware of judgmental thoughts about oneself or someone else, or a painful, distressing emotional reaction) . . . you can quickly apply a favorite tool that you have learned to be effective for you . . . to calm your system . . . and, once again, become the master of your reactions . . . and, so, in this moment in time . . . I'd like you to imagine . . . something . . . an occurrence . . . or a person . . . or a situation . . . that would typically elicit a reaction that is not in your best interest . . . and see yourself . . . practicing your favorite tool . . . see yourself doing that now . . . (Long pause) . . . And, now, allow yourself to feel the satisfaction that comes from honoring the importance of your own needs . . . and adhering to a disciplined practice . . . that will balance your inner being . . . balance your autonomic nervous system . . . and release fears . . . And make a promise to yourself . . . right now . . . a promise that comes from a deep place . . . of personal integrity . . . that each time . . . you are cognizant . . . of even the beginning of an overreaction . . . that you will commit to your practice . . . This is a process . . . a practice.

Commentary

The above script is designed to prepare the client to take a time out when he or she is triggered in the context of a relationship such as fighting with a spouse or feeling overwhelmed by kids. Additionally, a client might experience some type of overwhelming feelings that are not necessarily in the context of a relationship such as panic in anticipation of a job interview, excessive worry about the state of the world, or persistent fear of being in a car accident.

4. When Triggered or Anxious but Unable to Take a Time Out

Goals

- Select an appropriate tool for the desired response that can be used without a time out.
- Use an arsenal of tools discretely or in an emergency when circumstances prevent a formal time out.

Script

And we have worked on many tools together . . . tools for when you have time to really focus on altering your reaction . . . on increasing your sense of mastery . . . and others that require only a brief "circuit breaker" . . . for you and I know . . . that sooner or later . . . we don't know just when . . . your emotional reactions will inevitably be triggered . . . instantaneously . . . sometimes unexpectedly . . . quickly . . . likely at times when you are unable to excuse yourself to take a time out . . . maybe when there are other people around . . . or in some other way, you find that you don't have privacy . . . or perhaps you are in your car . . . stopped at a light . . . or you've pulled over . . . but need to continue rolling very soon . . .

At such times . . . in these kinds of situations . . . you can reassure yourself that you have learned several tools that you can use discretely . . . without anyone noticing . . . and quickly . . . Now I'm not sure if you'll select the (name the tools the person has mastered) or a modification of one of these . . . or another tool that I'm not mentioning. Take a moment to select one or two of these tools . . . Please let me know which tool or tools you have selected . . . (pause). Good . . .

And, so, in this moment in time . . . here and now . . . I'd like you to imagine . . . something . . . an event . . . an interaction with a person . . . or a situation that is typically uncomfortable for you . . . one that has . . . in the past . . . elicited a reaction from you . . . that was not how you would have ideally responded . . . that was not in your best interest . . .

And revivify that trigger . . . recreate it . . . experience it . . . (pause) but you recognize right then that you are not where you can take a formal time out . . . you aren't in a position . . . to use anything but the quick tool or tools you selected moments ago . . . so visualize yourself applying this tool . . . do that right now . . . (long pause). Good . . .

And . . . then . . . make a promise to yourself . . . right now . . . a promise that comes from a deep place . . . a place of personal integrity . . . that you will practice what you have just done . . . over and over again . . . so that you can be prepared . . . to automatically respond in this different way . . . using these tools . . . make that promise . . .

And, finally, I want you to picture yourself a few weeks from now . . . a month . . . or at some time you are looking forward to . . . and imagine that you have practiced using these tools . . . and that you are responding in a less reactive . . . more self-controlled way . . . and that you feel a greater sense of mastery . . . And allow yourself to feel the satisfaction of taking a more positive step . . . breaking a maladaptive pattern . . . providing yourself the opportunity to balance your inner being . . . to calm your autonomic nervous system . . . letting go of fears . . . of behaviors that can be used against you . . . and once again, honor yourself for adhering to a disciplined practice . . . give yourself credit for doing something that takes dedication . . . that's not easy to do . . . that requires discipline . . .

And (client's name), this is a process . . . a practice . . . one that becomes a part of your life . . . and will . . . in time . . . change your life . . . change your life in fundamental ways . . .

Commentary

Obviously clients cannot always take a formal time out every time they feel anxious or experience the start of an over-reaction. For example, someone may experience a panic attack while driving and may have to wait until he or she can pull over, or someone may be in the middle of a corporate board meeting and become extremely angry at a colleague. It is simply not always convenient or possible to leave every situation without creating additional stress. The advantage of the tools is that they can be used quickly and immediately without a prolonged time out or an extended session of self-hypnosis, although the ideal situation is to take a time out period.

Time outs give the client time to pause and gain perspective on a response and to give the body adequate time to calm and diminish the excessive autonomic nervous system response. If a client practices taking regular time-out periods, the brief tools will be paired with associations to these previously experienced extended calm states, thus re-eliciting the desired response more quickly and more easily.

Indeed, clients are instructed to practice quick tools any time that they are aware of the need for self-regulation, even when they are in a public situation without the option of privacy. For example, the Tight Fist from Tier 3 is sufficiently subtle enough to be used without drawing attention to oneself in a work or social situation. It will serve first to release tension and can then be followed by a few slow, deep breaths to relax the system further. Also, simply looking upward, a component of the Eye Roll, can quickly segue to the Self-soothing Imagery, Safe Place–Nature Scene and Safe Room from Tier 2. Sensory cues mentioned in Tier 3, such as touching the thumb and forefinger together in an OK signal, can also quickly remind the person that he or she is really OK despite transitory discomfort. Please note that the rehearsal scripts can be adapted as needed.

The above script might be an add-on to a trance following the behavioral rehearsal of a tool that requires extended time. It may also be a self-standing behavioral rehearsal after working on one of the brief tools during the session.

Conclusion

Chapters 4 through 7 have presented an array of powerful therapeutic tools that enable individuals to alter patterns of reactivity, something that is otherwise very difficult to accomplish in psychotherapy. Don't allow yourself to become discouraged if you don't have immediate and optimal results when using these tools. Mastery of the tools takes practice, both for the client and the practitioner. Be patient with yourself and be sure to take the time to rehearse using the tools on your own before using them with a client. In addition, I certainly encourage you as the therapist to experience hypnosis yourself before becoming a practitioner. This will help you become more sensitive to the subtleties and nuances required to be an effective hypnotherapist. Mastering delivery of the tools is one key to success, but knowing how to apply the tools to specific conditions is equally challenging.

CHAPTER 8

Application of Tools with Common Anxiety Disorders

═══════════

"I seem to worry about everything, the kids, the house . . . I wasn't always this way," said Melinda, a married, 25-year-old, full-time homemaker early in our first session. She sat at the edge of the chair, leaning forward as she continued. "I may have always been somewhat high strung. My parents said that I was nervous as a kid, but until recently, I certainly could function alright. But now I feel like I'm constantly on edge. It's especially bad when Rick, my husband, is out of town, which he is frequently . . . and I worry that my irritability and impatience is affecting the kids."

In addition to chronic worry, Melinda presented with a host of physical symptoms including abdominal distress, muscle tension, and occasional heart palpitations. The symptoms would quickly intensify to the point where she feared for her health and had an ill-defined yet intense fear of impending doom. And although she reported being chronically tired, Melinda had difficulty falling asleep. The heart palpitations prompted her to submit to a series of medical evaluations that revealed no organic basis for her complaints. Her family doctor concluded, "It's just your nerves, honey. Get some therapy."

The symptoms Melinda described are characteristic of someone who experiences generalized anxiety disorder or GAD. Born with an anxious temperament, she was now experiencing environmental stressors that intensified her anxiety. Indeed, it wasn't until life overwhelmed her with stress that her symptoms emerged. Melinda had good cause to be stressed: eight months earlier she had given birth to twin boys when her older children were only two and four years old. Her husband traveled for his work and was often away, so Melinda frequently found herself alone with four preschool-aged children. Further, the sleep deprivation she was experiencing as a result of her insomnia exacerbated her conditions.

Melinda is an example of the condition described by David Sheehan in his book, *The Anxiety Disease* (1986). Unlike Melinda's physician, who viewed her condition as purely psychological in origin, Dr. Sheehan argued that the constellation of symptoms that clients like Melinda present is, in part, biologically based. Sheehan is one of many mental health professionals who have recognized that anxiety disorders arise from a complex interaction of genetic, biological, behavioral, and environmental risk factors. Sheehan and others, including Barabasz and Watkins (2005), generally recommend a treatment strategy that integrates both medication and behavior therapy.

Great strides have been made in understanding anxiety disorders over the last few decades. For instance, we now recognize anxiety disorders as the most common type of psychiatric illness affecting both children and adults. According to the National Institute of Mental Health (2004), an estimated 19 million adult Americans suffer from anxiety disorders. Anxiety disorders are highly treatable with psychosocial therapies, medication, or both, yet only about one-third of those suffering from an anxiety disorder receive treatment. "The Economic Burden of Anxiety Disorders," a study commissioned by the Anxiety Disorder Association of America (ADAA) (Greenberg, Sisitsky, Kessler, Finkelstein, Berndt, & Davidson, 1999), found that anxiety disorders cost more than $42 billion a year, much of which is due to misdiagnosis. In fact, Americans are reported to have spent more than $22.84 billion in repeated visits to health care facilities, complaining of physical symptoms that turn out to mimic those of anxiety disorders. Individuals with anxiety disorders are three to five times more likely to seek out a doctor and six times more likely to end up hospitalized for psychiatric disorders than those who do not have anxiety disorders. Across the board, anxiety disorders are characterized by a perceived temporal disturbance. Individuals who suffer from anxiety are focused on the future, specifically *what could go wrong in the future*, to the degree that they cannot experience the here and now. Nor are they able to recognize the inevitable truth that they are indeed adequately or even successfully handling whatever life is presenting in the moment. This robs them of any experience of joy, satisfaction, or trust in their innate coping mechanisms. One objective of the tools in the Toolbox is to bring these individuals back to the present. In fact, one of the phrases that I use most frequently with anxiety disordered clients in hypnosis is "Everything is OK in this moment. Because it is."

Individuals with anxiety disorders tend to fixate on the future, suffering from *anticipatory* anxiety, which is experienced in two ways. The first is anticipatory anxiety that they experience before a potentially stressful event. The second is anticipatory anxiety specifically related to their fear of future manifestations of their symptoms. For example, individuals who have had panic attacks spend an inordinate amount of energy ruminating about if and when their next episode will manifest.

Different Types of Anxiety Disorders

Anxiety disorders may develop from a complex set of risk factors, including genetics, brain chemistry, personality, and life events. The following information illustrates the range, depth, and complexity of these disorders. Anxiety disorders that will be examined in this chapter include the following:

- generalized anxiety disorder (GAD)
- specific phobias
- social phobia/social anxiety disorder (SAD)

They are categorized in the DSM-IV-TR (APA, 2000) as follows:

Generalized Anxiety Disorder (GAD)

GAD is characterized by excessive, unrealistic worry that lasts six months or more; in adults, the anxiety may focus on issues such as health, money, or career. In addition to chronic worry, GAD symptoms include trembling, muscular aches, insomnia, abdominal upsets, dizziness, and irritability. The symptoms are severe enough to impair work and social and family life.

Specific Phobias

People with specific phobias suffer from an intense fear reaction to a specific object or situation (such as spiders, dogs, or heights); the level of fear is usually inappropriate to the situation and is recognized by the sufferer as being irrational. This inordinate fear can lead to the avoidance of common, everyday situations.

Commentary on Specific Phobias

People with specific phobias are particularly responsive to the tools in the Toolbox. It may be that individuals who develop phobias are particularly imaginative and hypnotically responsive by nature. Indeed, three different studies have indicated that those who develop phobias tend to be highly susceptible to being hypnotized (Fromm & Nash, 1992).

What may be presented as a specific phobia by the client can sometimes occur with co-morbid symptoms such as agoraphobia or panic disorder. These cases are often more complex than they initially seem. For example, a particularly common therapeutic consultation is for clients who fear expressway driving. Although clients typically focus initially only on the fear of driving on the expressway and the inconvenience the phobia causes in their daily lives, after a thorough assessment, we often discover that there is an underlying panic disorder and/or agoraphobic condition. The realization that one cannot quickly exit from the freeway is often the common thread of those suffering from this particular phobia.

The application of the Toolbox has led to mastery of fears of elevators, spiders, dogs, public speaking, flying, and driving for a number of my clients. One unusual case involved a man who was afraid of pigeons. He was planning a trip to Rome and anticipated that his phobia would interfere with his enjoyment of the city. I taught him tools from each phase of the Toolbox, with a special emphasis on kinesthetic cues paired with safe-place imagery and self-statements linked with relaxation responses. He called me after an enjoyable vacation and reported that he had felt neither anticipatory anxiety nor actual distress relating to the pigeons; he was able to appreciate the beauty of the fountains in Rome because he could finally look beyond the birds.

Social Phobia/Social Anxiety Disorder (SAD)

Social anxiety disorder is characterized by extreme anxiety about being judged by others or behaving in a way that might cause embarrassment or ridicule. This intense anxiety may lead to avoidance behavior. Physical symptoms associated with this disorder include heart palpitations, faintness, blushing, and profuse sweating.

Treatment of Anxiety Disorders

A variety of treatments can be used for treating the many aspects of anxiety. Treatment modalities include cognitive behavioral therapy (CBT), relaxation therapy, insight-oriented psychotherapy, hypnosis, as well as medication. Drugs used to treat anxiety disorders include selective serotonin reuptake inhibitors (SSRIs), tricyclic antidepressants, benzodiazepines, beta blockers, and monoamine oxidase inhibitors (MAOIs).

Why the Toolbox Is Helpful with Anxiety Disorders

Hypnotic focusing techniques can be especially useful with a number of different anxiety disorders. For example, the relaxation response in a trance state can be effectively paired with behavioral tools such as systematic desensitization in the treatment of phobias. Wolpe suggested that relaxation is incompatible with anxiety (1958).

Hypnosis also increases the effectiveness of cognitive behavioral treatment (Lynn, Kirsch, & Rhue, 1996; Schoenberger, 2000) and can help to alter cognitions. It is difficult for an individual to listen to his or her own constructive self-talk when he or she is overwhelmed with physiological arousal. Hypnosis can calm the person enough that rational, non-reactive, cognitive self-statements can be heard. For clients with inadequate emotional self-regulation, hypnosis can empower them to notice early warning signs and prevent full-blown panic attacks.

In terms of managing the many physical symptoms commonly associated with anxiety disorders, hypnosis focuses attention inward, thus assisting the client to note somatic symptoms. The client can be trained to observe somatic manifestations that were initially framed in a negative light with less reactivity. Hypnosis is also effective for the sensory alteration of uncomfortable physical or psychological feelings. For example, hypnosis may be especially useful for suggesting numbness to parts of the body to alter an individual's perception of acute or chronic pain. It can be effective for clients to reinterpret pain as a curious sensation or mild pressure. Edgette and Edgette, authors of *The Handbook of Hypnotic Phenomena in Psychotherapy* (1995), have used hypnoanesthesia to elicit changes in emotional sensitivity as well. Additionally, clients can elicit a dual perspective with hypnosis, thus helping them access a wise and rational side that knows that they can tolerate the transient discomfort of anxious episodes (Brown & Fromm, 1986; Frederick, 2005). This can be useful for anxious clients, as it is more realistic for a person to elicit another voice that is more metered and in control than to completely eliminate the worried part of the self.

Finally, the Toolbox can provide an opportunity for skill rehearsal. It has been suggested that when one practices hypnosis, one is being conditioned to activate newly learned response patterns in the future (Humphries & Eagan, 1999). In several of the hypnotic strategies that follow, clients are instructed in trance to rehearse cognitive tools or exposure to targeted situations in a calm and non-reactive manner.

Assessing Anxiety

When a client comes into treatment complaining of stress or anxiety, I first assess the prominent characteristics of the presenting symptoms. Current symptoms are observed and recorded. Below are some of the key actions involved with assessment:

- Rule out physical disorders, side effects of medications, and food and environmental allergies (see below).
- Identify dysfunctional behaviors that interfere with daily functioning and/or relationships.
- Determine problematic emotions.
- Identify negative thought patterns.
- Identify recurring or overwhelming body sensations.
- Identify problems with daily habits such as sleep, eating, etc.

In addition to these, a formal anxiety assessment tool such as the Beck Anxiety Inventory may also be useful. It is a brief, inexpensive, and thoroughly validated instrument developed by Aaron Beck (1990) and published by Harcourt Assessment.

Often Missed Yet Critical Aspects of Assessment

During the assessment, it is particularly important to rule out physical disorders that may be the source of the anxiety such as hyperthyroidism and cardiac arrhythmias. Mild food allergies that have previously gone unidentified can also be a compounding factor in the presenting anxiety.

I have found that all too often therapists fail to consider the client's use of prescribed or over-the-counter medications, psychotropic street drugs, or the daily use of other stimulants such as caffeine or nicotine. Such substances could exacerbate or even cause the symptoms of an anxiety disorder. For example, headache medicines containing acetaminophen and caffeine are frequently abused.

One of my clients dramatically illustrated the need to be watchful for the effect of medications. Clare is a 29-year-old single woman who presented with a rapid heartbeat, cardiac palpitations, irritable bowel, and generalized anxiety. When I reviewed her medications, she told me that she was taking four: one to slow her heartbeat, one to soothe her GI distress, one SSRI for her anxiety, and thyroid medication for a hypothyroid condition. At the end of the first hypnotic session, she reported that although she enjoyed the experience, her heart still raced during the session, she had palpitations, and she continued to feel "revved up." Curious about this persistent agitated response, I encouraged her to have her thyroid checked. She stated that her internist had recently checked it and that her thyroid functioning was normal. Nevertheless, I emphatically told her that I would like her to have it rechecked.

The next session, she informed me that her thyroid levels were at the toxic level and that her doctor had significantly reduced the dosage of her medication. Within a month, she was able to get off both her cardiac and stomach medication. Feeling much improved, she soon weaned off her SSRI and reported that she had no troubling symptoms of anxiety. Indeed, there was no indication that she continue in psychotherapy. I encouraged her to call me again in the future if she had troublesome symptoms but told her that she need not continue at this time.

I have also found that many of my clients whom I have diagnosed with anxiety disorders demonstrate a hypersensitivity to caffeine. Drinking a few cups of coffee a day seems in no way excessive to the average adult. For some individuals suffering from anxiety disorders, however, this can be too much. I have seen many clients' presenting symptoms significantly lessen when their daily intake of caffeine is curtailed.

Therapists should also be aware that clients are often in denial concerning the effect that drug use is having on their mental and physical well-being. In the event that a client is aware that his or her use of a particular substance is problematic, this vital information might be withheld until a greater trust is established between the client and therapist.

Assessing if Anxiety Is State or Trait

The terms *state* and *trait* as related to anxiety refer to whether or not the source of the anxiety is internal or external. Most people experience anxiety in reaction to sufficient levels of life stress. Spielberger (1969), recognized for developing the Spielberger Trait Anxiety Inventory, defined *state* anxiety as anxiety that occurs in response to threatening and clearly identifiable triggers. According to Sheehan, "Tension and symptoms of [state] anxiety occur only in response to immediate, clear-cut, identifiable stimuli. The onset of each attack is not very sudden or unexpected but [is] related to immediacy of [the] triggering stimulus" (1986, pp. 110–111). For example, anticipation of surgery would be likely to elicit anxiety for most people.

Trait anxiety, however, refers to an anxious temperament. It is a personality characteristic that remains stable over time, suggesting that there is no readily discernable trigger that elicited the symptoms (Spielberger, 1972). In such cases, individuals who are consistently sensitive and reactive may have a more biologically based condition. Melinda, for example, described herself as always having been high strung. In reality, individuals with anxiety disorders are usually able to identify a trigger, even if it is one that would not elicit the same reaction in others who are not prone to anxiety. For example, I knew one college student who started to worry persistently that the plants in his dorm room were not getting enough light. In other words, the anxiety will find a target, even if one is not readily available.

Treatment Goals

For each anxiety client, there is a set of predetermined treatment goals that I aim to achieve, although I also clearly adapt and individualize treatments based on each client's needs. Below is a list of common treatment goals for anxiety disordered individuals with anxiety disorders. At the end of treatment, the client will have:

- skills to interrupt negative, irrational, or obsessive thoughts
- mastery over self with ability to produce calming responses
- diminishment of worry
- elimination of fear of future anxiety reactions
- increased resiliency in face of short- or long-term stress

- diminishment of restlessness, irritability, and insomnia
- diminishment of somatic expressions of anxiety such as racing heart, sweating, and stomach distress
- hopefulness about recovery

Psychoeducation as a Critical Aspect of Treatment

A well-executed first session educates clients on the nature of anxiety and their own subtype of anxiety, clarifying the genetic and biochemical components of the disorder. Psychoeducation conveys to the client the three major components of the anxiety disorder: genetics, temperament, and environmental stressors. I begin treatment for all clients with psychoeducation, but it is especially important for anxiety-disorder clients. In fact, I see as much as a 20% decrease in anxiety symptoms immediately after the psychoeducational session because clients begin to relax upon hearing that they are not "going crazy" and that their symptoms are relatively common and treatable.

All too often, therapists treating anxiety disordered clients gloss over the critical aspect of providing thorough and targeted psychoeducation. I have found that this form of psychoeducation helps to normalize clients' experiences and validate their perceptions, thus mitigating the shame so often associated with their symptoms.

Genetics

It is rare that clients who present with anxiety disorders do not have a first-degree relative who also has or has had problems with anxiety. Current research indicates that inherited genetic tendencies play a role in establishing each individual's normative level of tension or anxiety (Eysenck, 1967; Gray & McNaughton, 1996; Leonardo & Hen, 2006; Middeldorp, Cath, Van Dyck, & Bloomsa, 2005). Some individuals are genetically predisposed to be more anxious than others. Clients need to hear that being overly anxious is no more their "fault" than if they were short, tall, blond, or brunette. This seems to normalize anxiety and reassures them that it is not a disorder that reflects weakness of character.

Temperament

The second component of the anxiety disorder that should be addressed in the psychoeducation phase is the role of temperament and the variability of people's responses to the anxiety. Some individuals seem to be more resilient and more determined by nature than others despite being saddled with an innate tendency to be anxious. As suggested by Aaron Beck (1984), recognized for his cognitive treatment approaches to anxiety and depression, differences in personality styles account for the varied reactions to stress. For example, Claudia, who suffered from panic disorder with accompanying specific phobias, had a fear of elevators. When asked how often she used an elevator, she said, "Every day. I work on the sixth floor, but I wouldn't quit my job because of my fear." Claudia grew up in a healthy, supportive family and had well-developed ego strength despite her anxiety disorder. Her fairly well-developed level of mental health and ego strength helped her to manage her phobia more effectively than a more fragile client might.

Stress

The third component of psychoeducation relates to the need to address the ubiquitous nature of stress in our culture and its impact on the anxious condition. The increasing sense of time urgency alone is creating burdens on our emotional and physical systems. The expectation that we be available 24/7 by cell phone, e-mail, or fax leaves us no time for rejuvenation. When the unexpected stress occurs such as a computer crash, a family illness, or a job loss, we are all subject to that stress, triggering any number of equally unexpected responses in us. There is truth to the notion that we find out what we're really made of when under pressure—quite often our deepest fears emerge in less than pleasant forms—and sometimes those fears take on a life of their own. The individual with an anxious temperament and genetic vulnerability is less resilient to the inevitable stress that we encounter. Thus, it is wise to advise the anxious client to be particularly careful not to take on too many burdens that may be unrealistic in view of her condition.

Case Study 1: Application of the Toolbox with Generalized Anxiety Disorder

Background

Donna, age 49, was referred to me by another therapist who had been seeing her for 18 months. The referring therapist had primarily been using supportive psychotherapy. Both Donna and her therapist felt that she had not been making sufficient progress in therapy.

Donna's natural, genetically based tendency to be anxious was worsened by an unsafe, chaotic family environment and poor modeling. She described herself as a scared, lonely child who felt unsafe and unwelcome in her family of origin. Believing that she was unwanted by her mother and being physically and verbally abused by her father, Donna grew up anticipating that harm would come to her. Her nervous system was on constant alert, vigilantly watching for danger. Without having had the benefit of soothing, nurturing parental figures, she failed to internalize a mechanism of self-soothing. In addition, a recent divorce after 29 years of marriage, an uncertain employment situation, and the departure of her 25-year-old son to his new home in Oregon had left her feeling burdened with financial responsibilities while experiencing isolation she felt incapable of handling.

Presenting Problems

The referring therapist reported that Donna suffered from generalized anxiety disorder (GAD); she was frequently overwhelmed by anticipatory anxiety, ruminating on possible personal catastrophes. Donna tended to be chronically anxious, but her tension escalated to intolerable levels if there was a tangible, perceived external threat to her safety. For example, the governor of our state had recently announced that there were going to be some cutbacks in state services due to a downturn in the economy. Donna, a state-employed auditor, suffered severe anticipatory anxiety as she waited to hear if she was going to be laid off. She reported poor sleep, chronic fatigue, and inadequate concentration. Physically, the anxiety was taking its toll as well. She reported a number of somatic complaints including headaches, irritable bowel, and intermittent, unexplained rashes. The constant release of stress hormones, chronic muscular tension, and repeated increase in respiration and heart rate are all somatic reactions to stress. This over-reactivity presents physiological challenges to the body which in turn lead to diminished immune capacity and increased vulnerability to systematic breakdown (Kiecolt-Glaser & Glaser, 1992; Rossi, 2002).

Treatment Plan and Clinical Considerations

Initial Assessment

When I assessed Donna, it was also my impression that she had classic symptoms of GAD. She was a habitual worrier, her focus regularly shifting from concerns about work and health to money and her children. She was generally pessimistic and anticipated negative outcomes to her concerns. There was a kind of temporal distortion in that many of her thoughts were focused on the future, thereby leaving her unable to enjoy present pleasures. In addition, she had numerous somatic complaints, including stomach pains and headaches. She reported that she had difficulty sleeping and was always fatigued.

Donna suffered from both trait anxiety and situational or state anxiety. Like most individuals with anxiety, Donna was born with a sensitive temperament, a genetic disposition that made her vulnerable to anxiety and depression. She reported that her mother had numerous phobias, was prone to anger, and had numerous psychosomatic complaints. She further stated that her maternal grandmother rarely left her home and may have been agoraphobic.

It could be argued as well that as with other anxiety cases that her anxious style could be learned behavior. Right from the womb, children are powerfully linked to every emotion a mother feels. If a sensitive child picks up on her mother's anxious emotional state, she might learn to mimic that just as she might learn to mimic angry outbursts or displays of patience.

Treatment Goals

- Develop proportional emotional reactions to triggering events.
- Diminish focus on the future.
- Develop self-soothing skills.
- Distract from worry by focusing on imagery.

- Diminish somatic expressions of anxiety through sensory alterations.
- Enhance positive thinking and development of gratitude.
- Focus on the here and now of daily situation.

In the first session, the goals were to normalize the anxiety reaction, validate and empathize with the stress Donna was currently encountering, and create positive expectancy. As this particular client seemed very fragile, it was essential to create a safe holding environment. An additional theme of this session was to alleviate any shame she carried in having the symptoms. It was also devoted to assessment and teaching her the basic hypnotherapeutic techniques of Tiers 1 and 2 of the Toolbox. For instructional purposes, a review of the goals for these preliminary tools is provided here but will not be repeated with each case in order to avoid redundancy.

Tools Used with Donna

Tool 1: Recognizing Somatic, Cognitive, and Emotional Cues

Goals
- Quickly identify and interrupt the somatic, cognitive, or emotional precursors of an inappropriate reaction such as worry.
- Reframe these cues as opportunities to practice self-regulation and build in a regimented habit of diffusing tension.
- Develop a curious, nonreactive stance when the cues emerge.
- Prevent accumulation of anxiety from day to day.

Tool 2: Time Out

Goals
- Pause before reactivity escalates.
- Identify and relax muscular tension.
- Establish a habit of taking time-out periods as needed.

Script
Donna, you and I have often discussed that you become upset very easily, particularly when you are worried about something that is not in your

control . . . You've learned in our work together that you often suffer unnecessarily by becoming very reactive . . . perhaps thinking that future situations would be unmanageable or that you would not be able to handle or cope with what may or not come up. You've learned that you are somebody who worries in advance . . . overestimating the likelihood that something bad will happen. We all say words to ourselves when we find ourselves to be upset . . . and then we start to react . . . or perhaps over-react . . . and you and I know you often say the words "what if" when you're worried . . . particularly about your job or your health. Sometimes, you notice your muscles get tense or your stomach hurts or you feel sad or scared.

These words and feelings in your body, along with your emerging emotions can be used as warning signs, they can warn you . . . advise you . . . that a time out is indicated. And you can acknowledge these warning phrases with a gentle, nonreactive welcoming . . . as if to say, "There you are again. Come on in . . . we'll sit down and rest together. We'll take a time out to calm down."

Commentary

Because Donna was a chronic worrier who experienced excessive anxiety, the importance of taking regular breaks to rebalance her system was emphasized. She was directed to listen to an audiotape each morning and to take a scheduled break every 90 minutes to practice one of the tools. The preceding script incorporated several themes of cognitive therapy, including overestimating the possibility of a bad circumstance occurring while underestimating her coping skills (Beck, Emery & Greenberg, 1985; Bourne, 1995; Burns, 1981; Yapko, 2003). The script suggested that Donna take a time out when she recognized cognitive, somatic, or emotional precursors to excessive reactions.

Tool 3: Breathing—Attending and Deepening Breath

Goals
- Focus attention on the breath as a means of self-soothing.
- Use deep, calming breaths to elicit relaxation.

Commentary

After teaching Donna how to use tools 1 and 2 from Tier 1, I led her through the first of the focusing and calming tools from Tier 2 to prepare her for the more specific tools from Tier 3. Donna was taught a standard, deep diaphragmatic breathing exercise to provide her with an immediate mechanism to diffuse distress. She was encouraged to be aware of her breathing and to note if she was breathing diaphragmatically, a more effective style of breathing associated with the relaxation response (Benson, 1983; Woolfolk, 1984). Her relaxation was further deepened with Tool 9, the Stairway.

Tool 8: Self-soothing Imagery, Safe Place—Safe Room

Goals
- Gain mastery of anxiety or counterproductive impulses with self-soothing.
- Distract from worry by focusing on visual imagery.
- Create an easily revisited context that will create a sense of safety.
- Have a venue for the Dialing Down Reactivity tool.

Script
And so perhaps you can imagine that as you are walking down the hallway, you see a door with a doorknob . . . And perhaps you can mentally sense touching the doorknob and turning it to open the door . . . And I wonder if you'd like to open the door and discover that you are entering a special room . . . a safe room . . . a retreat room. And you can look around this room, and as you do, you can enjoy decorating it so it will be especially pleasing and comforting for you. Take some time to decorate the room just as you'd like. (Pause.) You are the creator, the designer of this image, so perhaps you can take a special enjoyment in selecting the décor, furnishing it however you like . . . just the right colors, just the right textures . . . just the right furnishings that are pleasing to you. And can you see the colors, hear the sounds, feel the feelings you'd like to feel in this room? . . . Look around your room. And perhaps now you might like to sit down in a comfortable chair . . . or couch . . . or bed. Taking a special enjoyment in discovering how nice it is to sit or lie down and to rest. And as you mentally sense yourself resting . . . in this lovely room, you can experience a feeling of soothing comfort . . . And isn't it a pleasure to have a room . . . a safe and welcoming room of your own? And as you rest in your room, you can continue to go inside to that place of quietness, of safe solitude . . . safely alone with a voice guiding you along as you slide along more smoothly, deeply, more and more deeply . . . and you can rest . . . Yes, rest. Resting your mind, resting your mind . . . and the rest of your body . . . deeply down into the quiet . . . That's right. And now even deeper if you wish, and can you appreciate the stillness, the absolute stillness that allows you to retreat from the world in your room for a few minutes, which can seem like a few hours . . . ? This experience can give you the benefit of hours of rest. That's right . . . Donna . . . resting comfortably in your room.

Commentary

There are two aspects of this script to note. First, I chose to have Donna create an imagined safe room rather than trying to access an actual memory of a safe place because she had such a limited memory bank of positive experiences. Since negativity and self-pity about what she did not have in her life were so dominant in her personality style, an attempt to access positive memories might have elicited a resistant reaction and a worsening of the focus on what she was missing in her life. Therefore, a safe room was created to be used in conjunction with later tools. Second, note that kinesthetic awareness was incorporated into the script. Since Donna was particularly sensitive to bodily sensations, using kinesthetic awareness in a positive way seemed fitting. The suggested bed or chair or couch is comfortable. That goes along with an opportunity to create detailed visual imagery. The theme of rest was particularly important for this client, as she, like many anxious clients, had intermittent insomnia and was frequently tired.

Tool 21: Dialing Down Reactivity

Goals

- Calibrate appropriate level of reaction to life event.
- Visualize an image that will help "dial down" a reaction.
- Reinforce ability to diminish anxiety with self-statements.

Script

The following is an especially long script. Although it was presented as a whole unit to the client, I have subdivided it into three components for the benefit of the reader.

1. Identification and Diminishment of Reactivity

Now I'd like you to think of an event or situation, Donna, that has you worried . . . something that is coming up in the future that concerns you. Nod your head when you think of it. (Donna nods.) Good. And now let all those worried, tense feelings come up. And again return to your safe room . . . Let a finger come up when you can re-elicit the image of your safe room. And in that room is a desk with a large dial on it . . . a dial with a needle that points to your current level of tension [or reactivity] on a scale of 0–11 . . . and when you can see the needle registering on the dial, please nod . . . (Nods.) OK . . . Good . . . And now . . . as you think of this event, notice what number the needle of the dial is registering. And connecting to a very logical part of yourself, you might ask if the number is higher than it really should be? If so, you can utilize the power of imagination to dial the number down, dial the number down to just where you . . . when you really stop to really think about it . . . where you think it should be . . . where you would like it to be . . . to be in alignment with just the right level of tension that this concern merits. A less-reactive part of your mind, perhaps the deeper part of your mind will advise you as to just the right level of reaction this concern needs for you to be effective and focused and yet relaxed . . . It may be that no reactivity is in your best interest, or maybe you need just a little bit of tension to handle the situation . . . And now take three deep breaths slowly. In and out . . . Slowly in and slowly out. In and out . . . relaxing again and a little bit more. 5, 4, 3, 2, 1 . . . more, more, and more deeply relaxed and think about the situation that was upsetting or worrying you and see the needle moving down now, moving it down to where it should be, moving it down, maybe even sensing that your fingers are turning a knob that moves the needle down now. OK . . . and, if the needle is not in that optimal range . . . if it's on a middle-range number . . . or if it's in the upper zone . . . utilize your power of imagination to dial the number down . . . to move the needle into that optimal range . . . Again, nod when you have been able to move the needle into that range . . . focus on your breathing . . . deep, relaxed breaths . . . waves of relaxation . . . slowing your pulse . . . lowering your blood pressure . . . moving that needle down into the optimal range . . . nod when you are there . . . (nods) Very good . . . Dialing it down. That's right. And now nod your head when it's dialed down. (Wait for the nod.)

Commentary

Inherent in this tool is the flexibility of the client to adjust the reaction to just the right level of emotionality that is reasonable for the situation. It acknowledges that the client can connect to a logical, less-reactive part of the self: "And connecting to a very logical part of yourself, you might ask if the number is higher than it really should be." Note that kinesthetic suggestions, "maybe even sensing that your fingers are turning a knob that moves the needle down now," are used along with visual imagery to make the experience more vivid.

2. Self-efficacy and Self-statements

And isn't it nice to know, to discover, that you are in charge, that you can dial down your fears with the power of your mind, the power of your imagination? And from time to time, you may notice that the stress of an event or a relationship or some unavoidable challenge has come into your life, and you can be comforted to know that you can determine how much you'll worry . . . or even if you'll worry at all. And each time you dial down, dial down, it will become easier and easier to feel in charge, to be in charge. And you might say the phrase, "I am in charge of my response." Say that phrase to yourself now three times, and as you do, remember it, or you may choose another phrase that is exactly what you need to hear from yourself . . . So go ahead, and it really doesn't matter if it's my phrase or your phrase, just say your phrase now, three times. Repeating the affir-mation, "I am in charge of my response" helps to embed the suggestion and to reinforce it. And every event that is stressful or challenging provides you with an opportunity. An opportunity for you to practice your ability . . . to be in charge of your reactions, to dial down your reactions to an appropriate level.

Commentary

The preceding section of the script aims to increase self-efficacy ("You are in charge") and seed the possibility of change with phrases such as, "I don't know just when you'll start feeling you are more resilient, more resilient to life's inevitable challenges." Supportive self-statements such as, "I am in charge of my response" are first introduced to Donna in this session as part of this protocol to use along with the visual imagery.

3. Post-hypnotic Suggestions for Integration of the Tool

And you can take a moment now to anticipate practicing self-hypnosis several times a day. And particularly on those occasions when you can feel that your ten-sion level is higher than you wish . . . Now I am going to be quiet while you see yourself practicing . . . practicing the calming breath . . . visualizing your quiet room with its desk, with its dial . . . and seeing yourself intentionally dialing down, dial-ing down once again, and as you continue to relax, deeper and deeper into the stillness . . . and continue to learn more and more how to let your mind go still, rest quietly . . . and even luxuriate in the stillness. Take some quiet time now to just enjoy connecting with this wise, receptive part of you. (Long pause.) That's right. That's right . . . and it is particularly comforting to know that you have a tool that you can use whenever you wish . . . learning to use the power of your mind to change the way you think . . . the way you feel, the way you act and react . . . and inoculating yourself to handle whatever comes forward in your life. And sooner or later, I don't know just when . . . you'll start feeling you are more resilient, more resilient to life's inevitable challenges. But I do know that each time that you dial down your anxiety, you will connect to your innate ability of your mind to control your reactions . . . and you will continue to discover your emerging power to manage your emotions. (Pause.) Now you can begin the process of returning to normal consciousness. Perhaps you can move your fin-gers and wake them up a bit, followed by your arms, discovering that your arms can wake up, too. And when you are ready you can open your eyes and come all the way back . . . alert and refreshed and relaxed.

Commentary

Included in the intervention is behavioral rehearsal of practice sessions. I waited to use this tool with Donna until she was very relaxed. For clients who are highly susceptible to being hypnotized, it could be used without as much deepening. Note that this tool allows the client to determine how much reactivity the trigger merits each time he or she visualizes the anxiety dial. Please note that Donna was directed to rehearse her at-home practice, a component of Tier 4.

Tool 19: Self-statements

Goals
- Develop supportive and positive self-statements to counter catastrophic thinking.
- Enhance self-regulation.
- Use breath to diminish tension.

Script
With every inhalation, internally state the following phrase while inhaling, "I breathe in safety." With every exhalation, subvocally state the phrase, "I breathe out fear."

Commentary
The concept of developing supportive and positive self-statements was initially introduced in the previous protocol. In this session, a truncated version of the self-statement tools was presented to Donna as she took slow, deep breaths. Pairing new cognitions with breathing created a context that would facilitate the incorporation of a healing theme of safety. Because Donna had felt chronically unsafe since childhood, the words *fear* and *safety* had special meaning for her. As a result of living in a highly charged home environment as a child, Donna's body learned to remain in a state of hyperarousal, causing her to perceive a variety of daily threats as an adult in response to what many would consider mundane activities or occurrences. For example, she would typically get anxious if her paycheck was late, if her son didn't call, if she had an unexplained physical symptom, or if her boss seemed disapproving. I chose the self-statements, "I breathe in safety" and "I breathe out fear," paired with breathing, as a simple, concrete tool that she could draw upon easily, even at work.

Tool 32: Gratitude

Goals
- Shift focus from negative events, thoughts, or fears to the multitude of positive aspects of the client's life.

- Diminish focusing on the future.
- Diminish irritability.
- Elicit positive affect.

Script

When you really stop to think about it . . . gratitude is really not compatible with fear . . . because your worries seem to be about the future and gratitude brings you back to the present, doesn't it? Some time ago, Donna, I read a book called, *Learned Optimism*. It was written by Martin Seligman, the world's leading expert on explanatory style. Your explanatory style, Donna, is how you interpret life events. And in recent years, Dr. Seligman has been studying the differences between pessimists and optimists. His research has shown us clearly . . . what you and I know intuitively . . . that optimists have more satisfaction in life than do their pessimistic counterparts. Optimists are not only happier but healthier . . . And wouldn't that be nice for you . . . to begin to be happier . . . to be healthier? To have more satisfaction in your life? And did you know that research has shown that happy people live about eleven years longer than unhappy people? And you don't need a world-famous psychologist to tell you that optimists see life from a positive perspective . . . You are insightful enough to know the logic of the advantage of looking at things positively . . . And you know yourself well enough now to acknowledge that whenever you look at the resources that you have . . . your friends, your children, your home, or your intelligence with appreciation, you do start to feel better. And in a moment you can give yourself an opportunity to feel better . . . right now and later on . . . And won't that be nice?

So with your permission, I'd like you to use your imagination to have an opportunity to shift your thinking in such a way that will surely . . . inevitably soften your fears . . . and increase your satisfaction with your life. And I want to suggest to you to imagine a glass. You can be curious as to just what glass your intuitive mind will select. And nod your head when you see that glass appear before you. (Donna nods.) And what does your glass look like?

> **D:** A large brandy snifter.
> **C:** Good. A large brandy snifter, what a good choice . . . a glass big enough to hold so many things to be grateful for. And out of all the things in your life that you are blessed with, I wonder which will come to mind first. And when it does, just nod your head again. (Pause.) (Donna nods.) And now using that creative mind of yours, transform that blessing into a concrete representation that you could place in the glass. Perhaps you might write it down on a piece of paper or select a symbol to represent it . . . the good thing, the piece of good fortune, the resource, the loved one. And now I'm going to be silent

while you enjoy the ability of the deeper part of your mind to fill the glass . . .

Commentary

After induction and deepening, the client was told that anxiety was incompatible with gratitude. I then introduced the glass-half-full metaphor preceded by an introduction to the concept of optimism. Please note that I refer to Martin Seligman as an "expert" on optimism. This was done to join with Donna, as she was a voracious reader with a special interest in psychology. This is an example of Erickson's individualization principle at work. She was encouraged to envision her own glass and was reinforced for the choice she made. Note also the permissive language: "I wonder which (grateful thought) will come to mind."

Tool 14: Sensory Alteration—Breathing in the Light

Goals

- Enhance awareness of where the body holds tension when stressed, particularly muscle tension that accompanies high anxiety levels.
- Calm the muscles, as well as the nervous system, through visualization.
- Deepen into a relaxed state by accessing a memory of comfort.

Script

Donna, you've just been talking about how worried you are about possible cutbacks in the state budget affecting your employment. I'd like you to take a minute and focus on the worry. Let those worried feelings come up . . . all the way up . . . and nod your head when you feel the worry and experience the tension in your body that accompanies it. And now . . . scan your body to identify exactly where you are experiencing your stress, that tension . . . and place your hand on that place where you feel the tension . . . Good . . . and now imagine a light in a soothing color emerge in front of you. The color doesn't matter; just allow the intuitive part of your mind to choose the right color for you . . . Now I would like you to breathe in that colored light . . . and let it spread all around that area of the body where you placed your hand (pause 60 seconds). You can soothe your body and mind with the colored light at any time, whenever you notice the tension or stress in any part of your body, whenever you find yourself worrying or upset. This simple tool will help you . . . soften your muscular tension . . . and soften your response . . . enabling you to very quickly regain control and balance.

Commentary

As mentioned previously, Donna's anxiety was expressed somatically. Therefore, it was crucial that she learn to identify and alleviate psychosomatic tension quickly. I asked her to place her hand on the part of her body that felt the tension in an attempt to train her to become aware of just how much tension she held in her body. Suggesting that she could trust herself to choose the right color light in the visualization implied that she could rely on her intuition.

Outcome

It took about a month for Donna to schedule regular practice sessions. Once she did, her progress was significant. She was a quick student and learned to identify and interrupt her worried thoughts. Later in the treatment she was taught Tool 11, Mindfulness with Detached Observation, with the goal of helping her to experience how attending to the symptom inevitably softens its intensity. She was also taught Tool 13, Sensory Anesthesia, to further diminish somatic symptoms. At my suggestion, she joined a mindfulness meditation group, which not only reinforced the therapeutic teachings, but also served as a good social connection for Donna. She enthusiastically worked at becoming more focused on present awareness in her daily life. Donna has terminated regular treatment with me but schedules occasional appointments if she experiences any setbacks.

Case Study 2: Application of the Toolbox with Specific Phobias

Background

Sally, a 34-year-old, impeccably dressed woman, said, "You've got to help me get over my fear of needles." She told me that from the time she was a child she had been afraid of needles. Fortunate to have had good health, she generally avoided going to the doctor's office. She described herself as a determined, ambitious woman who had always achieved any important goal. She was a graduate of a prestigious East Coast law school, an employee in a large, successful law firm, and a happily married wife for the past five years. "This is so unlike me to have any fears much less such a juvenile one. I typically tackle anything. I was an athlete in college and a good student. I was raised to not let anything get in the way of my goals. I'm so embarrassed about this fear that I've hardly told anyone about it but my husband, my best friend, and now you."

It is always important to determine if there were any traumas related to the phobia. In Sally's case, she recalled one early event when she was about 12 going to the doctor for a pre-camp physical and blood was drawn. She began to cry as she recalled how traumatic the experience was for her. She remembered becoming dizzy, her heart was racing and she felt like she was going to faint. That incident was the last time she had exposed herself to needles. It is important to note that Sally's fear of needles, unlike the example of needle phobia given in Chapter 2, generalized from the initial blood draw to any type of injections or further blood work.

Presenting Problems

I asked her why she was seeking treatment now. She said that she and her husband had been trying to get pregnant for ten months and that her physician recommended that she get some blood work done to determine if there were any hormonal imbalances affecting her fertility. Her disappointment in not conceiving quickly was compounded by her anticipatory anxiety of any impending medical evaluation. Worse yet was the thought of actually initiating fertility treatment, which would involve repeated injections since the treatment of infertility necessitates injections that superovulate the woman.

Treatment Plan and Clinical Considerations

Initial Assessment

In the initial session with Sally, it was also important to rule out any medical conditions that may have been concurrent with the needle phobia. The fear of needles is not uncommon, however, it is not frequently addressed clinically. For example, *vasovagal reflex reaction*, a reflex of the involuntary nervous system that slows down the heart and causes fainting, happens on occasion with exposure to needles. In this case, unlike most other phobias, exposure therapy can lead to an actual medical problem such as fainting. Although a *vasovagal faint* is typically not serious, it is important that clients disclose their phobia to their doctors and other medical staff. A client wouldn't know if he or she were going to have this response, but the professionals should be prepared just in case. Sally reported that recent visits with her ob-gyn revealed no problems other than her as yet to be explained basis for infertility. She stated she had never had any fainting episodes or knowledge of cardiovascular problems.

I encouraged Sally to inform her team of medical professionals about her needle phobia. The disclosure would serve two purposes. First, if there were any untoward reactions when she initiated medical attention, the medical personnel would be prepared. Second, anticipatory anxiety often diminishes simply by admitting the problem to another person in the feared situation.

Psychoeducation

After the initial assessment was done, she was provided with psychoeducation about her condition. Again, as with all clients, the groundwork for positive expectancy of a good outcome was established. I told Sally about my experiences treating needle phobia and that everyone I had worked with had recovered. Further, I told her about research on the positive relationship between hypnotizability and individuals who are phobic (Crawford & Barabasz, 1993). Sally said that she was surprised to hear that research and feared that she might be an exception. She doubted that she was very hypnotizable because she was a "control freak." I assured her that the hypnotherapist does not control the client, that all hypnosis is really self-hypnosis, and that a hypnotherapist cannot make someone do something against his or her will. As mentioned earlier, I have found that reviewing the common myths and misconceptions of hypnosis delineated by Yapko (2003) is a good starting place with all clients. I reflected the commonly held view that the therapist is simply a facilitator who creates a context for trance.

I proposed a treatment plan for Sally, explaining that her therapy would involve two phases. First, she would learn to elicit a relaxation response in our sessions that she would practice daily in between appointments. Second, as she became more skilled at eliciting a relaxation response, we would use this skill to help her overcome her fear of needles in progressive increments through visualization and exposure therapy. She seemed eager to initiate the treatment and stated that she was committed to the requisite practice sessions.

Treatment Goals
- Diminish sympathetic nervous system over-reactivity.
- Develop mastery in eliciting a relaxation response both in and out of the office.
- Gain mastery over needle phobia.
- Diminish avoidance of necessary medical interventions.

Sally was introduced to the opening tools of the Toolbox with instructions to practice two time-out periods daily. The following tools were used to focus attention and diminish psychophysiological arousal.

Tools Used with Sally

Tool 3: Breathing—Attending and Deepening Breath (with eye fixation)

Goals
- Focus attention on the breath as a means of self-soothing.
- Use deep, calming breaths to elicit relaxation.
- Mitigate fear of losing control by incorporating eye fixation.

Script

I'd like you to keep your eyes open. Take a moment to focus on your breath. You don't need to change your breath, simply notice it, and as you do, perhaps you can notice sensations that accompany your breath. With a gentle curiosity, you can notice the texture of your breath, the rhythm of your breath, and even the temperature of your breath. And as you now take a deeper breath in and hold it for a moment, you can begin to experience a letting go of tension as you exhale.

And I'm going to be quiet while you allow yourself to become very focused on your breath. Very focused on your breath . . . becoming very curious about what you observe as you look at the painting on the wall in front of you. And you can discover how pleasant it is to sit and stare and enjoy . . . noticing the colors and shapes in the picture. And as you look at the scene in front of you,

you might comfortably enjoy immersing yourself in that scene . . . becoming curious about what you see . . . beginning to enjoy the absorption . . . (Sally's eyes begin to blink) and yes, your eyes just naturally begin to blink . . . that's right . . . blink. That's right your eyes are beginning to blink . . . blinking is such a normal reaction when we stare. And blinking is a phenomenon that you don't have to think about . . . it happens naturally . . . just like breathing or digesting your food. Of course, you can volitionally blink, but it's so much easier to trust the wisdom of your body to take care of that automatic reaction for you while you simply become more and more comfortable sitting in this chair listening to my voice and staring off at a picture on a wall in a room with nothing else you need to do. And you can keep your eyes open or half open or when and if you wish . . . all the way closed. (Sally closes her eyes.) That's right.

Commentary

Eye closure can be extremely anxiety provoking for some individuals because one can feel vulnerable and less in control. For clients with anxiety disorders, it is often a good idea to give them a choice whether or not to close their eyes, especially for clients like Sally for whom the need to be in control is a dominant issue. With this in mind, I used a variation of this tool that includes eye fixation; she was directed to stare at a painting in my office while she observed her breathing.

Directing Sally to keep her eyes open until they closed naturally helped her maintain a sense of being in control. Utilizing the blinking response served to help her feel that she was being carefully attended to, which provides a feeling of safety and further establishes rapport with the therapist. Suggesting that she could trust the wisdom of her body was seeding the idea that she could trust her body to function without vigilance.

Tool 8: Self-soothing Imagery, Safe Place—Nature Scene

Goals

- Regulate affect.
- Gain mastery over anxiety or counterproductive impulses with self-soothing.
- Dissociate from worry by focusing on visual imagery.

Script

And you can return in your mind's eye to that delightful memory of lying on that hammock . . . feeling a gentle movement of the hammock . . . shifting back and forth . . . the hammock . . . cradling you . . . Can you feel yourself held gently in the hammock with a slow, rhythmical movement? Maybe enjoying the feeling of a soft ocean breeze across your face and arms and shoulders . . . And you can look at the ocean in front of you and see its colors and the image of the water becomes more and more detailed . . . an ocean that is blue or turquoise . . . or whatever colors that please you . . . to stare at . . . to take in . . . to smell . . . to hear perhaps . . . that exquisite sound of the waves touching the shore . . . And perhaps you feel as if you are bathed in an ocean of calm . . . an ocean of comfort . . . in the light of the Caribbean sun . . . That's right, soaking up the warmth of the sun . . . and the light.

Commentary

In the interview, Sally told me about vacations that she remembered fondly that could easily be elicited to calm her system and help her feel comforted. For clients who can access actual memories of times when they experienced comfort and relaxation, it is often easy to revivify the relaxation response with visualization.

Sally chose an image of lying on a hammock on a Caribbean island. The scene was an actual memory from her honeymoon, a time in her life when she felt especially content and safe. She was guided to use all of her senses to revivify the experience.

In subsequent sessions, she became comfortable closing her eyes, so the eye fixation technique was no longer necessary. Once she was able to experience deep relaxation in the office and replicate it at home between sessions, it was time to desensitize her of her needle phobia.

Desensitization Hierarchy Combined with Sandwich Technique

The next segment of the therapy combined hypnosis with systematic desensitization, drawing heavily on the four-step protocol of Dr. Joseph Wolpe (1958), who is often considered the father of behavioral therapy. Dr. Wolpe developed the Systematic Desensitization Approach to the treatment of phobias that is still widely employed today and which has been empirically validated a number of times (Rimm & Masters, 1974). Wolpe's approach combines a relaxation response with gradual exposure to the feared objects or situation. A hierarchy is constructed beginning with the least anxiety-provoking stimuli and leading to the most frightening. The client is then desensitized in small, incremental steps. The Systematic Desensitization Approach has four steps:

1. Relaxation.
2. Exposure to mildly provoking aspects of the feared event from least frightening to most frightening.
3. Great detailing of the fear-inducing scenario.
4. Rehearsal of behavioral exposure in the office and then finally practice in real life.

Wolpe's standard systematic desensitization was incorporated into the Sandwich Technique tool in Sally's case of needle phobia. With this modified desensitization approach in mind, Sally and I created an individualized desensitization hierarchy as follows:

1. Look at a picture of a syringe with a needle.
2. Look at a picture of a nurse giving someone a shot.
3. Look at a real syringe.
4. Visit an acupuncturist with me to observe acupuncture treatment.
5. Watch a diabetic friend give herself an injection.
6. Visit the Red Cross with her husband and watch him give blood.
7. Go to the doctor's office with her friend and role-play getting an injection.
8. Go to the doctor's office with her husband and get her blood tested.
9. Go to the Red Cross with her husband and give blood herself.
10. Allow her husband to administer prescribed fertility injections in my office.
11. Allow her husband to administer injections at home.

Tool 24: Sandwich Technique

Goals
- Build an imaginary "sandwich" that alternates between exposure to soothing images and phobia-related images.
- Gain mastery of using a safe place for affect regulation.

- Increase tolerance of uncomfortable affective states.
- Diminish intensity of fearful or avoidant response to needles or images of needles.

Commentary

This session began with an explanation of the sandwich technique. Then Sally was asked to close her eyes, and she was guided into a deeply hypnotic state. In hypnosis, I directed her to open her eyes and look at a legal-sized piece of paper with a life-sized photograph of a needle. Looking at the needle was the first step in the desensitization hierarchy. She was told to memorize the image for 30 seconds and then to close her eyes and see the visual image of the needle in her imagination. I checked in with her and asked her to rate her anxiety level from 0 to 10 (0 meaning no anxiety and 10 meaning panic). On the first step of the hierarchy, she responded that she ranked her subjective unit of distress to be between a 6 and a 7. I then directed her to return to her safe place, in the Caribbean on her hammock with directions to re-elicit the relaxation response. I encouraged her to sustain the relaxation response with great sensory detail for about one minute. Then I showed her the photograph with the needle and again asked her to rank her anxiety level. It had now gone down to a 3. Once again the sandwich tool was used and on the third trial her subjective unit of distress was at 0. In subsequent sessions, we used the same protocol to complete all of the steps in the desensitization hierarchy.

Outcome

I continued to see Sally weekly for 10 more weeks in succession, during which she successfully progressed through the desensitization hierarchy. In one session, I took advantage of the fact that there is an acupuncturist down the hall from my office. With my colleague's cooperation, Sally and I went together to observe an acupuncture treatment. In this same session, she was also able to visualize, in a hypnotic state, going to the Red Cross with her husband. The next levels of the hierarchy were confronted hypnotically in my office and then actually, in vivo, out of the office. I was able to enlist the cooperation of her physician's office to allow the role-playing step of the desensitization. Steps 8 and 9 were the most challenging for Sally and each required an extra session practicing the tools and visualizing the procedures. I assured Sally that although this process was very challenging, I had no doubt that she would be able to overcome her fears with repeated practice and persistence. At this point she felt ready to proceed with the infertility treatment, steps 10 and 11 on the desensitization hierarchy. I saw her one more time, one month later. She reported that she had begun the treatment for infertility that involved both blood work and repeated injections by her husband. Sally stated that she experienced only minimal anxiety when she underwent these procedures and utilized the self-soothing imagery to soften any remaining distress. Ten months later she called me to tell me she was pregnant with twins.

Case Study 3: Application of the Toolbox with Social Phobias/Social Anxiety Disorders (SAD)

Background

Brian was a 21-year-old college student who suffered from social phobia. Brian functioned adequately in most aspects of his life: he performed well in school, had a few close friends, and reported a satisfactory relationship with his family. Yet many areas of his life were unbearable to him. For example, he was unable to go out with his friends or socialize with other students in his classes or dormitory. Friends frequently invited him to parties, but the thought of being observed by others at social gatherings was too daunting to endure. He worried that he wouldn't know what to say if someone approached him at a party or that he would be judged by the others for being silent, awkward, or for making simple conversation.

Brian made sure that he sat in the back row of all his lecture courses so that when class was over he could scoot out as quickly as possible and avoid interaction with other students. When asked if he had a girlfriend, Brian shook his head and admitted that he was attracted to a girl in his history class but was afraid to initiate contact with her. Like others with anxiety disorders, he focused on the future, specifically on what could go wrong in the future. In this instance, he worried that if he asked the young woman out that he would eventually have to take her out to a restaurant. Eating in public was particularly frightening to Brian. Just the thought of eating in a restaurant on a date made him tense, so he decided to avoid the situation entirely by avoiding dating entirely.

Presenting Problems

Brian decided to enter therapy when his anxiety began to interfere with his academic achievement. During the past semester he had dropped two classes after he found out that in one he had to present his research in front of his classmates, while in the other he would have had to attend frequent small group meetings as the class incorporated small group projects. He finally admitted to his parents his reason for dropping these two classes, which he had originally been very enthusiastic about taking. They offered to help him find a therapist. Brian readily agreed to see me.

Treatment Plan and Clinical Considerations

Initial Assessment

In the initial assessment, Brian was very self-critical, the social phobia obviously having chipped away at his self-esteem for quite some time. Hence, it was important to include ego strengthening, even in the first session. With this in mind, I pointed out his generally good academic record and made an effort to identify Brian's many capabilities and well-developed inner resources that he often overlooked.

Treatment Goals

- Enhance self-esteem and diminish self-deprecating cognitions.
- Diminish avoidance behaviors.
- Lessen concern about being judged.

Tools Used with Brian

The tools from Tiers 1 and 2 were presented in the first session, along with Tool 5, the Arm Drop and Tool 10, the Elevator.

Tool 10: Elevator

Goals

- Relax sympathetic nervous system response and deepen the relaxation response by associating it with descending movement.

- Easily remember a deepening technique that is transferable to situations outside of practice sessions.

Script

Now I'd like you to imagine entering an elevator . . . it could be an ultra-modern elevator . . . or an old-fashioned elevator . . . it doesn't matter . . . you can be curious about just how creative you can be as you imagine your elevator. The only requirement is that the numbers above the door are lit up . . . and in a moment I'm going to count downward from 20 to 1, and as I do, you imagine the numbers shifting . . . down from 20 to 1 . . . each number a cue for you to develop a sense that you are descending down. OK, the doors close and can you see the number 20? (Continue counting downward, linking suggestions for comfort and muscle relaxation with every number.)

Commentary

My goal with Brian was to help relax his sympathetic nervous system response and deepen his hypnotic level so that he would be more open to suggestions that might normally be resisted in a waking state. This allowed the suggestions to be incorporated at an unconscious level.

Since elevator phobias are common among people with anxiety disorders, it is important to ask clients if they have this particular fear before using this simple method of deepening. The advantage of the elevator technique is that it incorporates visual cues designating the floors as the client descends so that he or she kinesthetically experiences a downward motion. In the third session, I proceeded with the following tools specific to social phobias.

Tool 26: Computer Screen

Goals

- Strengthen the ego.
- Replace negative cognitions with positive self-statements.
- Enhance relaxation response.
- Revivify calm state quickly.

Script

CD: You can use the power of your imagination to envision a computer in front of you. And when you see the computer, Brian, let me know by allowing a finger on either one of your hands to lift. (Pause and wait for a response.) And imagine that you see a statement typed on the screen that reflects your self-consciousness . . . I'm not sure what statement will occur to you . . . Maybe one of the statements that you have shared with me previously, like, "They can all tell I'm nervous," or "Everyone is looking at me." Your conscious mind can be curious as to which statement that plagues you will appear on the screen, while your unconscious mind will know just which self-statement is the right one to come forth . . . And let that finger come up when you see your statement on the screen. (Pause until the finger is lifted.) And what do you see?

B: They're all looking at me, and I feel like an idiot.

CD: Now I'd like you to lift your right hand and pretend that you are push-ing the delete button on your computer . . . Let your finger come up when the statement is deleted . . . (finger comes up). Good . . . And in its place is a beautiful image on the screen . . . A beautiful scene that serves as your screen saver . . . And what is that image?

B: It's a forest . . . with big, old trees and light streaming in. (Brian smiles.)

CD: And as you smile, you can really enjoy the forest with those big . . . old trees . . . and the light streaming through the forest . . . Your per-fect scene . . . Your perfect screen saver . . . And now the screen is blank again, and you can lift that right hand and type in another statement. I'd like you type in another sentence . . . "I'm fine as I am . . . I am perfectly acceptable . . . My close friends like me and these people will, too." (Pause.) Now take a deep breath . . . And go back to the screen saver . . . back to the forest . . . and you can relax . . . deeply . . . And whenever you find yourself with self-critical thoughts . . . all you have to do is go to the screen saver . . . see your forest . . . and bring your right hand up and delete the incor-rect and antiquated message. Your forest will automatically reap-pear, and then you can type in the correct messages.

Commentary

Since Brian had a special interest in computers, computer imagery with messages of self-esteem enhancement seemed fitting. This is another example of individu-alization, of incorporating the client's strengths and interests to establish rapport and facilitate trance. The use of conscious/unconscious dissociation was also used in this protocol to communicate that there is a part of Brian that can be more rational and less self-critical, even if he is typically disconnected from it, in this way suggesting that he already possesses positive coping mechanisms. Note also that several modalities were used, including visual, kinesthetic, and sub-auditory (self-talk). Since I didn't know which modality he would be most responsive to, I exper-imented with several.

Tool 23: Switching Channels

Goals

- Develop an ability to have two disparate emotional states at once.
- Access alternative responses to a trigger.
- Use imagery to enhance positive self-perception and visualize an ideal response.
- Use imagery to soften and diminish negative self-perception.
- Enhance ability to be in control of affect.
- Increase flexibility of thinking.
- Develop an ability to reduce the impact of a feared emotional reaction.

Script

I wonder if you would be open . . . to learning how to develop your capacity to overcome your self-consciousness in school. To help you gain mastery of your discomfort, you can learn to experience two opposing thoughts or feelings at once . . . Let me show you how . . . Imagine that you're sitting in front of a large TV screen . . . Imagine further that you have a remote control in your hand . . . that you can use to change the channels on the screen . . . You have a remote control that can zoom in to see details of the images . . . or you can brighten the image . . . diffuse it . . . or even turn it off. Now, push "power" on the remote control . . . feel the tip of your index finger as it presses down on the power button . . . hear the click . . . and see the screen illuminate as the power comes on . . . Now, press the number one . . . and let yourself become more and more aware of a mental image . . . or even a partial outline of an image . . . of a situation that you're afraid of . . . perhaps attending a group meeting with your class-mates to prepare for a class project. You see yourself feeling self-conscious and fearful that you are being scrutinized, which represents yourself when you feel out of control . . . Now push the number two . . . switching the channel . . . and a picture of your ideal self appears . . . retaining complete self-control . . . control of your reactions and how they appear . . . and imagine yourself as you would ideally perform, speaking fluently to your classmates, comfortably . . . even laughing with them. Hold that image. (Pause for 20 seconds.) . . . Yes, and hold onto that image. Let yourself experience how positive it is . . . to see yourself performing in this ideal way. (Pause for approximately thirty seconds.)

Now push the number one again and switch channels . . . to the image of your self-conscious self . . . This time the picture is blurrier . . . (Do not pause long.) Now, immediately push the number two and switch to the scene where you are confident and comfortable in the class . . . Enjoy zooming in on this image of your ideal self . . . while you let it become crisper . . . bolder . . . brighter (pause for one minute).

Now push number one again and see the image of the scene where you are self-conscious . . . becoming smaller and blurrier . . . the color has faded . . . perhaps you see it in black and white now. . . . Then, quickly press number two . . . and once again . . . view yourself . . . your ideal self . . . interacting or responding the way you would most like to . . . Hold that image . . . resonate with it . . .

And, I'm going to be silent for a few moments . . . while you firmly connect to that image of you . . . responding with containment . . . maturity . . . equanimity . . . (long pause) and I encourage you to practice this channel switching daily . . . so that you can look forward to using this Switching Channels tool automatically . . . reflexively . . . whenever you find yourself afraid before class.

Commentary

In my experience, it is often easier to develop a juxtaposition of the feared response with the ideal response rather than attempt to eliminate the anxious reaction entirely at first. In Brian's case, it was effective to have an ideal image paired side by side with the self-conscious response. Since the initial goal was to prevent academic problems, the theme of this tool focused on attending group meetings with classmates. Because Brian responded so well to the Switching Channels tool, it was used repeatedly with other themes, including eating in restaurants, asking a young woman on a date, and engaging with other students in the dormitory.

I directed him to continue shifting back and forth, holding the ideal image for longer periods of time. With each shift, the ideal image was seen as larger, bolder in color, and more detailed, whereas the self-conscious image became smaller and cloudier.

Outcome

Brian reported that this next semester at college went more smoothly. He enrolled in a class that required group projects, joined a fraternity, and started dating a young woman. He stated that his self-consciousness had lessened considerably.

Conclusion

In conclusion, there are numerous therapeutic tools from the Toolbox that are especially effective with the most common of anxiety disorders such as generalized anxiety disorder (GAD), specific phobias, and social phobias. Since these are among the most frequently presented types of psychological disorders, it is especially important for mental health professionals to have available as many tools as possible to offer hope and relief to these clients. One benefit of these tools is that they offer an alternative or an adjunct to psychopharmacological interventions. In addition, they enable the client to take charge of his or her own reactivity, which should be the ultimate goal of any solid, well-balanced psychological treatment plan. In Chapter 9, we will apply the tools from the Toolbox to more complex, incapacitating anxiety disorders such as panic disorder, posttraumatic stress disorder (PTSD), and obsessive compulsive disorder (OCD).

CHAPTER 9

Application of Tools with Severe Anxiety Disorders

─────────

Among the range of anxiety disorders, there are several that typically cause considerable disruption in the functioning of the sufferer. These disorders incorporate a constellation of intrusive symptoms and are generally the hardest anxiety disorders to treat. Application of the tools, integrated with cognitive behavioral therapy and psychotropic medication, when needed, has led to a number of successful outcomes.

Anxiety disorders that will be examined in this chapter include the following:

- panic disorder with agoraphobia
- posttraumatic stress disorder (PTSD)
- obsessive compulsive disorder (OCD)

They are categorized in the DSM-IV-TR (APA, 2000) as follows:

Panic Disorder

People with panic disorder suffer severe attacks of panic—which may make them feel like they are having a heart attack or are going crazy—

for no apparent reason. Symptoms include heart palpitations, chest pain or discomfort, sweating, trembling, tingling sensations, feeling of choking, fear of dying, fear of losing control, and detachment from reality. Panic disorder often occurs with features of agoraphobia. People are so afraid of having a panic attack in a place from which escape would be difficult that they avoid these places.

Posttraumatic Stress Disorder (PTSD)

PTSD can follow an exposure to a traumatic event such as a sexual or physical assault, witnessing a death, the unexpected death of a loved one, or natural disaster. There are four main symptoms associated with PTSD: "reliving" of the traumatic event (such as flashbacks and nightmares); avoidance behaviors (such as avoiding places related to the trauma); emotional numbing (detachment from others); and physiological arousal such as difficulty sleeping, irritability, or hypervigilence.

A hallmark of PTSD is acute episodes of panic known as "flashbacks." In these intense emotional episodes, survivors will often become immersed in both the physical and emotional state in which their trauma occurred, even becoming attuned to physical sensations experienced during the time of their trauma. The reliving of their trauma on a regular basis in the form of both flashbacks and nightmares can interfere significantly with daily functioning and normal sleep patterns. It is important that survivors learn to ground themselves fully in the present when flashbacks occur, as well as work to alleviate the hyperarousal and hypervigilance that interferes with sleep patterns and daily functioning.

Individuals with PTSD often report feelings of detachment or alienation from themselves and others; thus, it is common for people with a diagnosis of PTSD to concurrently suffer from depression. It is also common for individuals with PTSD to present with a number of other conditions such as substance abuse, memory and cognition issues, and/or other various physical or mental complaints.

Obsessive-Compulsive Disorder (OCD)

In OCD, individuals are plagued by persistent, recurring thoughts (obsessions) that reflect exaggerated anxieties or fears; typical obsessions include worry about being contaminated or fears of behaving improperly or acting violently. The obsessions may lead an individual to perform a ritual or routine (compulsions) such as washing hands, repeating phrases, or hoarding to relieve the anxiety caused by the obsession.

OCD is a particularly difficult condition to treat. With OCD there are no quick fixes. Unlike other individuals with anxiety disorders who tend to be highly hypnotizable, individuals suffering from OCD are often poor hypnotic subjects, thus contributing to the challenge of treating them. Some clients with OCD, though, do respond quite well to the Tools. An exceptionally challenging case that was responsive to the Toolbox will be presented in this chapter.

I encourage therapists to utilize a wide variety of tools from the Toolbox in their efforts to help OCD clients because this greatly increases the likelihood of success. The treatment of OCD often requires therapy of longer duration than treatment for some of the other anxiety disorders. If some of the tools prove ineffective, try others, as most all of them are appropriate to use with these clients. With passionate patience and persistence, I have witnessed significant alterations in patterns with some of my most challenging OCD clients.

Case Study 1: Application of the Toolbox with Panic Disorder

Background

Diane, a 43-year-old mother of two young children, had recently moved with her husband and children from Washington State to Michigan when she first came to see me. In Washington, she had worked as a nurse in a hospital. She was unemployed after recently leaving a part-time nursing position in Detroit due to her difficulties with anxiety. When Diane came to see me, she began by voicing what she had identified as the precipitating event in the daily battle with anxiety she now endured: Diane experienced what appeared to be an acute panic attack while she was attempting to purchase household goods at Sears.

Presenting Problems

Diane described her first panic attack as follows. As she browsed the aisles pushing her shopping cart, her heart began to race. Her breathing became rushed and shallow. Although her grip on the cart's handles tightened, her hands began to slip, her palms had become sweaty. Diane found herself urgently searching for an exit. She desperately wanted to get out of the store, and as each second passed she became more confused, disoriented, and alarmed.

Leaving all of the items in her shopping cart, Diane raced through the aisles until she finally found an exit. This single encounter with a full-blown panic attack led to a generalized avoidance response that caused Diane to alter her life significantly. She began to spend a considerable amount of psychic energy anticipating panic attacks and strategizing different ways to prevent such events. She not only began to avoid Sears, but any crowded, public environment from which a fast escape might be difficult. She avoided shopping malls, restaurants, movie theatres, and even PTA meetings. She was also uncomfortable driving.

Over the next four months, her symptoms worsened, and her daily activities became more and more restricted by her intense fear. By the time Diane came to see me, she had become very depressed and had begun to lose hope that she would ever recapture her "old self." She relentlessly feared and anticipated the sudden onset of a panic attack. The acute anxiety she experienced while driving to and from work proved so disruptive that she found it necessary to quit her job. At this point, Diane decided that it was finally time for her to seek outside help. It was then that she came to see me.

Treatment Plan and Clinical Considerations

Initial Assessment

I diagnosed Diane with panic disorder coupled with agoraphobia. Because the initial panic episode at Sears was so severe, she suffered from significant anticipatory anxiety, fearing that another panic attack would overtake her at any moment. Although the first attack was the most intense, Diane continued to experience additional attacks, often without clearly identifiable triggers. Her anticipatory fear had a profound effect on her subsequent psychological well-being and daily functioning. Diane was showing symptoms of agoraphobia as well, and was becoming increasingly reluctant to leave the house without her husband or her neighbor, whom she also identified as a support figure. In addition to agoraphobia, Diane displayed a number of classic panic disorder symptoms.

Michael Otto and Thilo Deckersbach (1998) delineated several typical characteristics of panic disorder that Diane exhibited, including the following: fear of losing control, looking for escape routes, interpreting ambiguous somatic reactions as harmful, and overestimating the likelihood of future panic attacks. Diane experienced a global fear that something awful was likely to happen but could not be concrete about what the feared scenario or stimulus was. During the episodes in which Diane experienced severe panic, she became intensely aware of bodily sensations that registered alarm. On a cognitive level, Diane understood that her fear was irrational, as was her level of reactivity. Despite this knowledge, Diane was unable to subdue her distress. Feeling she had no alternative but to curtail her life to accommodate her fears, Diane experienced self-doubt and depression. Her overwhelming anxiety challenged Diane's sense of herself as a competent, capable adult.

Treatment Goals
- Establish mechanisms to discharge anxiety quickly.
- Establish ability to elicit feeling of safety.
- Develop capacity for detached observation of somatic, emotional, and cognitive over-reactions.
- Instill hopeful expectation of recovery.

In the first session, Diane was provided with psychoeducation concerning the general nature of anxiety disorders, specifically panic disorder, and was reassured that people *do* indeed recover from panic disorder. Because of the severity of her condition, I also recommended that she see a psychiatrist to be evaluated for psychotropic medication.

Like many clients with anxiety disorders, she was reluctant to take medication, as she was afraid that medication would make her feel even more out of control. "I don't even take aspirin. I don't want to put drugs into my brain," Diane stated. I told her that we would put that particular issue on hold and reexamine it later.

I often recommend that my clients with panic disorder ask their physicians about psychotropic medication as an adjunct to psychotherapy. The knowledge that a panic attack can be aborted very quickly can greatly diminish the anticipatory anxiety that plagues these clients. It can be reassuring to have the fast-acting benzodiazepines such as Xanax, Ativan, and Klonipan on hand as a safety valve to be used in a crisis. In my experience, most of my clients with anxiety disorders do not abuse these medications. Diane is typical of these individuals who are often fearful of any mind/body altering substances and have a low probability of abusing them. I have found that clients with PTSD are often an exception and are at greater risk for drug abuse. However, it is crucial that clients on the aforementioned drugs are monitored carefully for signs of dependence or abuse, particularly if the client has any history of substance abuse. Psychiatrists prescribe antidepressants such as Paxil, Zoloft, Lexapro, and Celexa, among others, as psychopharmacological interventions to treat panic as well. It is wise for therapists to develop a good relationship with a psychiatrist that is characterized by mutual respect and frequent exchanges regarding clients' status.

I instructed Diane in the tools from Tiers 1 and 2 before using the tools from Tier 3 to address her panic disorder. Further, she was given strategies from Tier 4 so she could be prepared to implement the tools in her daily life.

Tools Used with Diane
Tool 18: Tight Fist
Goals
- Establish a mechanism to discharge anxiety quickly.
- Establish a sense of confidence and self-efficacy if panic occurs.

Script

CD: I'd like you to imagine being in a situation where it might be likely for you to have another panic attack . . . Nod your head when you identify such a place and circumstances . . . where you are afraid you might panic.

D: (Diane nods.)

CD: Where are you?

D: At the grocery store.

CD: Now go to the part of the scene, in the grocery store, where you would feel most distress and let me know when you are there.

D: I'm at the check-out counter . . . with a shopping cart full of food.

CD: That's right . . . you are at the check-out counter with a basket full of food . . . Take a moment to really experience the distress . . . the panic . . . Feel your heart racing . . . the dizzy feeling in your head . . . the urge to bolt . . . allow yourself . . . Diane . . . to elicit these uncomfortable feelings of anxiety . . . It's safe right now . . . here with me . . . So you can make the feelings very vivid . . . distressing, disturbing . . . (Diane shifted in the chair; tears were in her eyes, and her face was flushed.) OK, I can see the panic . . . tell me . . . what do you notice in your body right now? . . . (long pause) . . . What are you thinking? . . . I'm right here with you . . . you're OK . . . continue to let the feelings come up . . .

D: My chest is tense . . . My heart is racing, and I'm feeling dizzy, and I want to run out of the store.

CD: Now, Diane, you can learn an intervention that will quickly, very quickly . . . calm your system so that in just a moment or two you can take charge of your reaction and calm yourself . . . Now imagine that all that tension in your chest is going into your hand . . . and make a fist with your hand . . . squeeze it tightly . . . feel the tension . . . that's good. And imagine that the tension is transformed into a liquid . . . in a particular color . . . a color of your own choosing that represents the terror . . . the distress . . . the panic . . . and the uncomfortable feeling in your chest or anywhere else in your body . . . and imagine that all of the colored liquid is in your fist . . . in your fist right now . . . the fist absorbing all the color . . . all the fear . . . Hold your fist tightly . . . (pause for 10 seconds) . . . and then slowly relax the fist . . . and all the fear is released down through your fingers onto the floor where it instantly evaporates . . . That's right . . . it's gone . . . and you can take a deep breath . . . and you say to yourself . . . "It's only panic . . . I can handle it . . . I am safe . . . " And isn't it comforting to know that you have this tool available . . . and that you can develop it further with practice? And you can keep the tool in your pocket in the event you need it.

Commentary

I cannot stress enough the importance of teaching a client to interrupt an over-reactive response with a tool when she or he is *actually* experiencing manifestations of panic or anticipatory anxiety. I purposely did not initiate a calming response at the start of this protocol, as I wanted her to experience the anxious feelings in the session with *as vivid an affective experience* as possible. Teaching the tools in the abstract without eliciting the stress response is typically insufficient. In traditional talk therapy, the client is not actively engaged with the external trigger. I explained to Diane the importance of recreating the feelings that she experienced in her panic attack so that she would have an opportunity to intervene and self-regulate using the Tight Fist tool. My intention was to teach her that although panic was uncomfortable, she could indeed handle it, first in the safe environment of my office and then outside.

The intervention began with providing a suggestion that assured Diane that she would learn to intervene rapidly if panic arose. Phrasing the suggestion in this manner addressed the time urgency for relief that panic sufferers experience. The tensing and relaxing inherent in the tightening of the fist in this tool releases muscular tension. Transforming the tension to an image of a colored liquid employed another modality to enhance the intervention.

Diane was pleased with her response in the office but expressed concern that the techniques would not work with a "real" panic attack. I again reassured her that we would persist with a variety of interventions until she felt confident of mastery. At this point I felt it was an opportune time to revisit the issue of psychiatric consultation for medication. Although Diane still expressed some hesitation, I told her that I had a very conservative and trustworthy psychiatrist colleague who would not prescribe if she deemed it unnecessary. Medication can initially expedite treatment of debilitating symptoms such as Diane suffered.

Next, Diane was directed to re-elicit a relaxation response with the Hand Warming and Self-soothing Imagery tools from Tier 2. Then Diane was introduced to Tier 4 and rehearsed practicing her daily affect regulation protocols while she was still in trance. She was provided with written instructions describing the focusing attention, calming, and deepening phases from Tiers 1 and 2 of the Toolbox, along with instructions for the Tight Fist tool from Tier 3. The whole protocol was recorded on audiotape and given to her as well. A structured plan for and commitment to at-home practice sessions was also established. In the next session, Diane reported that she had kept her commitment to practice at home. She stated that she found the Tight Fist tool to be particularly to her liking. She also reported having seen the psychiatrist I had recommended who prescribed a small dosage of Paxil to be taken daily, as well as Ativan to be used as needed until the Paxil became effective.

She was then introduced to two additional tools, also from Tier 3, which were different in nature from the Tight Fist tool: Mindfulness with Detached Observation and Mindfulness and Releasing. I chose these tools so that she could begin to develop a more nonreactive stance to her cognitive patterns of anticipatory anxiety and catastrophic thinking.

Tool 11: Mindfulness with Detached Observation

Goals
- Become a detached observer of somatic reactions.
- Become a nonreactive observer of worried thoughts.
- Eliminate self-criticism when negative emotions or thoughts emerge.

Script

CD: Take a couple of deep breaths . . . simply feeling the air as it enters your nostrils . . . and as you do, you can go inside for awhile . . . directing your attention inward . . . drifting deeper within . . . so you can have an opportunity to learn something new . . . to learn a process called mindfulness . . . that involves standing back and watching your feelings. . . . Now I'd like you to ask yourself what the feeling is that is coming up for you right now? And as you identify that feeling . . . simply observe it . . . without judgment . . . without self-recrimination . . . like a detached observer . . . like a scientist observing an interesting phenomenon. And what do you notice now?

D: I notice tension in my shoulders.

CD: Tension in your shoulders. Just sit with the tension . . . just notice it with curiosity. (Pause.) And what do you notice now?

D: The tension is almost gone.

CD: That's wonderful.

Commentary

Mindfulness involves finding an internal, silent witness to observe emotions from a place of detachment. In doing so, the client is less likely to feel overwhelmed or engulfed by an emotion or a sensation. Exercising mindfulness is particularly helpful when people are experiencing severe emotional reactions such as panic or intense pain. When Diane appeared to be in an agitated state, I instructed her to pause, direct her attention inward, and simply attend to the feelings as they emerged. I encouraged Diane to disengage from the emotion or somatic reaction, observe it, and asked her to do so without judgment or self-recrimination. Note that in this intervention, I tell her that she "can have an opportunity to learn something new." (See Chapter 3 for a discussion on learning as a theme in the protocols.)

Tool 12: Mindfulness and Releasing
Tool 15: Sensory Cue/Anchor

Goals

- Identify feelings.
- Reduce intensity of feelings through breathing.
- Release uncomfortable feelings.

Script

I'd like you to have an opportunity to experience a simple but powerful way of acknowledging your feelings . . . just being with them . . . even when the feelings are uncomfortable. So as soon as you begin to experience that fear of losing control or that discomfort in your chest or stomach . . . or perhaps a thought that something awful is going to happen, that can be a cue for you to take a moment for yourself . . . that will support you . . . and mindfully . . . nonjudgmentally . . . just accept what is . . . in that moment . . . And I suggest that you begin to say these comforting phrases in your mind: "I am aware of the panic. I breathe through the panic. I flow through the panic. I release the panic." And in this way, you will let your body and mind express itself and do what it needs to do . . . And you can be reassured and comforted . . . knowing that all feelings come and go, they are time limited . . . fleeting . . . and will pass . . . soon. They will pass . . . And as you wait for the anxious feelings to pass . . . you can choose to repeat the phrases over and over again . . . simply saying: "I am aware of the panic. I breathe through the panic. I flow through the panic. I release the panic." Now take your thumb and forefinger of either hand and make an OK sign. This OK symbol can remind you that you are really OK, that you are safe and secure and strong . . . And you can use this OK symbol anytime in the future when you need it, to reconnect to your capacity to handle whatever comes up for you.

Commentary

Tool 15, Sensory Cue/Anchor, was included as an adjunct to the mindfulness tool so that Diane could quickly remind herself that she was indeed able to manage her feelings. Once Diane was trained in mindfulness, I was easily able to introduce a type of self-talk characterized by a detached style that de-escalates the catastrophic reaction. The goal was to calm her system sufficiently with the mindfulness approach so that she could tolerate the distress and to remind her that every episode of panic is time-limited. In the event that Diane was unsuccessful in preventing a panic attack, she was provided with the following phrases that could help her ride out the emotional storm: "I breathe through the panic. I flow through the panic. I release the panic."

Diane was in many ways an ideal client, and it was easy to establish a good relationship with her. She was open and communicative and practiced the tools on a daily basis. After two months of therapy, she reported that she had had no further panic attacks since the onset of treatment. However, she also reported that her activities were still restricted and that she remained too dependent on her husband to drive her places and accompany her to activities.

Tool 31: Age Progression (Short-term)

Goals

- Experience the satisfaction of positive feelings elicited by imagining symptom relief.
- Instill confidence in her ability to use the tools to relieve symptoms of panic.
- Incorporate the positive feelings into the present affective state.
- Emphasize the limited duration of a panic attack.

Script

CD: Do you know, Diane, how long the average panic attack actually is?

D: I don't know, but it feels like they last forever.

CD: Actually, most of my client's panic attacks last about twenty minutes.

D: That's all?

CD: That's the average, although some episodes last just a bit longer but not very long in real time. And you can endure twenty minutes of distress . . . knowing that the distress, even if it is intense, is time limited and that it will pass fairly quickly.

Now, Diane, I would like you to imagine the upcoming PTA meeting that has you worried. I want you to think of being at your son's school, in the cafeteria for the meeting, where you might be when the anxious feelings are emerging . . . Imagine feeling the symptoms you associate with your panic attacks beginning . . . when your body begins to feel tense . . . You might imagine that spaciness and shortness of breath, the rapid heart beat, that discomfort you've felt before . . . and remember that it is OK to feel this right now, because I am here with you. And Diane, I would like you to nod when you are there . . . (Diane nods.) And where are you now?

D: I'm with my husband in the cafeteria, and it's filled with parents.

CD: Good, Diane, that's very good. And what do you feel in your body?

D: My hands are beginning to get sweaty, and my forehead feels hot, and I'm getting dizzy. I'm glad I'm sitting down.

CD: Alright . . . and now, Diane, I would like you to imagine that you're at the PTA meeting . . . your palms are sweating . . . you're becoming dizzier and dizzier by the moment . . . and now "fast-forward" in your imagination to when the imagined panic attack is dying down. See yourself using your Tight Fist tool and releasing all the fear and tension. And practice it here and now just as you would there and then. (Diane initiates the Tight Fist tool.) (Pause.) And now also practice your Mindfulness and Releasing Tool. Repeat the phrases: "I am aware of the panic. I breathe through the panic. I flow through the panic and I release the panic." Repeat these phrases three times to yourself. (Pause.) And now go ahead in time to when the 10 or 20 minutes have passed and the panic attack is over. Let a finger come up when it's over. (Diane lifts her finger.) Isn't it nice to know that you can trust your ability to intervene and support yourself recognizing that you have tools that can help you . . . that you have access to multiple strategies to intervene effectively? To recognize that the episode really wasn't that long, was it? . . . And whenever you wish, you can fast forward to when the panic episode has wound down . . . is over . . . has no more energy. Diane, let yourself feel the secure satisfaction in trusting that you will remember to use your tools, your interventions, whenever or wherever you need them . . . And as you practice the tools, the Age Progression tool and the others that you have learned, you can allow yourself to begin to feel very hopeful, with very satisfying feelings washing over you. You are the master of your fears, building resiliency and courage, once again in control.

Commentary

As was mentioned previously, clients with panic disorder suffer from anticipatory anxiety, as well as the actual episodes of panic. Because Diane, like most clients with panic disorder, had a profound sense of hopelessness regarding her condition, it was especially important to use this tool to enable her to envision a time when she was able to intervene successfully with effective self-regulation. In this version of the Age Progression tool, Diane was given an opportunity to walk through an anticipated panic attack and see herself intervene with a combination of three tools. I encouraged a belief that she could survive a panic attack, hoping that confidence in affect regulation would diminish anticipatory anxiety.

Tool 31: Age Progression (Long-term)

Goals
- Build positive expectancy regarding changes resulting from therapy.
- Diminish hopelessness and depression.
- Experience the satisfaction of positive feelings elicited by imagining symptom relief.
- Incorporate the positive feelings into the present affective state.

Script
So now as you experience that comfortable relaxation again, you can begin to become receptive to creating strategies in your imagination that will . . . in turn . . . become realities in the course of time . . . for you to comfortably use when and if they are necessary . . . And perhaps you can imagine going into the future to a time when things are better for you. Better because of the diligent work that you are doing here right now in my office . . . and later . . . during your practice sessions at home. And I wonder if you can imagine yourself in the future . . . some months from now and with this perspective . . . notice all the ways your life is better because of the work you did in therapy. Perhaps you can take a deep breath and let it out slowly . . . As you do, you can feel a profound sense of relief as you acknowledge permanent shifts in your reactive style . . . the permanent changes in your nervous system that are truly yours as a result of the healing that you've achieved.

Commentary
At this point, I had the immediate goals of increasing Diane's positive expectancy that her condition would indeed improve. With this goal in mind, I taught her the tool of Age Progression to increase her optimism about recovery. This intervention focused on moving forward in time to when she was no longer plagued by her anticipation of future panic.

Outcome
Treatment with Diane was not limited to the tools described above. As therapy continued, Diane was instructed in most of the tools from all of

the tiers of the Toolbox. With challenging cases like this one, it is wise to offer the client as many interventions as possible. She found Tool 6, Arm and Leg Heaviness, and Tool 7, Hand Warming, to be easy to master and very effective in quicky eliciting a relaxation response. Diane responded beautifully to therapy. She was able to fully resume all of her normal activities and was no longer dependent on her husband to accompany her on errands. The combination of psychotropic medication and application of the tools resulted in a calming of the autonomic nervous system and the psychophysiologically-based reactivity that was out of control when she first started treatment. Diane was able to stop her medication under the supervision of her psychiatrist after adhering to drug therapy for fourteen months. She continued in regular treatment with me for a total of two years and still consults with me as needed for support.

Case Study 2: Application of the Toolbox with Posttraumatic Stress Disorder (PTSD)

Background

Suzanne's mother died when she was 9 years old. She and her three sisters were left to be reared by an alcoholic father who managed to provide financially for the family but abandoned the family emotionally. At age 14 in her freshman year of high school, Suzanne had stayed after school for a choral rehearsal one rainy afternoon. Her father was supposed to pick her up at 4:00 P.M. After waiting two hours for him to arrive, the custodian had to lock up the school doors. Suzanne was allowed inside to call home one last time, yet there was still no answer. Rather than stand out in the rain, Suzanne called for a taxi to take her home. About halfway between her school and her house, the cab driver turned off onto a road Suzanne had never seen before. He parked the car, slid in next to Suzanne on the cab's back seat, and raped her. When she finally arrived home, bruised and crying, Suzanne found her father in a drunken sleep on the couch. He had been too drunk to remember to pick her up from school, and now he was too drunk to even notice her arrival. Not only had Suzanne been severely traumatized, but there was no one to comfort her or to help her process the trauma. Unfortunately, Suzanne suffered further trauma two years later, experiencing yet another violent rape by several neighborhood boys. Again, her trauma went unacknowledged and unaddressed.

Twenty-three years later, Suzanne was driving down Woodward Avenue in Detroit on her way home from work. She saw a taxi in the next lane and began to panic. Intellectually, she understood that she was not in danger. The cab was in another lane, and her car doors were locked. Nevertheless she experienced an overwhelming feeling of distress as adrenaline flooded through her body and terror struck. Suzanne could only find one thought that calmed her anxiety enough so that she could keep driving: the minute she walked in her front door, she would mix herself a drink.

Presenting Problems

Suzanne suffered from severe anxiety, panic attacks, and alcoholism. It is also not a surprise that she had a volatile and unstable marriage. The most dramatic of her symptoms, however, was the cancer of the adrenal glands that she developed at age 24. Adrenal cancer is typically an aggressive cancer that is characterized by excessive production of hormones. One can speculate that the stress response resulting from Suzanne's repeated traumas had an influence on the development of this life-threatening illness.

Treatment Plan and Clinical Considerations

Initial Assessment

Suzanne was diagnosed with PTSD. It is typical for clients with PTSD to be retraumatized by a relatively innocuous trigger such as what happened to Suzanne when she saw the taxi on her way home from work. Early in the treatment, I confronted Suzanne's increasing dependence on alcohol to self-soothe. She willingly joined AA and maintained sobriety throughout her therapy. It would have been difficult to treat her successfully if she had continued to drink.

Like most survivors of trauma, Suzanne was highly hypnotizable. Clients with PTSD are experts at slipping into dissociative states and thus are highly talented hypnotic subjects. With these clients, a sufficient depth of trance often develops quickly so the standard deepening steps can be truncated. Although these clients' dissociative tendencies are conducive to treatment, this hypnotic talent is a double-edged sword: relief of specific symptoms can be established quickly (e.g., insomnia or somatic complaints), but special care should be given when eliciting hypnosis to individuals who have experienced childhood trauma so that untoward responses such as maladaptive dissociation or abreaction do not ensue. It was important that Suzanne establish mastery of self-soothing rituals that can be rapidly engaged in and that emphasize affect regulation to prevent excessive and uncontrolled dissociation while she was undergoing hypnotic treatment. In order to accomplish this, I introduced Suzanne to many of the calming techniques from Tier 2 of the Toolbox.

I have found Yvonne Dolan's (1985) interventions for creating resources particularly helpful during the early phases of treatment for clients with PTSD. As suggested by Dolan, establishing a symbol for the present and developing a cue for comfort and security is highly efficacious. In Dolan's Symbol for the Present intervention, the client is directed to select a symbol that represents her adult life functioning (e.g., car keys). The cue for comfort and security helps the client access an experience of comfort (e.g., a safe place) and then directs the client to develop a cue to help her quickly revivify the secure state (Dolan, 1991).

Because excessive dissociation often occurs with trauma survivors in response to fear or any feeling of vulnerability, it is especially important that trust is developed between the client and the therapist before hypnosis is ever initiated. When trust exists, the client's awareness of safety is enhanced, giving the client one more defense against the tendency to engage any maladaptive coping mechanisms during trance.

Suzanne was also instructed in the preliminary tools of identifying precursors and taking a time out (as delineated in Chapter 4) in the first session and in all subsequent sessions. She was also always taken through the usual trance induction, including focusing attention, calming, and deepening before using the tools from Tier 3 of the Toolbox. We closed each session with tools from Tier 4, emphasizing rehearsal, transfer, and practice.

Treatment Goals

- Diminish feeling of abandonment.
- Diminish hypervigilance.
- Access and develop healthier parts of self.
- Diminish feelings of helplessness.
- Stop dependence on alcohol to self-soothe.

Tools Used with Suzanne

Tool 27: Imaginary Support Circle

Goals

- Elicit a sense of protection and safety.
- Promote a sense that she is not alone.
- Recognize a network of real or imagined people or entities who care for her personal safety.

Script

And we have been talking about how alone and unprotected you felt as a child . . . that all too often . . . no one was there . . . to nurture and protect you . . . to guide you . . . to wash away any discomfort . . . and we also know that . . . even though . . . as an adult . . . you have your husband . . . your colleagues . . . and friends, sometimes that younger part of you feels small and alone . . . So . . . with your permission . . . we are going to create a support circle for you . . . so that you never need to feel alone again . . . (long pause) So now . . . I'd like you to return to your safe place . . . and you know how to go back there . . . and you can be pleased how easily and how naturally you can recreate your safe place . . . notice how nice it is to be back in the familiar setting of safety and security . . . and you can make any modifications or additions to your safe place that you like . . . and when you are settled in and ready . . . experience yourself there with all your senses . . . the images and colors . . . soft carpeting . . . soothing colors of paint or wallpaper . . . special decorations [incorporate information from previous descriptions of her safe place] . . . any sounds or physical sensations . . . even pleasant aromas . . . allow yourself to enjoy being back in your safe place . . . enveloped in a cozy, comfortable, snug protective environment . . . some place where you feel utterly safe . . . and let me know with a finger rising . . . when you have fully immersed yourself in that place of safety and security (Suzanne's finger rises.) . . . Very good . . . And I wonder if you can arrange a sitting area of couches or pillows . . . a circle that can be expanded to perhaps five to ten people . . .

And . . . as you sit there . . . I'd like you to imagine someone very wise and kind walking up toward you . . . and this person can be someone you've met in your lifetime . . . someone who has had a profound impact on your life . . . someone alive or dead . . . a person you regard with love and admiration . . . perhaps someone you've told me about . . . just let a finger come up when that first person is there . . . (Suzanne raises a finger.) . . . Good . . . and now another person is coming to join the first person . . . and this person might be someone else that comes to mind immediately . . . someone important in your life . . . or it might be someone famous from history . . . or fiction . . . the only requirement is that this person be wise and kind . . . and once again . . . raise a finger when he or she has arrived. (Suzanne raises a finger.) Now think of some others to join your circle . . . I don't know if you will choose any or all of them before your personal support group is fully assembled, and now . . . it might be time to bring someone you associate with strength and courage . . . and I'm not sure who that might be . . . but you can trust your unconscious mind to bring just the right person who is strong and will protect you . . . OK, that's good . . . Now . . . you can be curious about who else might join the circle . . . Some people select favorite teachers or coaches . . . uncles and aunts . . . grandparents . . . mentors . . . childhood friends . . . Others include angels or other religious figures . . . Or maybe you would like to ask your mother to join the circle. (Suzanne nodded and began to weep softly.) Yes, your mother who made you feel so loved and safe . . . would you like her to be with you? (Suzanne nods.) You choose whomever is important to you . . . people who bring balance to your support group . . . and I'm going to be quiet while you complete the group . . . You could bring any friend or relative . . . co-workers and confidantes . . . And you are welcome to bring me . . . if you wish . . . into the circle . . . and I'll be silent now for a few moments while you bring in other people to the circle . . . and . . . when you are finished . . . raise a finger . . . (long pause). Good . . . and now . . . I'd like you to look around your circle . . . feeling the support . . . taking in the wisdom . . . the strength . . . the genuine caring . . . and . . . you can appreciate with wonder . . . the peaceful energy that each special person brings to your circle.

And what a nice thing to know . . . that you can return to your safe place . . . and imagine your support circle . . . and what a relief it is . . . is it not . . . just simply to experience this support . . . to let go with faith . . . that this support group will stand behind you . . . serve as a safety net . . . and this support circle restores you . . . and replenishes you . . . and you can be pleased that you are being bathed in this warm bath of caring . . . and love . . . and probably everyone . . . from time to time . . . gets scared . . . feels alone . . . and isn't it nice to know . . . that you have a tool for when you get scared or feel alone . . . your inner support circle . . . that you can summon . . . whenever you need to . . . and each time you imagine creating your imaginary support circle . . . you will become more skilled . . . at creating this healing imagery . . . whenever you need it . . .

Commentary

The tragic and premature death of Suzanne's mother and the secondary abandonment by her negligent father resulted in a failure to internalize safety; therefore, a core wounding for Suzanne was abandonment. The Imaginary Support Circle was taught to Suzanne to help her create imagery that elicited a sense that she was safe, protected, and not alone. With her highly developed hypnotic skill, the images of protectors were easy to evoke. Suzanne was able to establish a Safe Place easily, although some clients with PTSD have difficulty accessing a memory of a place where they felt safe. For some, the best safe place is my office.

Tool 28: Parts of Self

Goals
- Recognize innate ability to comfort more vulnerable parts of self.
- Identify a more mature developmental state with adult nurturing abilities.
- Enhance ego strength of the adult part of the self.

Script
And when you stop to think of it . . . we are all made of many different parts, including very young adolescent, or adult, or parts that are mature . . . scared . . . vulnerable, confident, and strong . . . so many different parts . . . that reflect our developmental shifts, as well as our experiences . . . And it certainly makes sense that when you are experiencing fear, you can access a mature part, a strong part of yourself that can take charge of the parts of you that feel exposed or in danger . . . A strong mature part that can not only comfort the younger self but can take charge of situations in a reasonable way, a nonreactive way . . . a courageous way . . . Because you know, Suzanne, there is a part of you that is always with you that is strong, that is balanced, that is mature, that is all grown up . . . It is always there . . . even if you temporarily overlook it . . . It is always there. And this is a perfectly good time to access that mature and evolved part of yourself . . . So take a minute to get in touch with her now . . . that part of yourself that is your adult part of self, a part that is strong and balanced and courageous. And let a finger come up when you can feel her coming to the surface. (Pause.) . . . (Suzanne's forefinger elevates slowly.) Good.

Now wait for the words that come from the wisest part of your being . . . that part of you that is most developed . . . strongest and most solid . . . or even most spiritual . . . or maybe images rather than words will come to mind . . . Allow your unconscious to connect to that part of self that is wise and strong and all grown up. And really feel it . . . your strength, your maturity . . . your compassion . . . And with all those strong qualities . . . you can look into the eyes of a younger, more helpless part and touch her hand and reassure her that she's OK . . . that you'll handle the rough spots for her. That she is not alone . . .

Commentary

The Parts of Self tool is based on Ego State Therapy, a parts model that emerged from the field of hypnosis. Ego State Therapy involves the client's recognition of the many different emotional and developmental states that reside within each individual's conscious and unconscious mind. Although states are different aspects or energies of the self, some are more mature than others. During flash-backs, survivors often revert back to their developmental state at the time of their trauma; thus, Suzanne could be sitting in my office and experience the same fear that she had experienced back in the taxi cab when she was fourteen. She could recognize intellectually that the fear was from the past, but emotionally, she was locked into the terror and pain of her previous experiences, as well as in younger developmental states. Using an ego state intervention, I guided Suzanne to rec-ognize a mature, actualized ego state of the present. Once Suzanne found this ego state, I asked her to provide comfort and reassurance to her scared, younger self from the past. It was important for Suzanne to recognize the competence and maturity she expressed in her present life and her ability to free herself from the pain and fear of the past.

Outcome

Suzanne continued treatment with me for two years, during which time she remained sober and cancer free. The course of her recovery involved some setbacks in the first six months of treatment in which she was inconsistent in her adherence to practicing the tools in between sessions. I hypothesized that the self-soothing that she experienced in the office was at odds with the state of vulnerability and anxiety that she had felt for most of her life. There was resistance to letting go of that which was familiar, albeit uncomfortable.

As a result of the strong therapeutic relationship we developed, Suzanne was eventually able to trust the process and become more and more comfortable with self-soothing on a regular basis. It took the bet-ter part of a year before Suzanne was truly able to consistently access and maintain feelings of safety and well-being. Once this was achieved, we were able to address other goals, particularly her chronic hypervigilance and exaggerated startle response. An adaptation of the Watchman tool (Tool 29) and the Self-statement tool (Tool 19) was helpful in this regard. About 18 months into therapy, she reported that the flashbacks had stopped and her hypervigilance had significantly diminished. Further, Suzanne became very skilled in nurturing her more vulnerable parts of self. She was particularly responsive to the Parts of Self tool.

After two years, Suzanne decided to take a break from therapy. Her life functioning was good and her symptoms less severe. She acknowledged that she still had unfinished work in her recovery process and anticipated inevitable setbacks, particularly under times of stress, but wanted a break from the intensity of the therapeutic process. I was supportive of this decision but assured her that I would continue to be available for consultation and treatment, especially in the event that she experienced any setbacks or life challenges for which she needed support.

Case Study 3: Application of the Toolbox with Obsessive Compulsive Disorder

Background

Derek reported that he had always been a meticulous child. He told me that his mother still told her friends about all the cute little routines he used to put her through: there was a certain way she had to make his peanut butter and jelly sandwich each morning, or she would find it in his lunchbox, uneaten, when he returned from school. He was the only one of her three children who insisted not only that his bed be made daily but that he be the one to make it. Whenever she made his bed, she would inevitably do it "wrong," and her little 8-year-old would completely strip all the bedclothes from his bed and remake it from scratch. More than once this had resulted in his getting to bed over an hour past his set bedtime. Derek conveyed to me that his mother had always enjoyed what she called his "antics." But now he was 32, completing his post-doctoral work in structural engineering and thinking about marrying and starting a family. His "antics" were beginning to severely interfere with his daily functioning.

Presenting Problems

Derek came to treatment at the insistence of his fiancée, Lisa, who accompanied him to our first session. She stated that unless Derek recovered from his OCD, she couldn't go through with their marriage plans. Lisa reported that his last visit to the grocery store made her realize how developed Derek's symptoms had become. She stated that he would only buy food that was spelled with an even number of letters. Peanut butter with 12 letters and fish with four were safe to buy, but almonds with seven letters were not. Further, Derek would separate all of the evenly priced grocery items from the oddly priced ones, relegating each category to opposite sides of his shopping cart. Because of his various peccadilloes, Derek would often spend up to four hours in a grocery store just to select ten grocery items.

In addition, Derek's sleep had become so severely disrupted due to his obsessive thought patterns that he was only able to sleep a few hours a night. Even when the bed was made correctly, Derek would be kept awake by the nagging sensation that some portion of the bedclothes had been tucked in improperly. More than once he had woken his fiancée so that he might remake the bed. No amount of shuffling, folding, or fixing would ease his discomfort. He would toss and turn throughout the night in an agitated state. His fiancée had finally said that if he could not stop fumbling with the sheets, she would begin sleeping in a different room. She could handle the grocery shopping, but Derek's inability to cope with her bed-making skills was unacceptable.

Treatment Plan and Clinical Considerations

I have found that OCD is the hardest anxiety disorder to treat successfully. It may therefore require that the therapist search for a variety of interventions. Cognitive therapy and the affect regulation tools, along with psychotropic medication, can have a synchronistic relationship. When used in combination, they work well in these challenging cases.

Initial Assessment

In the initial assessment, I met with both Derek and his fiancée. Derek stated that he was under the care of a psychiatrist who had tried a number of antidepressants in an attempt to treat his OCD. Although Derek reported that his mood had improved once he had been on medication for about a month, the OCD symptoms had not abated. After taking a history of the presenting problem, I devoted much of the session to providing psychoeducation about the nature of OCD to the struggling couple. There was particular emphasis on creating hope for a positive outcome of treatment.

In the next session, Derek was instructed in the preliminary tools of identifying precursors and taking a time out and was guided through the usual trance induction and deepening before using the tools specifically for OCD. At the end of every session in which a tool was taught, Derek was instructed to rehearse his practice sessions using the tools from Tier 4.

Treatment Goals

- Interrupt intrusive thoughts.
- Postpone obsessive thinking.
- Interrupt compulsions.

Tools Used with Derek

Tool 29: Watchman

Goals

- Feel in control of the therapeutic process.
- Know that the observing protective part of the self is accessible in the hypnotic state.

Script

And you and I both know that you are very analytical and educated and make thoughtful decisions in your life . . . so I wouldn't expect someone with your kind of intelligence to immediately jump in with both feet until you are ready . . . until you are more certain of the process . . . and I think of a famous researcher named Ernest Hilgard . . . who wrote a scholarly analysis of the hypnotic process . . . and coined the term the "hidden observer" . . . And his work makes me think of how people process information on two levels simultaneously . . . consciously and unconsciously . . . So your hidden observer . . . that conscious part of you that is split off . . . that you can always count on . . . that remains in the corner of this experience . . . gently watching . . . monitoring whatever happens . . . making certain that this hypnotic experience is in alignment with your needs and values . . . and that observing self . . . the conscious mind . . . can change my words or images seamlessly while the unconscious mind can notify the conscious mind if this transformation is relevant . . . and the conscious mind can give permission to your unconscious mind to change my words to your words . . . my images to your images . . . so you can really let go . . . trusting your ability to achieve this wonderful state of relaxation . . . allowing your unconscious mind to drift . . . yet assured that you are in control . . . And it can be very reassuring, can it not, that this wise and adept observer of the process is there as a guide? . . . as a resource when you need him . . . and as you become more comfortable . . . more competent . . . trusting more and more . . . this observer can rest . . . can suspend . . . almost like that state everybody has experienced before they go to sleep . . . not really awake . . . but not fully asleep . . . At those times your body may be asleep while your mind is awake or your mind is asleep while your body is awake . . . or perhaps the right side of your body is sleepier than the left, which leaves the right side left to rest later . . . or maybe the left side of your body is the right side to fall asleep first . . . and you can experience a hypnotic sleep, different than nighttime sleep but so relaxing . . . And that observer will eventually even be able to sleep, as well . . . ever ready . . . on call, if needed . . . But you don't need to think about that right now . . . so much better to just enjoy this moment of sitting in a comfortable chair . . . with a voice . . . my voice . . . with part of your mind . . . while the other part of your mind floats . . . going wherever it wants to go.

Commentary

This tool is useful for people who are wary of the trance process. It was especially useful to address Derek's need to be in control before he proceeded with the process. I employed an intervention that allowed him to feel that he was in control, assuring him of his observing part of self. I felt it was important also to acknowledge his intelligence.

Tool 16: Thought Stopping

Goals

- Interrupt intrusive thoughts.
- Use cognitive, visual, and kinesthetic tools to reinforce thought stopping.
- Utilize previously demonstrated successes in learning new skills.

Script

As you continue to sit comfortably in the chair . . . listening to my voice . . . taking the opportunity to learn how well you can manage your mind . . . just like you've learned so many things before . . . you learned how to spell your name . . . how to write it . . . how to ride your bike . . . and . . . recently . . . you learned how to do that statistical analysis for your dissertation . . . which was very difficult . . . but you've already had the experience of something being very complex and challenging . . . when you've had serious doubts as to whether or not you could ever be comfortable . . . be comfortable understanding advanced statistics . . . the analyses of covariance . . . and you learned that there's a variety of strategies . . . there's a possible variance as well of just how quickly you can learn to master thoughts, interrupt thoughts, stop thoughts that are not in your best interest . . . and one of the variety of tools that I know to be helpful is a tool called Thought Stopping . . . and when you drove here today . . . you probably passed a stop sign . . . right before you turned into the entrance to my office . . . and take a moment right now to visualize that stop sign . . . And it's interesting that stop signs all over the country look the same . . . a symbol that anyone can easily recognize . . . and you can see in your mind . . . an octagonal red sign with white lettering . . . and raise your finger when you can see it (Derek raises a finger.) . . . Good . . . and now I would like you to put that stop sign down beside you on the chair for a moment or two . . . and direct your mind to a worried thought . . . perhaps a thought of something bad happening . . . in your house . . . after you've left for work . . . or perhaps you'd like to select another worried thought . . . and when you have that worried thought, let a finger come up in your right hand so I'll know . . . (Derek raised a finger.) OK . . . very good . . . and take a moment to really let yourself feel that tension . . . that anxiety . . . And you can be interested in just how quickly you can revivify the tension . . . when you worry . . . really let it come up now . . . OK . . . And now I'd like to teach you three things for when you are feeling this way . . . I'd like you to bring your right arm up as if you're stopping traffic . . . see that stop sign . . . and say "Stop it!" . . . Bring your right arm up as if you're stopping traffic . . . see that stop sign . . . and say "Stop it!" . . . (Derek raises his arm and says, "Stop it!") . . . Good . . . well done . . . And now . . . take a deep breath in and return to your safe place and say to yourself, "Everything's OK right now" because it is . . .

Commentary

It is noteworthy that the Thought Stopping tool employs visual cues of a stop sign, kinesthetic cues of the arm lifting, and a vocal cue verbalizing the words, "Stop it." Using several modalities makes the intervention more powerful and engaging. In addition, there is a reference to both past learning and mastery of other difficult challenges that he successfully met. The reader should note that the script was individualized to utilize Derek's experience in graduate school. The reference to his previous self-doubt regarding his ability to master statistics parallels his current doubt in his ability to overcome his obsessions and compulsions. I also made sure to advise Derek that he may need to practice several repetitions of the Thought Stopping tool at home to successfully interrupt undesirable thoughts.

Tool 20: Postponement (of Obsessive Worry)

Goals
- Enhance mental flexibility.
- Enhance ability to redirect obsessive thoughts.

- Compartmentalize reactions such as worries, obsessions, or grief.
- Create a time-limited window for engaging in obsessive thinking.
- Diminish chronic rumination.

Script

CD: And you came to see me to do something about your obsessive thinking . . . and now that you are . . . in a comfortable, relaxed state . . . you have access to a kind of mental flexibility . . . which is a good thing because . . . one of the things we know about obsessive thinking is that there is too much rigidity . . . in the rumination . . . in the thinking . . . and I've learned that one of the benefits of this relaxed state is that in a hypnotic trance, you have the mental elasticity to interrupt rigid patterns of behavior . . . And your rigidity is reflected by you going over and over the same thoughts . . . which then blocks your ability to focus on the things you need to at that time . . . and what is really important is for you to connect to the part of your mind that can choose what you wish to focus on . . . at any given time . . . and you already have prescribed times to focus and do other things, other tasks . . . you have prescribed times to wake up . . . to get to work . . . and maybe when you eat lunch, though it may vary day to day . . . but, generally, lunch is in the middle of the day . . . and you have these prescribed times because you have chosen them . . . and you've developed the habit to do those things at those times . . . and, in the same way . . . you can create a prescribed time to worry . . . to obsess about your worries . . . so you can have the freedom to enjoy your day . . . knowing that . . . at the end of the day . . . you have created a space in time . . . to focus on the accumulated worries and thoughts . . . and you can even make notes for that worry time . . . so that you can let go of the worries now . . . secure in the fact that you can get back to them later . . . (long pause) So . . . I want you to select the time that will be your prescribed worry time . . . and nod your head when that time appears to you. (Derek nods.)

CD: What time is good for you to set aside?

D: 8:00 at night.

CD: And now imagine where you will do this thinking . . . (Derek nods.)

D: In my den.

CD: OK . . . very good . . . and at least at first . . . I want you to allow twenty minutes for worrying . . . so . . . you will be in the den from 8:00 P.M. to 8:20 P.M. . . . And it can be such a relief to know that the thoughts and worries will be attended to at that time . . . in that place . . . (long pause) and during the day . . . inevitably . . . there will be seeds of thought as a worry begins to emerge . . . and when this happens you can take a deep breath . . . and you can see the time you have selected for the worry . . . and you can see yourself even writing a note to remind you later of the thought or worry . . . and this can be an even greater relief to realize such a burden has been lifted from your mind by not having to worry about these things throughout the entire day . . . (long pause) and when the pre-scribed time comes this evening . . . I'm not sure you'll be in the mood to worry at that time . . . sometimes people aren't . . . or the worries might not seem very big at that time . . . and some people even report that when they get back to the worries . . . the worries have often shrunk . . . but your worries have been with you for a long time . . . so it wouldn't be right to let them go completely . . . yet . . . all at once . . . because they deserve proper time on a daily basis . . . so, even if you don't feel like worrying . . . or it doesn't seem like there's much to worry about right then . . . I would like you to honor the decision to abide by the prescribed worry time . . . (long pause) and won't that be nice for you to be in control . . . to know there is a time and place for everything you need to take care of . . . and you are in control . . . in charge.

Commentary

This intervention incorporates the standard cognitive behavioral supposition that the postponement of obsessive rumination leads to a progressive weak-ening of the response. With this in mind, I walked Derek through the process of postponing his obsessive worry to a preselected time of day in which he could engage in his worries for a set length of time. Edna Foa, Ph.D., and Reid Wilson, Ph.D., recognized for their work with anxiety disorders, have incorpo-rated postponent in their work with obsessive compulsive disorders (2001). The script includes the theme of mental flexibility in the hopes of mitigating the cognitive rigidity that accompanies obsessive thought patterns. Further, the imposition of prescribed worry times can create a paradoxical response in which the client may choose to rebel against the directive and decide to ignore worry time all together. He may discover that even the allotted, pre-scribed worry time is no longer necessary. Note that Derek is directed to honor his worry time even if he doesn't feel inspired to do so. This strategy is another example of Ericksonian utilization, in which the troublesome symp-tom is used as a resource in the treatment (Rossi, 1980). This creates a win-win double bind for him as he can view himself as successful whether he complies with the worry time or not (Erickson & Rossi, 1975). If he complies, the implication is that he is successfully adhering to therapeutic suggestion; if he rebels because he isn't worried, he is also successful because his symptom is abating.

Tool 20: Postponement (of Compulsive Behavior)

Goals
- Interrupt pattern of ritualized compulsive behaviors.
- Delay impulse to react compulsively.

Script

CD: And as you experience that renewal of comfort . . . having reconnected with the gentle feeling of deep relaxation . . . in this comfortable state, this deeply relaxed state, you can use the power of your imagination to visualize . . . I wonder if you can imagine yourself in a theater looking up at a screen . . . And on this screen perhaps you can see yourself lying in bed at night. (Derek nods his head.) Good. And let's imagine that it is 2:00 A.M., and you awaken with a yearning to adjust the sheets . . . just as you have many nights before . . . And you see yourself staying in bed for just a little while . . . postponing that ritual for a short period of time. As you continue looking on the screen, how much of a delay can the Derek on the screen tolerate?

D: Two minutes.

CD: Two minutes. That's good. Now I'd like you to count your breaths backward, starting with the number two-hundred and forty . . . counting backward in increments of two . . . one number for every second of the two minutes . . . And nod your head when you get to zero. (Two-minute pause.)

D: (Derek nods.)

CD: And when you get to zero, you can visualize yourself getting up slowly . . . Now see yourself . . . very slowly and deliberately adjusting the bottom left side of the bed, tucking in the sheet, making the necessary adjustments that feel right to make . . . that will stay just as you've set them for the rest of the night . . . Staying still and motionless just like *you* will be before you drop off to sleep again . . . Good . . . now see yourself going back to bed . . . becoming very still . . . resting . . . quietly drifting off to sleep. (Long pause.) That's right . . .

Commentary

Please note that the previous script incorporates a combination of the behavioral rehearsal component from Tier 4, a movie screen, and another variation of the Postponement tool from Tier 3, which in this case serves as a form of pattern interruption. Pattern interruption was introduced by Milton Erickson, who suggested that a dysfunctional behavior could be altered by changing one component of the pattern. Several strategic Ericksonian approaches referenced by O'Hanlon (1987) and delineated by Gafner and Benson (2003) were included in my work with Derek as we sought to interrupt his compulsive rituals. They included altering the frequency, time, quality, and sequence of the problematic patterns. In working with challenging cases of obsessive compulsive disorder, I have found that including pattern interruption in treatment can yield significant changes.

Incorporating this approach to pattern interruption, I first directed Derek to postpone the sheet-adjustment ritual. Derek was to determine how long he could comfortably postpone the remaking of the bed and then delay the ritual for this amount of time. Then, he was directed to change the pace and the order of the ritual. He had reported that he always started the ritual in the middle of the night, quickly making adjustments on the bottom right side of the bed. ("You can visualize yourself getting up slowly . . . Now see yourself . . . very slowly and deliberately adjusting the bottom left side of the bed.") Derek was instructed to observe the sequence of the altered bed-making pattern by visualizing the new behavior on a movie screen. In the hypnotic intervention, he was directed to shift the sequence of the behavior and retuck the sheets on the bottom *left* side of the bed. These pattern interruptions were incorporated in the behavioral rehearsal tool, using a screen to watch his altered behavior as presented above.

Note that Derek was also directed to initiate the repetitive, tedious process of counting his breaths backward. In so doing, his compulsive style was utilized to focus his attention and to help him relax. I directed him to count backward using even numbers only, as he initially presented with the symptom of being uncomfortable with odd numbers. In subsequent sessions, the postponement tools were used again successfully to address his discomfort with odd numbers and his need to have a particular arrangement of food in the shopping cart.

Outcome

Derek made considerable progress with all of the initial treatment goals. He also made strides in his ability to successfully interrupt obsessive thinking and postpone compulsions. He was able to continue to postpone his nightly bed-making ritual in slowly increasing increments of time. The Watchman tool was particularly appropriate for Derek, as it helped him to feel sufficiently protected so he could more easily engage in the process. I noticed an acceleration of his progress after it was introduced.

Derek's compulsive nature was utilized in the treatment and served him well, as he rigidly adhered to practice sessions. He continues to take his medication and schedules regular appointments with his psychiatrist. Further, during the course of treatment, he and Lisa married. Lisa remains very supportive, patient, and encouraging of Derek's taking regular time-out sessions to practice his tools, as he works to curb his maladaptive responses. Derek continues to come to treatment bimonthly to reinforce and maintain his progress.

Conclusion

Among some of the hardest anxiety disorders to treat are panic disorders, PTSD, and OCD. It is not unusual for clients to be unresponsive to standard talk therapy and/or behavioral therapy when being treated for these disorders, thus leaving many therapists with little in the way of options. The tools in the Toolbox, however, have been utilized with significant success, albeit not without a passionate determination to continue trying different tools until progress can be seen. Clients with these deeply ingrained responses tend to require more time and effort before results can be measured; however, there is significant reason to pursue such a course. The tools hold true hope for change. The next chapter will apply tools from the Toolbox to over-reactivity in intimate couple relationships.

CHAPTER 10

Application of Tools within Marital/Committed Relationship Therapy

＝＝＝＝＝＝

Therapists who work with couples have long been challenged by the difficulty of teaching partners to react in a reasoned manner with appropriate affect regulation and focused communication without sacrificing emotional responsiveness and intimate connection. Clients who present with uncontained emotional responses have difficulty resolving conflict in their marital relationships. A number of communication formats have been designed for therapists to teach listening, focusing on the issue at hand, and selecting non-accusatory language, but clients still need to manage their reactions and sustain these new skills outside of the office. Research has shown that long-lasting changes of interpersonal patterns in couples are hard to effect (Jacobson & Addis, 1993). Hypnotic techniques used in couples therapy serve to interrupt the destructive, automatic psychobiological reactions, thereby decreasing escalation of conflict. Although primary, this is just one of the many advantages of using the Toolbox with couples.

This chapter will discuss the particular issues involved in couples therapy as well as the benefits of using the tools, before delving into the practical application of the tools with couples in three case studies. Please note that the structure of this chapter and Chapter 11 is somewhat different than the other chapters. I have included case studies that demonstrate the benefits of combining a number of different tools because I thought it would be instructive to demonstrate the manner in which many of the tools can be integrated in typical sessions.

Frequently, an individual initiates therapy to address a personal condition but often this uncovers deeper issues within that individual's intimate relationship. This then launches the individual and his or her partner into couples therapy. These case studies will reflect some of the themes and behavioral goals of Gottman's approach to marital therapy, selected principles of Imago relationship therapy developed by Hendrix, and clinical experiences of the author, as well as a presentation of the tools. It is important to stress that the hypnotherapeutic tools are not necessarily used in isolation from other approaches and theoretical models; on the contrary, especially in couples therapy, it is not uncommon for me to combine them. First we will address some of the damaging behaviors in relationships as defined by Gottman.

Destructive Behaviors in Relationships

Since it always takes two over-reactors for conflict to escalate in a relationship, it is safe to assume that both people in a couple are contributing to the problems in one form or another, even if the destructive behavior of one seems more overt than that of the other. These behaviors have been narrowed down by Gottman (2000) to four primary ones. These core destructive behaviors tend to be automatic and are often accompanied by intense emotional responses such as anger or resentment. Gottman describes what he terms "The Four Horsemen of the Apocalypse" as the destructive behaviors that are often evident in failing marriages:

1. Criticism: Complaining with blaming.
2. Defensiveness: A counterattack when an individual feels criticized, belittled, or misjudged.
3. Contempt: Expressed when one partner implies that she or he is better than the other.

4. Stonewalling: Emotional withdrawal, distancing, giving the "silent treatment," and ultimately pulling away from the relationship.

Hendrix's (1988) view is that marital problems stem in part from a lack of consciousness of the unfinished business or wounding from childhood that is being replayed in the current relationship. He also asserts that our early caretakers create images that influence our selection of partners; we are unconsciously drawn to a partner who can readily bring in just the "right" or familiar qualities to re-elicit childhood wounding and dynamics. He further believes that the adaptation to stress in childhood results in defenses that are expressed in an individual's personality and must be addressed in the relationship therapy. I have been heavily influenced by my training in both the cognitive behavioral approach of Gottman and the more psychodynamic approach of Hendrix, but I have also observed a number of other dynamics that contribute to the challenge of successful relationships.

One of the biggest problems I have witnessed has to do with individuals having unrealistic expectations of their partners. It has been my experience that part of the process of developing a mature relationship is developing acceptance of the necessary, inevitable limitations of our partners. We expect our partners to be the ultimate lover, fun companion, effective co-parent, responsible business partner, good roommate, as well as best friend and confidante. That's a tall order. The reluctance to tolerate differences, to let go of unreasonable or grandiose expectations, and embrace idiosyncrasies as endearing, requires an attitude shift and a level of development that sometimes takes nurturing and training to achieve.

Solutions to Destructive Behavior in Relationships

Though there are a number of useful approaches to addressing the common issues that present in relationships, I have found that Gottman and Hendrix's principles combined with the Toolbox are by far the most effective. We will start with Gottman's theme of the "Four Horsemen of the Apocalypse" as applied to couples.

Gottman first helps the couple identify the "Four Horseman" behaviors and then replace them as follows:

1. *"Complaint without blame"* replaces criticism.
2. *"Accepting responsibility"* replaces defensiveness.
3. *"Culture of appreciation"* replaces contempt.
4. *Self-soothing or soothing by the partner* in order to stay connected replaces stonewalling (2000, p. 115).

Gottman's approach works directly with the immediate behaviors and does not tend to delve into the underlying, unconscious dynamics that were formed in childhood. The work of Hendrix, on the other hand, makes full use of the wisdom to be gained from each partner's early childhood wounding and nurturing, in addition to teaching the couple powerful communication tools.

Healing Childhood Wounds

Harville Hendrix's approach to couples therapy focuses on the etiology of the conflicts in the relationship. The emphasis is on heightened awareness of the developmental wounding that is recapitulated in adult relationships (Hendrix, 1988). Therapeutic interventions focus on repairing the developmental arrests in each partner. One of the most useful tools Hendrix offers is the "Couples Dialogue."

The communication format of Hendrix's Couples Dialogue has three initial components: mirroring, validating, and empathizing. Mirroring involves paraphrasing a message back to the partner, providing an accurate reflection of the content and feeling of his or her message. Validation consists of communicating to the partner that his or her thoughts make sense though it does not necessarily suggest agreement. Empathy conveys that the partner can understand and participate in the experience of the partner to a certain extent (Hendrix, 1988).

How the Tools Can Support Other Approaches

Use of the tools can greatly increase the effectiveness of Gottman's and Hendrix's approaches. For example, *age regression*, a commonly used hypnotic phenomenon, can provide clients with an opportunity to go back in time, and it can enhance consciousness of unfinished business from childhood. It is particularly helpful when utilized with Hendrix's "Parent-Child Dialogue," which is an exercise to help couples understand and empathize with their partner's developmental wounding. Additionally, age regression enables clients to retrieve overlooked resources and memories. Often, couples having difficulty have amnesia for their earlier sense of connection and joy with each other. Age regression can also elicit the "positive sentiment" that Gottman addresses, which has a very powerful impact on how a couple manages conflict (2000, p. 185). Teaching this tool is relatively easy.

To elicit age regression, the therapist suggests that the client use imagination to trigger the memory of past experiences (Yapko, 1988). To revivify positive affective states with age regression, the hypnotherapist might direct the clients to remember a more positive time in the relationship, typically early on before power struggles and conflict developed. They are encouraged to access a specific event that was particularly significant in its representation of his or her ability to experience joy and connection with each other. Both Phillips (2000) and Yapko (1988) contend that with visualization it is always advisable to use the senses to revivify the memory more compellingly. Ego strengthening can also be a useful component of this intervention as the client is reminded that he or she is a person who is capable of loving another person. Just as remembering the past can be a powerful change agent, so can imagining the future.

The hypnotic phenomenon of *age progression* (see Chapter 6, p. 103) can be effectively utilized to assist clients in identifying their hopes for the future (Hammond, 1990). Yapko recommends the use of age progression wherein the client visualizes himself in the future after the desired changes have been made "to build a positive response set regarding the future" (1988, p. 113). Age progression can also help the client to experience the satisfaction that accompanies healthier interactions with his or her partner. It also serves as a model for the couple; when each partner visualizes new behaviors, it is more likely that they will be manifested.

Benefits of the Toolbox in Relationship Therapy

At this point, it may be useful to revisit the primary benefits of the Toolbox that were presented in Chapter 1 and to elaborate on how the tools specifically address issues within relationships. Note that a new benefit for relationships has been added at the end of this list.

- Develop self-soothing skills.
- Change cognitions.
- Develop a dual perspective by working with ego states.
- Modulate emotions.
- Rehearse desired behaviors and skills.
- Develop internal focus.
- Enhance impulse control.
- Amplify positive affect.

Develop Self-soothing Skills

Diminishing physiological overstimulation and increasing a feeling of safety, which can facilitate ownership of issues in a power struggle, can enable one to act less defensively in an ensuing conflict. It is not the conflict itself that has a destructive effect on relationships but rather the inability to resolve the conflict with positive affect that is injurious (Gottman, 2000).

Change Cognitions

As stated earlier in Chapter 1, it is difficult to listen to one's own constructive self-talk when one is overwhelmed with physiological arousal, let alone clearly hear another's perspective without judgment or overreaction. Utilizing the tools in Tiers 1 and 2, in particular, helps partners become calm enough so that they can hear and respond to reasonable cognitive self-statements.

Develop a Dual Perspective

A dual perspective enables the individual to access a more reasonable, less-reactive part of the self, even while feeling disappointed, hurt, or angry. Using the Parts of Self tool or the Juxtaposition of Two

Feelings tool, among others, the partners can learn to re-elicit tolerant parts of themselves, as well as positive aspects of the partner, even when triggered.

Modulate Emotions

Skill at activating a relaxation response will enhance the ability to modulate emotions. For couples to remain connected, even when there is conflict, the ability to modulate emotions is critical.

Rehearse Desired Behaviors and Skills

The Toolbox can provide an opportunity for skill rehearsal in intimate relationships. It has been suggested that when clients practice hypnosis, the response patterns are being conditioned to activate in the future (Humphries & Eagan, 1999). In several of the hypnotic strategies that follow, clients are instructed to rehearse appropriate dialogue and reaction styles in trance. For example, the communication skills of active listening and validating are rehearsed, along with the practice of interrupting defensive reactions by intentionally directing their thoughts to positive qualities of the partner.

Develop Internal Focus

All too often partners erroneously point their fingers at each other as the source of their pain. As one focuses inward and relaxes, defenses soften. As one continues to maintain an internal focus, it becomes easier to comfortably "own" the realization that the problem in the relationship is not necessarily the other person, but rather how one chooses to react to the other person.

Enhance Impulse Control

The ability to stop the impulse to speak without regard for the partner's feelings is a mandatory skill in healthy, mature relationships. One must also be aware of the effect of negative nonverbal communication such as eye rolling, grimacing, smirking, or slamming doors. Impulsive, punitive reactions such as leaving the house in anger without communicating or leaving an angry voicemail need to be discontinued to prevent short- and long-term damage to the relationship.

Amplify Positive Affect

Finally, hypnosis provides an opportunity to generate and amplify positive affect. The tendency to view the history of the marriage negatively is often an indication that a marriage may be in jeopardy. Gottman asserted that the most important finding in his extensive research was that "more positive affect was the only variable that predicted both stability and happiness in marriages" (2000, p. 11). It is therefore incumbent upon the therapist to help the couple to focus selectively upon the strengths of the relationship.

Many relationships are in trouble not simply because of conflict but because people don't feel connected anymore. Some partners report feeling a sense of loss, that their intimate relationships feel more like those of platonic roommates than of lovers. Using the Age Regression tool, which focuses on remembering and revivifying earlier feelings of connection, as well as the Gratitude tool to attend to that which is positive now but overlooked and undervalued, can ultimately save a marriage lacking in passion and loving connection.

Case Study 1: Application of the Toolbox with Marital Conflict (Jonathon and Janice)

Background

At the first scheduled therapy session, Jonathon arrived alone at my office ten minutes prior to their 1:00 P.M. appointment. By contrast, Janice arrived at 1:25 P.M. While waiting for his wife to arrive, Jonathon shook his head wearily and said, "This is what I have to put up with all the time." When Janice rushed in breathlessly, she apologized for being late, explaining that it took longer than expected to get the children to her mother's house. Jonathon sighed and rolled his eyes, avoiding eye contact with his wife.

After validating each partner's reaction and highlighting this interaction as something we would likely come back to, I proceeded with obtaining history and background information. Jonathon and Janice were in their early thirties. They had been married for eight years and had three sons, ages 6, 5, and 1. Jonathon was employed as an engineer. Janice was a freelance writer. Jonathon presented as a handsome, meticulously groomed young professional. He spoke in a cerebral, logical manner, weighing his words carefully as he talked. In contrast, Janice was bubbly and effusive in an irrepressible, youthful way. She spoke quickly and readily went off on tangents.

When asked about the history of their relationship, Janice took the lead, reporting that she and Jonathon were introduced by their families and were pressured to marry. Everyone thought they were an ideal couple. Almost from the outset of their marriage, Janice and Jonathon had doubted the wisdom of that advice and questioned their suitability as partners. It seemed that they had had nothing but problems.

Presenting Problems

Jonathon stated that he found Janice's disorganization intolerable. He criticized her for her lack of time management, stating that she was always late for appointments. He complained that their house was in shambles and that their bedroom was so cluttered that he avoided entering it and preferred to sleep on the couch.

Janice in turn stated that her husband's communications to her were almost entirely limited to criticism and contemptuous remarks. "He never compliments me. When he isn't complaining, he ignores me." He retorted that she preferred talking to her mother and sisters than to him and that she could get a lot more done around the house if she wasn't wasting time on the phone with family members.

Janice reacted to this criticism by becoming defensive and then typically counterattacking. Jonathon responded to her reactivity by disengaging, eventually displaying "stonewalling" behavior (Gottman, 1999). When not at work, he "exited" or left the relationship as much as possible (Hendrix, 1988). According to Janice, he spent many evenings with his best friend, pursued hobbies, and went to sleep early in the evenings, doing whatever he could to avoid encountering his wife's emotionality. Jonathon admitted that he did tend to isolate himself but that his wife was exaggerating the amount of time spent away from the family.

Jonathon's behavioral patterns in the relationship reflected his struggles with flooding. In his research on couples, Gottman (1998) noted that men, for the most part, are "emotionally flooded" more easily than women and are unable to tolerate as much emotional intensity. Physiologically speaking, emotional flooding for men entails an increase in the sympathetic nervous system arousal, manifesting as increased muscle tension and heartbeat, agitation, and excitement, symptoms that are classically called the "fight/flight response," as addressed in Chapter 2. In other words, women have a greater capacity to tolerate intense emotions, endure strong feelings longer, and experience a fluctuation of emotions within a shorter time frame. Consequently, men may attempt to withdraw from their partners when conflict arises because, as Gottman stated, negative affect is harsher and physiologically more punishing for them than for women.

When met with his wife's confrontations or emotionality, Jonathon became flooded, experiencing excessive psychophysiological arousal such as racing heartbeat and inability to focus. He reported feeling overwhelmed at first, then powerless to cope with his wife's behavior. He typically responded by distancing himself from her, which only elicited more negative exchanges and harsh words from Janice. The couple described an insidious cycle of attacks and withdrawal, leaving them both exhausted and pessimistic about the outcome of the marriage.

Treatment Plan and Clinical Considerations

Initial Assessment

In addition to the problem of flooding and withdrawal, I also saw Hendrix's conception of the *minimizer/maximizer* dyad exemplified in this case. Janice was the classic *maximizer*, fitting Hendrix's description of a person who "is expressive and explosive . . . fighting to get what he [she] needs" (1992, p. 70). Jonathon, by contrast, was the *minimizer*, responding to stress by imploding and expressing his fears by fleeing from conflict. Although minimizer/maximizer themes are not delineated in the scripts that follow, they are typically addressed in relationship therapy. Another dynamic in the relationship was that Jonathon took on the role of parent while Janice reacted to him from a childlike ego state.

Treatment Goals

The specific behavioral goals for this couple were to diminish defensiveness by taking responsibility and owning their parts in conflict, to practice active listening or mirroring, and to validate and empathize. Another goal was to practice using visualization to rehearse effective communication. A further goal in the treatment was to help the couple learn from each other's adaptive style, wherein Janice, the *maximizer*, could use Jonathon as her teacher and learn to model his skill in containment, and Jonathon, the *minimizer*, could become somewhat more like his wife: expressive, assertive, and willing to communicate distress. Additional goals included the following:

- Contain verbally damaging exchanges.
- Increase empathy.
- Close "exits" (engaging in activities such as watching TV or talking on the phone with the express purpose of avoiding one another).
- Establish date nights together away from the children.
- Develop positive expectations about the relationship and experience positive affect on a regular basis.
- Increase awareness of impact of verbal and nonverbal communication.

Beginning Phases of Treatment

Once this couple was evaluated, and I had established a positive rapport with them, Janice and Jonathon were introduced to Tiers 1 and 2 of the Toolbox. They were led to identify triggers or reactions that could warn them of a possible over-reaction. In this case, the volatility that emerged naturally in the session provided a perfect opportunity for them to practice Tier 1 in the office. I interrupted their harsh, rapid-fire exchanges and asked them to close their eyes, focus inward, and scan their bodies for tension. They were then directed to place their hands on the parts of the body that felt tight or uncomfortable.

Further, they were asked to direct their attention to the thoughts and emotions that accompanied that somatic tension. I then explained the necessity of taking "time out" to provide them with an opportunity to interrupt their habitual reactive responses. I helped them to understand that it was unrealistic to expect that they could automatically alter their reactive patterns. Instead they needed a short time away from each other to calm down and rehearse appropriate responses. Readiness to engage in these protocols should, however, be approached with a word of caution.

I typically do not introduce the tools until the second session. Although rapport is essential for effective therapeutic work with any client, when using hypnosis, it becomes especially important. Closing the eyes in itself creates vulnerability and going "inside" can lower defenses. Hence, I do not recommend beginning this work without establishing sufficient rapport.

The tools that follow can be utilized in individual therapy with clients who are experiencing difficulty in their relationships. Alternately, they can be incorporated in couples therapy. If both partners are in the session, I induce trance in each partner and then individualize the hypnotic suggestions such as in the example below:

Script in Preparation for Using the Tools

Janice, you can comfortably remain in your safe place while I speak to your husband for a while, experiencing more and more relaxation as you develop an open-hearted, loving space inside . . . You can listen to the words I say to Jonathan . . . or you can drift away for a while listening to your own words . . . or you can listen to all of my words, or some of my words . . . or you can simply attend to the tone of my voice to guide you into a deeper state of being wherein you'll experience something new about yourself while I continue to speak to Jonathan . . . and your unconscious mind, the deeper part of your mind, will know just which messages to attend to . . .

The clients were introduced to all of these tools in session two, but they were repeatedly exposed to them throughout the therapy to ensure that mastery was affected. At the end of each session, they were then taken through Tier 4, a rehearsal of using effective communication strategies, including taking responsibility, apologizing, and reflective listening. Before the introduction to Tier 4 rehearsal, however, I facilitated the revivification of an intensely emotional exchange to set the stage.

As a start to the behavioral rehearsal of Tier 4, the couple was asked to close their eyes and recall an argument that they had referred to in the beginning of the therapy session. They were encouraged to allow all the negative feelings and thoughts to be revivified that accompanied this disagreement. It is important to encourage intensification of the negative affect in the therapy session so that the couple can experience how the focusing techniques can create the desired soothing response. Once they re-elicited the feelings that accompanied their argument, they were led through Tier 2 of the Toolbox to create a calming response and tools from Tier 3.

Tools Used with Jonathan and Janice
Tool 6: Arm and Leg Heaviness

Goals
- Focus attention and deepen relaxation.
- Identify muscular tension.
- Release muscle tension with sensations of limb heaviness.

Commentary
The development of arm and leg heaviness elicits physical relaxation and emotional equilibrium very quickly for most clients. In this intervention, heaviness in the limbs was linked to comfort, which was in turn linked to the suggestion of a more conciliatory and compassionate response.

Script
And so, you can begin to create a relaxation response by focusing on your hands. And as you do, can you imagine that there are lead weights on your wrists? Lead weights making your hands so heavy . . . so heavy, and as they become so very heavy, you can feel even more relaxed . . . even more relaxed than you were a moment ago . . . Allow your arms to become heavy, as well . . . following that comfortable heaviness in your hands . . . And maybe that heaviness will spread to your legs . . . nice heavy legs . . . so heavy that it would be difficult to move them . . . You could if you wished, but they can stay so very heavy and still. What a nice feeling it can be to experience that heaviness in your legs. And with that comfortable relaxed feeling that accompanies the heaviness in your limbs, you can create a calm and comfortably detached state that enables you to be very calm . . . calm enough to be more conciliatory and compassionate. And in this balanced state you feel that everything is OK . . . more than OK.

And because you are OK, Jonathan and Janice, this is a good time for you to see yourselves interacting with each other in an ideal way. And you might do this by taking responsibility for a part of what your partner is unhappy about. And I wonder how you might imagine doing this? Perhaps you would apologize for any hurts intended or unintended . . . or would you ask your partner about her/his displeasure or frustration and reflect back your understanding in slightly different words? Or do you have another idea of how to approach your partner respectfully . . . patiently . . . lovingly, validating her/his experience and showing your concern?

They had further rehearsal from Tier 4 to practice the self-hypnosis protocol daily in addition to any time they felt triggered. I told them that it would often be sufficient to use just one component of the protocol, for example, heaviness of limbs or the OK symbol, to successfully interrupt an overly emotional reaction. Note that the "comfort of trance" and feeling that that they are safe or "OK" is linked to the behavioral change.

Tool 28: Parts of Self

Goals
- Increase access to more mature parts of self.
- Encourage loving nonverbal communication.
- Develop "curiosity" rather than judgment of one another.

Script

So, take a moment now to wait for the words that come from the wisest part of your being . . . that part of you that is most evolved . . . most loving . . . or even most spiritual . . . or, maybe images rather than words will come to mind . . . perhaps an image of looking at each other with soft eyes or an understanding nod . . . or maybe touching each other's hands . . . and you already know that sometimes nonverbal communication can be more powerful than words . . . whether there are words . . . or images . . . or both which come to mind, allow your unconscious mind to formulate your ideal response. (Long pause.) And I will be silent now, and in the silence, these words or images will come to you to guide your reaction. (Another long pause.) And when you have the words or the image, I want you to nod so that I will know. (Wait for clients to nod.) That's right. And can you tell me what the words are or what the image is? Can you find your voice and share with me? (Following their responses.) So, Jonathon and Janice, ask yourselves now *if* you should react? And if you do choose to react, what reaction do you feel would be supportive? What reaction would convey compassion to the other?

And maybe you can take some time to see yourself talking to each other in a soft voice showing your curiosity about your partner's concerns . . . Or, perhaps, you might wait to react . . . and maybe even not say anything at all, just be quiet . . . present.

If in your sessions no positive response from clients is elicited, say the following. It is important to reinforce positive expectations by seeding the possibility that the desired response will eventually occur.

I'm not sure when these words or images will occur for you . . . it might be later today when you leave my office . . . or maybe in a few days . . . or they might occur to you spontaneously . . . effortlessly . . . the next time you feel irritated by or annoyed with your partner.

Janice and Jonathon were then taken through Tier 4 and rehearsed practicing their daily affect regulation protocols while they were still in trance. They were given written instructions describing the breathing, sensory alteration, and the development of a safe place with a cue.

Outcome

Highly motivated to save their marriage, initially for the sake of their children, Jonathon and Janice practiced the techniques conscientiously and experienced remarkable changes in the dynamics of the relationship. For example, although they continued to have conflicts in their relationship due to the strong differences in their personality styles, the disagreements no longer escalated. Janice consistently used the Time Out and Calming tools, which helped her be more metered in her exchanges with her husband. Jonathon, in turn, was able to stay connected to her even when he perceived his wife to be overly emotional. Both of them closed their "exits." For example, he reported spending less time with his friends, and she decreased the time spent on the phone with her mother and sisters. They established regular date nights with each other and made appointments to dialogue with each other when disagreements occurred. Therapy was terminated after eight months when the couple was able to consistently demonstrate an ability to transfer their newly acquired skills outside of the office setting.

Case Study 2: Application of the Toolbox with Marital Conflict (Don and Cara)

Couple's Background

Don, aged 53, and Cara, aged 52, had been married for 25 years. They had two children, a son, aged 20, and a daughter, aged 16. Don was a minister and Cara was trained as a teacher but was not employed when the therapy began.

Presenting Problems

The referring therapist who had seen the couple for approximately 10 months felt that the escalation of conflict was the most pressing problem. Don was extraordinarily sensitive to perceived criticism from his wife. Her body language or tonal inflections alone could often elicit a very strong reaction. Don would become flooded with a venomous rage and would counterattack.

Don admitted that his anger was out of control and that the contempt he expressed toward his wife was not only hurtful to her but to him, as well. Cara believed that he was over-reacting to her comments and that he was unfairly and inappropriately attacking her. She would typically respond by initially snapping back defensively, then shutting down or "stonewalling." Cara often withdrew from Don for days. During the periods of withdrawal, Cara would express her anger nonverbally with silence and glares (a form of contempt). These nonverbal reactions, quite painful for Don, further exacerbated his feeling of being criticized and devalued.

Cara's stonewalling served as a defense to protect her from his rage. This was a passive way to attack Don's need for recognition and fear of criticism and rejection. A destructive cycle of anger and cold, silent withdrawal by both partners was punctuated by Don's intermittent aggressive pursuit of a response from Cara. This dance of dysfunctional reactivity was replicated frequently. When I met the couple, both reported feeling exhausted by the emotional climate of the relationship. Both partners were discouraged. Feeling hopeless, Cara had been threatening to leave the marriage. In turn, Don was feeling depressed.

Treatment Plan and Clinical Considerations

Initial Assessment

In the initial phase of the treatment, Don and Cara were seen together. The joint sessions were conducted in order to observe their interactions and to determine whether or not hypnotic interventions would facilitate their ongoing marital treatment.

In the first session, it was apparent that Cara and Don had mastered active listening. As a result of their Imago therapy, they displayed familiarity with "mirroring," a form of active listening that requires the accurate reflecting of a message from the partner. In addition, they had considerable insight into the dynamics of their relationship and how earlier childhood wounding was being replayed in their relationship. Yet these skills were not sufficient to contain the considerable hostility that was present in their interactions.

Treatment Goals

- Break the cycle of defensiveness, contempt, and withdrawal.
- Increase tolerance of perceived criticism.
- Enhance positive affect.
- Increase connection.

Tools Used with Don and Cara

Tool 30: Age Regression

Goals

- Revivify positive memories.
- Increase positive affect.
- Increase a sense of connection.

Commentary

The aim of this session was to enhance Don and Cara's relationship. As aforementioned, couples with marital difficulties often have amnesia for their earlier sense of connection. They typically describe a lack of affect or an emotionally dead marriage (Gottman, 2001). I completed Tiers 1 and 2 before using the Age Regression tool in Tier 3 that took them back to a time when there was a sense of connection and joy with each other.

Script

I wonder if you can go back in time and see yourselves when the two of you first began to date. And perhaps you can orient yourselves to the possibility of rediscovering some pleasant memories with your partner, perhaps remembering a specific encounter that was particularly meaningful when you were first in love. Going back in time, can you form an image in your mind of a scene when you were spending enjoyable time together? And take a moment to remember this scene, experiencing this scene in as much detail as possible.

Using all of your senses as you remember this pleasurable time . . . looking around you, what do you see? Was it quiet, or were there sounds in the background? Was there a special fragrance you associate with this time? Perfume or cologne or the aroma of a shared meal?

And as you go back in time, perhaps you can savor fondly the feeling of excited discovery when you would encounter each other. And you can allow yourself the pleasure of recalling the caring behaviors you expressed, the places you visited, the exquisite pleasure of touch, of talk, as you remember those times and places where you first fell in love. And let yourself feel that love, really feel it. Feel it now. And simply let yourself feel that love more and more, feeling that joy and connection that is so intense, so vivid, so compelling.

And can you remember what it felt like in your body to be in the presence of your beloved? That's right, that delicious anticipatory feeling and yearning for connection, yearning for touch, the reward of the embrace, the kiss. Let yourself feel it now, here and now. That's right . . . relaxing into that memory, falling into that memory, falling into that love . . . again . . . taking all the time in the world to reflect and ruminate and enjoy the reencounter . . .

And can you take a special enjoyment in remembering? Let yourself once again connect to that spark of excitement that you can feel when you are in love, when it becomes clear to you that you are a person who is capable of deep feelings, of connection, of love, who can truly allow yourself to experience joy with another person, to let yourself love and to feel loveable . . . to be really loveable. And I'm going to be quiet for two minutes of clock time while you remember, while you transport yourself there with each other, your body and your mind, as you remember, remember, and enjoy this feeling now. (Pause.)

Tool 31: Age Progression

Goals

- "Try on" the feeling of satisfaction once changes have been made.
- Visualize new behaviors and more effective styles of interacting.
- Recognize the effort that is necessary for change.

Commentary

In the third session, the goal was to create a mutual vision of an ideal relationship. Hendrix suggests that it is necessary to have a common relationship vision. In Imago therapy, couples are directed to write out the components of an ideal relationship in order to firm up their intentions and common goals. They are encouraged to write the qualities that they wish to incorporate using the present tense. For example, "We have fun together" or "We have great sex" (Hendrix, 1988).

The hypnotic phenomenon of age progression can take couples into their future, envisioning this ideal relationship, incorporating themes of health, home, play, sex, children, interactions, friends, and free time. Earlier in their Imago relationship therapy, Don and Cara had created a written version of their "Mutual Relationship Vision." In the previous session, they had been directed to bring it to our next meeting. Don and Cara reviewed their notes and talked to me about which aspects of the co-created relationship vision were of most importance. An abbreviated hypnotic induction was elicited with breathing and suggestion to revivify the trance experience of the previous session. Then the following suggestions for age progression were made.

Script

With your permission, I'd like you to drift ahead to a future time when your relationship has changed, when all the changes you have worked on in therapy, all the changes that you have yearned for have been achieved. Perhaps you will have taken a special kind of enjoyment in your ability to see the realization of your mutual goals. And, of course, I don't know what you are visualizing, but I wonder if you can experience a feeling of satisfaction, of joy, as you imagine the ways your mutual dream has come into being. And can you hold this feeling of satisfaction . . . this joy . . . experiencing it fully and deeply?

And as you do, can you acknowledge with appreciation your effort . . . and your partner's effort in jointly creating this mutual vision? So take some time to see yourselves interacting in an ideal way incorporating the behaviors you wrote of in your mutual relationship vision . . . seeing yourselves able to compromise and see each other's perspective . . . enjoying the pleasure of a satisfying sexual relationship . . . supporting each other as you co-parent . . . showing each other appreciation . . . And I'm going to be silent for a moment or two while you reflect on this satisfying vision of your shared values and dreams. (Pause.) And now when you are ready, you can slowly open your eyes, look at each other, and share your experience.

Subsequent to the three initial sessions, I consulted with the referring therapist who noticed insufficient improvement despite their reported enthusiasm with the hypnotic experiences. Don agreed with his primary therapist that if there was to be any hope of making the relationship viable, he needed to master containment of his reactivity. He was quite amenable to proceeding on his own, and this plan was agreeable to Cara as well. Hence, Don contracted to work with me individually while the couple continued their marital therapy with their primary therapist. As emphasized by Erickson, I chose to individualize the treatment by allowing the client's responses to influence my treatment strategy.

Case Study 3: Application of the Toolbox with Marital Conflict (Don)

Don's Background

Don's parents separated when he was 3 years old and divorced when he was 4. He had one older sister. He remembered his father as highly intellectual, remote, and minimally involved with him. Don's contact with his father became increasingly infrequent, and eventually he stopped seeing his father. After the divorce, his mother worked part-time as housekeeper. Then she became a registered nurse and worked in a hospital.

Don reported that his father became a vilified figure in the family, his mother often attacking his character. She freely expressed her resentment of her ex-husband, disclosing to the children that their father was not only irresponsible but a womanizer. These were a few among other character flaws that she would repeatedly share with her children.

In addition, Don's mother would often tell him and his older sister that she believed that all men were untrustworthy. He reported internalizing this disparaging commentary about men quite literally. Although as an adult he didn't believe that his mother's intention was to undermine his self-worth, he believed that she was insensitive to the effect her condemnation of males had on his self-perception. Don's view of himself was further affected by the chronic illnesses he had had all his life. He was born with Ehlers-Danlos syndrome, a connective tissue disorder of the hypermobility type. People with this syndrome often have fragile skin and unstable joints, as they lack sufficient collagen to support many body parts. Throughout his life, Don experienced tenderness and pain as a result of damage to the soft tissue around his ligaments. He was also asthmatic and experienced life-threatening asthma attacks in childhood. He reported suffering from migraine headaches from ages 4 to 13, as well.

As a result of his physical fragility, Don felt a greater sense of dependency on his mother and was fearful if she was not quickly available to him. His closeness to his mother made it difficult to separate her perspective from his own. He grew up very fearful that she would be critical of him as she was of other men, thus Don developed a strong sensitivity to criticism. This self-contempt remained a major dynamic that clearly affected his marriage relationship. Not surprisingly, when Don perceived that his wife was irritated with him, he reacted strongly. This is what Hendrix would see as a recapitulation of the wounding from childhood being expressed in the marriage.

Presenting Problems

Don was very concerned about the viability of his marriage. He reported that he was particularly distressed about his own reactions to Cara when he perceived her to be either critical or rejecting of him. He would attack her verbally in a contemptuous manner and follow her from room to room in failed attempts to get her to connect. All too frequently, he would lose his temper and yell at both her and his 16-year-old daughter.

Treatment Plan and Clinical Considerations

Initial Assessment

When I first met Don, he appeared depressed, reporting feelings of hopelessness, insomnia, and self-doubt. He appeared to be well-educated, articulate, and eager to engage in treatment.

Treatment Goals

Short-term
- Identify somatic cues warning of an imminent over-reaction and inappropriate response.
- Interrupt expression of excessive reaction.
- Soothe somatic sensations to diminish physiological arousal that leads to flooding.
- Maintain feelings of positive affect juxtaposed with irritation (to soften the irritation).

Long-term
- Accept self when feeling criticized.
- Develop intentional, metered communication.
- Develop curiosity rather than over-reacting to perception of wife's criticism.
- Become less sensitive to criticism.
- Learn to validate wife's perspective.
- Interact with his wife in an ideal way, in accordance with his values.
- Amplify positive affect associated with wife.
- Develop mindfulness.

Beginning Phases of Treatment

To rehearse anticipated scenarios, Don was directed to elicit an image of an emotionally charged interchange with Cara, such as being criticized, that would typically elicit an over-reaction. As stated earlier, it is important that the client re-experience the agitation and distress triggered by the partner in the therapy session so that he can practice interrupting his reactivity. This is an especially important step to increase transfer of the therapeutic learning into real-life experiences in the home. In this case, as with many others, it is important that the client accept the fact that he can have a negative reaction without self-condemnation.

Script in Preparation for Using the Tools: Eliciting Negative Affect
Imagine that you are experiencing that irritated feeling that comes when your wife does something to disappoint you . . . Perhaps you can recall a specific time that

her behavior really bothered you . . . That's right, just allow that memory to present itself to you, and as you remember it, allow that uncomfortable feeling to come, and let yourself really feel the annoyance . . . and when you're aware of this feeling, nod your head so I'll know. (Don nods.) Now allow yourself to feel that impulse to criticize her, perhaps even to mock her. Just allow this feeling to come without judgment or criticism of yourself for feeling this way. See yourself retaining that feeling of comfort as you see her irritating you.

I then used the tools from Tier 1 and directed Don to tell Cara ahead of time that he would take a brief time out rather than stonewalling or over-reacting. I frequently suggest that the client go outside or to the bathroom, somewhere where he won't be disturbed. It is advisable to explicitly state to the partner that he or she is taking a time out so that the partner does not feel abandoned in the midst of an attempted communication. I then taught him the Arm Drop, Tool 5 from Tier 2, and suggested he use that tool to focus his attention in his time outs.

Tools Used with Don

Tool 19: Self-statements (paired with Deep Breathing)

Commentary

After leading Don through Tiers 1 and 2, Don was then directed to use self-statements done in conjunction with the deep breathing. The protocol is an adaptation of the script from Chapter 6 (see p. 89).

Script

In this relaxed, balanced, calm state of mind, you can hear and internalize a statement to remind yourself that you really are in control . . . It will give you a more reasonable view of the situation, the necessary perspective, to help you handle this situation in a way that puts you more in control . . . First, take five deep breaths and say to yourself, "With each breath in, I breathe in soothing comfort; with each breath out, I release fear and frustration."

And as I state these words, I'd like you to repeat them subvocally, quietly repeating them to yourself after you hear me state them. (Vocalize the self-statement that fits best with the client's concern.) Now, continue your deep breathing and state, "I am in control" and "I choose to express myself in a soft and controlled way." And as you repeat these self-statements, you can integrate them . . . store them . . . put them in a mental file . . . for any time that this is exactly what you need to hear from yourself . . .

Don was then advised to repeat the steps several times until the impulse to be critical, defensive, or contemptuous was gone. I then led him through Tier 4 and directed him to rehearse controlling impulsive statements with daily self-hypnosis while he was still in trance. He was further advised to utilize the self-hypnosis protocol any time he felt triggered.

Tool 11: Mindfulness with Detached Observation

Commentary

For my next session with Don, we used Mindfulness with Detached Observation (Tool 11), a particularly fast and effective tool. Please note that once a client has mastered Tiers 1 and 2 of the Toolbox, a quick focusing technique such as "focus on your breath" is often sufficient to prepare the client for the next intervention. As Don was interested in the spiritual practices of many religious traditions, he was open to the mindfulness approach. It is particularly helpful for individuals who are self-critical when ego-dystonic emotions are present. Don's angry responses to his wife were very much at odds with his preferred self-image, a minister who values kindness, compassion, and tolerance. The mindfulness intervention moved him away from judgment of himself, as well as from the judgment of his wife.

I first had Don elicit a recent memory of a strong emotional response triggered by Cara and had him focus on the somatic sensations. I directed him to recognize where he experiences the stressful feeling and suggested that he place a hand on the part of his body that was experiencing the tension. Don was directed to do this along with the following prompts.

Script

And as you feel that tightness in your chest, you can ask yourself, "What is the problem or feeling I have right now?" (Wait for the answer.) Almost as if you're just sitting next to your feeling without judgment, without condemnation, simply with gentle curiosity. And what do you notice now? (Encourage client to respond.) Stay in the now. In the quiet stillness of this moment, what do you notice now?

Once again Don was directed to practice the mindfulness tool at home and to apply this approach when he felt the escalation of strong emotions. Don was encouraged to use the somatic reaction expressed in the body as a cue to practice the exercise.

Tool 22: Juxtaposition of Two Feelings

Goals

- Tolerate the presence of two conflicting feelings.
- Enhance positive affect.
- Soften resentment.

Commentary

The goal here was to elicit and amplify positive affect toward Cara and to decrease his reactivity toward her, as well as to maintain feelings of positive affect juxtaposed with irritation, in other words, to maintain two conflicting feelings at once. To do this, Don was first guided to a state of comfort that he had experienced with his partner. He then sustained the feeling while imaging a time when his partner's behavior might have elicited an over-reaction. This protocol emphasizes the amplification and maintenance of positive affect (Brown & Fromm, 1986). After an induction and deepening, Don was engaged in an interactive trance.

Script

CD: And in this quiet state you can orient yourself to a time when you were comfortable with Cara . . . a time when you felt good about yourself and good about her. And when you are aware of such a time, you can indicate that to me by allowing a finger to rise.

It is advisable to ask the client what he or she is experiencing at this point so that you can utilize the images and emotions as the trance continues. One should check to be certain that the client can indeed access positive affect associated with the partner, and, if not, build on the pleasant memories he or she can retrieve.

CD: And what do you notice now?

D: (Smiling) . . . I see Cara smiling . . . I'm lying in bed. She's next to me . . . naked . . . I'm giving her a full body scratch . . . feet to arms to head. She loves being scratched. I'm pleased to be giving her satisfaction. I love that she's opening up to me in a full open way . . . not on guard at all. I like touching her.

CD: And what do you notice in your body as you scratch her?

D: I feel warm with a pleasant sensation in my abdomen. I feel relaxed and pleased (laughing). I like the little bulges in her body. They're attractive to me.

CD: And what else do you notice that you're noticing as you feel your attraction to her body?

D: I feel warm and contented . . . I'm feeling joyful. I feel close and connected to her. I see her smiling.

CD: Good. You see her smiling. And as you see her smiling, you can hold on to that feeling of closeness and connection as you imagine yourself scratching her from feet to arms to head. You can take a deep relaxing breath, that's right, and you can hold onto that image and that feeling of warmth and that pleasant sensation in your abdomen. That's right . . . and the contentment and joy. Allowing that warmth, contentment, and joy to grow, a good feeling that you can continue to feel . . . very strongly . . . breathing in her presence . . . there with you. Let that warmth and joy and contentment continue to build. And perhaps you continue to see her smiling or maybe another pleasant image emerges in your mind's eye. And a part of your mind can hold on to these pleasant feelings and images even if another part of your mind revisits times that are less comfortable.

     I'd like you to imagine a difficult moment with Cara. I'm not sure which moment will emerge for you, but I do know that you have suffered painful moments with her. And when an incident emerges for you, when there was conflict, when there was frustration or disconnection, let me know. And what are you aware of now?

D: I'm remembering a time when she contradicted my opinion in front of our daughter. And I'm feeling very angry with her. I'm disagreeing with her as well, and my voice is raised.

CD: And now take a deep breath again, and I'm going to count from 5 to 1, and at the count of 1, you can return your attention to the joyful connected feeling you had a moment ago. 5, feeling the tension beginning to dissipate, 4, letting go, 3, moving away from anger, 2, floating, drifting, comfortably letting go, 1, and now return to the joyful, contented warm feeling to revivify feeling so good, so connected to her. That's right. Now I'd like you to retain this positive feeling as you imagine Cara contradicting you. Isn't it interesting that you can have two feelings at once, and perhaps . . . see yourself retaining that feeling of comfort as you see her contradicting your opinion?

Don was then encouraged to re-elicit the scene that contained positive affect for his partner, in other words, when he was giving her a full-body scratch.

CD: And once again the image will come to your mind, an image of a time when you were very comfortable and at ease with Cara. And you can return to the image of lying in bed and scratching her from her feet to her arms to her head. And as you see this image, allow yourself to really feel the pleasure, the connection, the joyful spreading of pleasure that this memory elicits. And now a cue will come to your conscious awareness that will remind you of this scene. I'm not sure if it will be a visual cue of Cara lying in bed, or her smile, or perhaps a kinesthetic cue, perhaps that pleasant sensation in your abdomen as you touch her, or perhaps a word, just the right word will come to mind to remind you of your warm connection to her, but you can take a moment to allow that cue to emerge for you . . . now.

D: I see her lying in the bed, smiling as I scratch her.

CD: Good, and that image of her lying in bed smiling as you scratch her can be your cue to pull a part of yourself into feelings of goodwill and connection even while you are irritated by her. And now once again go back to the image of her contradicting you. And when that image emerges, tell me what you notice.

D: I'm feeling a relaxed irritation. I'm alert and calm and yet somewhat irritated. I'm irritated but with a softness. I feel like warm water has mingled with ice water.

CD: Irritated but with a softness. Warm water mingled with ice water. That's very good. Isn't it wonderful to know that you can soften the inevitable irritation with your wife when you remember to connect to a scene of connection? So there is a part of you that feels the reaction when she irritates you and another deeper part of you that is softer, calmer that will stay with you regardless of the interaction. So won't it be nice to pause and take a deep breath when you next feel irritated and see her lying in bed, smiling as you scratch her and allow for that softness to occur, the soft irritation . . . a soft irritation that is so much easier to manage . . . isn't it?

While still in trance, a post-hypnotic suggestion was given to practice the juxtaposition of these two scenes daily in self-hypnosis.

Tool 17: Quick Impulse Control
Tool 4: Eye Roll

Goals
- Quickly interrupt a destructive reaction.
- Enhance containment skills.

Commentary

The first part of this session was spent reviewing progress that had been made in Don's marriage, as well as focusing on some concerns about his 16-year-old daughter. Ultimately, however, the goal of this session was to teach Don to reinforce his ability to control his impulses and to quickly interrupt a defensive reaction. By now Don was an experienced hypnotic subject, having been thoroughly trained in the calming and deepening tiers of the Toolbox. He was a good candidate for brief interventions that would quickly interrupt an over-reaction and equilibrate his affective response. Tool 17 has a special advantage in that it does not need to have a lengthy induction and can be implemented rapidly as needed. The eye roll and the slow breathing provide adequate focusing of attention and calming. The procedure directed Don to focus his attention with tools from Tier 2, in this case the Eye Roll and Breathing tools. Then he was instructed to add a kinesthetic anchor, an OK signal, which he created by holding his thumb and forefinger together and at the same time make an assertive self-statement, "I am in control."

I advised Don to repeat steps one through five until his impulse to defend himself was gone. Toward the end of the session, as a post-hypnotic suggestion, I recommended that he use the OK symbol with his thumb and forefinger, a kinesthetic cue and state a self-statement, "I am in control," when feeling reactive. He was further directed to imagine using the kinesthetic cue and self-statement while he imagined himself interacting with his wife (Tier 4).

Tool 8: Self-soothing Imagery, Safe Place—Nature Scene

Tool 28: Parts of Self

Goals

- Contain counterproductive impulses with self-soothing.
- Distract from distressing feelings by focusing on visual imagery.
- Diminish defensiveness.
- Encourage validation.

Commentary

This combination of tools, Self-soothing Imagery, Safe Place, and Parts of Self in one script aims to interrupt a defensive reaction in a few minutes by rehearsing the skill of validation. After these, we did a rehearsal from Tier 4 of the validation skill that had been taught in the Imago therapy used in previous couples sessions with his wife. In this example of rehearsal, I used a blank movie screen so that he could see himself practicing his skill. After an induction and deepening, we did the following intervention. After completing these interventions, I led Don through Tier 4 and had him rehearse his practice sessions while still in trance.

Script

You can now access your safe place (previously determined in another session) where you are so at ease and so at peace that it is easier than before to allow for your partner's feedback. Take a deep breath and, as you exhale, reassure the more vulnerable part of you that it doesn't need to be afraid of criticism. And you can breathe through your fear; you can breathe through your defensiveness.

And as you breathe into the stillness, you can imagine a large, blank movie screen in front of you. And as you imagine sitting in front of that screen, I'm going to count down from five to one. A scene will emerge on the screen of your partner criticizing you. And as you follow the breath, watch yourself validating her perspective, owning your piece in her complaint. Perhaps you might say, "I can see how you think that because it's true, I do that." Or maybe you'll say, "It makes sense that you feel that way."

I'm not sure just which validating words will come to you, but I do know that as you follow the breath and watch the screen, just the right words to validate your partner's views will come to you. That's good. (Pause.) And isn't it nice to know that there is a part of you that is so generous and loving and courageous that you can let go of that antiquated need to be defensive and to simply accept that you can meet her on a higher plane, a noble plane, that helps you both to grow? Now visualize yourself practicing these techniques. And as I sit here with you, this is a perfectly good time to visualize yourself practicing.

Case Study to Date

It has been three years since Don and Cara have terminated both the individual and conjoint therapy. Don checks in with me several times a year and reports on his progress. The marriage is still intact, and he states that the relationship is much more comfortable and satisfying. He practices the quick interventions derived from the Toolbox regularly. These sessions were audiotaped so that Don could recapitulate the themes that were given in previous sessions, including self-soothing, active listening, empathy, and diminished reactivity to criticism. He was advised to listen to the tapes daily for a month and then three times a week subsequently.

He reports that he is much less reactive to criticism than before treatment. Furthermore, he states that he is quickly able to identify somatic sensations that are precursors to angry or defensive reactions and that he is able to self-soothe with the brief hypnotic interventions.

Conclusion

Brief hypnotic interventions that focus on modulating emotional reactivity can be an effective approach to helping individuals who have had an impasse in marital therapy. I have consistently found the benefits of collaborative therapy to be considerable and the incorporation of hypnotic focus and suggestion in the treatment of couples or individuals in troubled relationships to improve the outcome markedly. It is suggested that the therapist be flexible in incorporating an individualized treatment plan for each couple, determining whether this aspect of the relationship work be done in individual treatment, conjoint treatment, or both.

CHAPTER 11

Application of Tools within Parent/Child, Sibling, Work, and Friendship Relationships

Judy, a 42-year-old social worker, maintained a full-time private practice and had two children still in grade school. In attending to the needs of her clients along with those of her children, she often found herself running ragged and juggling multiple responsibilities yet always feeling that she came up short. Housekeeping and cooking, not to mention taking time for her own self-care, were way down on the "to do" list. So when her husband Bob suggested that they have a dinner party to reciprocate friends' invitations, she reluctantly agreed with considerable ambivalence.

Judy immediately called her best friend Nancy, one of the people they had invited, and shared her doubts concerning her ability to pull off the dinner party with some degree of aplomb. She was therefore delighted when Nancy, an excellent cook, generously offered to help. "I'll come over in the morning and help you set up. And I'll bring the appetizers. So don't worry! Everything will be great."

On the day of the party, Judy called Nancy to check on what time to expect her. Nancy responded, "Oh, my gosh, I forgot all about coming over, and I just can't. The kids are in two games today, and

I'm running from one to the other. But I do have time to fix the appetizers, and we'll get there early to help set them up."

"That's OK," Judy responded, trying to hide her disappointment, "but please come no later than 7:15 since the others will be here at 8:00."

Annoyed at her friend's forgetfulness, she went back to her house-cleaning and last-minute shopping and cooking. She telephoned her husband four times, reminding him to pick up items she had forgotten, irritably displacing her frustration with her friend onto her husband.

As 7:30 approached, Judy looked at her watch. Her guests were coming in just a half an hour, and there was no sign of Nancy. At 7:45 she tried her cell phone and her home number with no success. By the time her first guests arrived soon after 8:00, Judy was barely able to contain her stress and frustration. She had a hard time composing herself to act as a gracious hostess as she apologized profusely to her guests for the lack of appetizers.

Nancy and her husband finally arrived at 8:40, appetizers in tow, as the guests were already starting to eat their salads. Nancy apologized again and said that their youngest son had had a "melt down" and her mother-in law had phoned and that she lost track of time. Judy was so angry that she avoided making eye contact with Nancy all evening. Nancy attempted to make up for her absence by offering to do the dishes, but Judy coldly told her that she really didn't need anymore of her help.

Judy's irritation at her friend was understandable in view of the fact that she had counted on her friend's support. However, Judy was unable to lay this issue to rest. Indeed, five days later, Judy was still fuming, replaying incidences from the dinner party over in her mind. Her sleep had been interrupted, as well as her husband's, when she would awaken, fantasizing confrontations with her friend. After five days of hearing multiple recapitulations of his wife's struggles resulting from Nancy's inconsideration, Bob finally said, "Nancy has been your friend for nearly 20 years. Can't you just let it go?" The problem was that Judy couldn't.

Judy is not unlike many people who are fine on a daily basis and/or with most of their relationships but who cannot seem to manage their over-reactivity with certain family members, close friends, or even fellow workers. As was mentioned in the discussion of Hendrix's work, when adult relationships trigger unresolved wounding from childhood, this can result in unconsciously projecting onto others the characteristics of our earlier caretakers, which often causes an over-reaction. This over-reactivity arises particularly when there is a conjoined task to be accomplished such as when siblings need to make decisions for the care of aging parents.

This chapter will provide applications of several key tools used for over-reactivity in the following types of relationships:

- parents who have conflicts and control issues with their adult children
- middle-aged adults dealing with their aging parents
- adult siblings
- friendships and work relationships

It is beyond the scope of this book to provide applications of the tools for dealing with over-reactivity within the parent/young child or adolescent relationship. However, these tools can be used to control impulses and destructive reactions frequently engaged in by stressed and harried parents. They can also be used by child and family therapists to teach young children and adolescents to self-regulate.

Please note that the purpose of this chapter is not so much to demonstrate new tools as it is to illustrate further applications of how the tools can be used to resolve challenges in other kinds of relationships. As mentioned before, whereas most of the tools can be used with many applications, I do try to select tools that seem to be a good fit for a particular presenting problem, as well as for the needs of the individual with whom I am working.

Common Barriers to Effective Relationships

We have already identified some of the common issues at work in intimate relationships in the previous chapter. This chapter will briefly address some of the common themes that emerge in other types of relationships that also have a significant impact on our lives. I have selected case examples that represent some of the most frequently presented relationship struggles that I see in my practice. These general themes are as follows:

- desire to fix or control others
- illusion of fairness
- overentitled versus underentitled

Desire to Fix or Control Others

The realization that we can't get others to change or to adhere to our advice can be frustrating and sometimes lead to overly reactive emotional responses. Yet as Marianne Williamson said in *A Return to Love*, "We are not here to fix, change or belittle another person. We are here to support, forgive, and heal one another" (1996, p. 116). The following anecdote illustrates how most of us feel about getting advice from others.

When my son Dan was in the seventh grade, he casually mentioned that he had an algebra test the following morning. As he spoke, he was drawing in his sketchbook with an occasional glance at the TV in the background. Incredulous at his cavalier attitude toward his studies, particularly since math was not his academic strong point, and with rising frustration, I said, "Well, you know, if you would turn off the TV, put your sketchbook down, and review your algebra, you might have a fighting chance of doing well on your exam." Without acknowledging this reasonable counsel from his mother, he returned to the art project that was capturing his interest.

A year later, when Dan encountered the mysteries of geometry, he said to me enthusiastically as if he had come to an astounding conclusion, "Mom, I've discovered that if I review the chapter before the test, I really do better!"

I smiled at him and commented, "That's great, honey . . . good idea! But you know, it occurs to me that last year when you were taking algebra, I made that identical recommendation to you."

Dan replied, "You know, Mom, it takes about a year for one of *your* ideas to become *my* idea, and until it is my idea, I just can't use it."

Most of the people I see who present with relationship problems are eager to offer opinions and suggestions to others. They want to "fix" or control their partners, their friends, their co-workers, and family members until he or she "gets it right." Most people, however, are like my son, preferring to come to their own conclusions in their own time. We can only plant seeds and offer soft suggestions and hope that the seeds of influence bloom later.

Illusion of Fairness

Another theme that leads to emotionally laden power struggles relates to the implicit contract in relationships that life's burdens and responsibilities will be shared equally. In reality, one person in a relationship often shoulders more of the load, though this division of labor can shift during the course of the relationship. In addition, it is common for one person in a relationship to carry more of the emotional load than the other, and this disparity can lead to resentment and a breakdown in relationships.

Overentitled Versus Underentitled

Most of my clients have personality characteristics on a continuum that ranges from the moderately overentitled to the full-blown narcissistic personality disorder, as well as the mild or extreme codependent. The criteria for diagnosing the narcissistic personality disorder is in the DSM-IV and requires the expression of at least five distinctive characteristics, all of which reflect "a pervasive pattern of grandiosity, need for admiration, and lack of empathy that begins by early adulthood and is present in a variety of contexts" (2000, p. 658). In her groundbreaking book, *The Wizard of Oz and Other Narcissists*, Payson writes that the "significant dividing line between the neurotic and the character-disordered has to do with the capacity of the individual for self-observation, as well as for real empathy of others" (2002, p. 19). Rather than the narcissistic personality disorder, however, it is more common for me to see those who display sub-clinical features of this personality style. They are what I call the overentitled. They tend to expect special treatment, are insensitive to the needs of others, and are often overly sensitive to perceived injuries to the self. The overentitled client is also typically deficient in the ability to reflect upon his or her actions or attitudes and is quick to blame others.

In contrast, those who are underentitled have many features of the codependent. I prefer to call these clients underentitled rather than codependent because most of us have these characteristics to a certain degree. The term *codependent* implies an extreme constellation of behaviors typically associated with excessive caretaking of those who are addicts and/or narcissists to the detriment of one's own functioning and well-being. The underentitled are often motivated by a need to please others, have fears of abandonment, and are undeveloped in acknowledging the importance of their own needs. There is often a rigidity that characterizes their interpersonal patterns.

Overentitled Behavior: Contempt

A particularly destructive style of interaction used by the overentitled falls under that of contemptuous behaviors. This is one of the four behaviors delineated in the last chapter that were identified by John Gottman (1994). They include criticism, defensiveness, contempt, and stonewalling. At a workshop I once attended, Gottman described contempt as "the sulfuric acid of relationships." Contempt is expressed when one person in a relationship implies and/or believes that he or she is better than the other. The overentitled judge with abandon their children, parents, siblings, and co-workers, as well as their spouses. They directly or indirectly suggest that "I think better than you, I behave better than you, I am smarter, kinder . . . etc., because I *am* better than you." Harville Hendrix also observed that "In our partnerships, we're . . . anxious to stake out our territory, [because we are] so wary of being dominated" (1994, p. 177).

Underentitled Behavior: Avoidance

The underentitled hide resentments and typically avoid direct confrontation. They fail to set boundaries, become overly responsible, and focus excessively on the needs of others. They accumulate resentments like green stamps to be "cashed in" with an abrupt ending of relationships. Eventually, like their overentitled counterparts, they can become judgmental and critical of others.

Benefits of Toolbox with Other Relationships

Use of the Affect Regulation Toolbox benefits these other relationships just as much as the intimate marital, romantic relationships we examined in the previous chapter. To recap, the hypnotic tools in the therapist's Toolbox can help diminish reactivity within all relationships in the following ways:

- self-soothing
- changing cognitions
- developing a dual perspective by working with ego states
- modulating emotions
- increasing loving connection and positive affect
- rehearsing desired nonreactive behaviors
- linking desired nonreactive behaviors with inevitably occurring triggers

Case Study 1: Application of the Toolbox with Parent/Adult Child Conflict (Marianne and Laura)

Background

I received a call from Laura, a 28-year-old former client of mine, who told me that she would like me to see her mother, as well as herself. In fact, she felt it would help her immensely if I saw her mother *first*. I was about to inquire as to the issues that she and her mother would want to address with me, when Laura interrupted, stating that "Someone's *got* to talk some sense into her—she'll explain it to you when she comes in."

Later that day, Laura's mother, Marianne, called to schedule an appointment. I had seen Marianne and her second husband three years earlier in couples counseling. When we met for our session, Marianne was gracious and happy to see me. Once we sat down and began to talk about her daughter, however, Marianne's tone and demeanor changed to that of exasperation, and her body tensed. "I've really had it with Laura this time. I don't know what that girl is thinking." Laura and Marianne had recently come into conflict concerning some life decisions that Laura, an adult and mother of a 4-year-old child, was making.

"When Laura chose to pursue a divorce two years ago, I supported her. I didn't like the idea of her raising her child alone, but I remember the circumstances under which I got a divorce when Laura was 7. It was tough, but I knew it was for the best. But what Laura's doing now . . . it's just ridiculous! Laura claims she's in love with this boy who is only 21 years old, has never worked, never gone to college, lives with his parents, and has this pie-in-the-sky dream of becoming the next Steven Spielberg—if only he gets the right break." Marianne paused momentarily to roll her eyes. Before I could get a chance to respond, she resumed.

"And, *and*, to make matters worse, she's planning on quitting her teaching job because she finds it boring—whatever that means. I don't care whether or not she finds it boring, she's got a daughter to think about—my grandchild—and with the teaching job, she has a short work day, holidays that coincide with her daughter's school schedule, and summers off. She's a mother now. She can't be making irresponsible decisions as if she were only 16—or the age of her little boyfriend. I can try 'till I'm blue in the face, but I can't talk any sense into her. She just won't be rational." Marianne's eyes began to tear as she looked down to her lap, fiddling fitfully with her purse strap in an effort to redirect some of her agitation. "I worry so much about how her decisions are affecting my granddaughter. I was hoping that you could help me figure out how to get through to her."

Presenting Problems

When it appeared that Marianne was finished speaking, I began by calmly validating her concerns, emphasizing that her reaction was natural of any mother who was watching her child make decisions that she believed to be unwise. I assured her that it made perfect sense to want to impart the wisdom that she had accrued in life in order to guide her daughter, and further, that it made sense that she had a strong emotional reaction in response to her fears for her granddaughter's well-being and felt that some intervention was urgently needed.

But, I asserted, it was just that: a *reaction*. I asked Marianne what she could actually *do* about this situation. All her behaviors had been directed at changing her grown daughter's attitudes and actions, an endeavor that was likely to yield disappointing results. This was something that she didn't have the power to do.

In an alert, waking state, I addressed these themes with Marianne to help her embrace the inevitable truth that she's powerless over controlling her daughter's decisions. I talked to her about the inevitable limits of a parent's capacity to influence adult children. Indeed, if a parent is perceived as too controlling, the parent actually weakens his or her influence with the adult child, as the adult child is more likely to withdraw in response.

I further suggested that it is only through closeness and connection that parents have influence. Criticizing adult children and aggressively confronting them with one's own perspectives regarding how they should live their lives is at cross purposes with the goal of maintaining an amicable relationship. In Marianne's case, if she is perceived as being too controlling and intrusive by her adult child, she may actually weaken her influence. Her daughter may end up pushing her away or stonewalling her (the destructive behavior identified by Gottman that was mentioned in the previous chapter). If control creates conflict, conflict leads to withdrawal and thus ultimately lessens influence.

Marianne and I scheduled a follow-up appointment in which I would reiterate these themes and introduce her to the tools so that she could communicate with her daughter without excessive reactivity and fight the impulse to be controlling. In the second session, Marianne was introduced to Tiers 1 and 2 of the Toolbox. I explained that it was unrealistic to contain her reaction and control her impulse to confront her daughter without taking time to calm down. Tool 3, Breathing—Attending and Deepening Breath, was followed by the Thought Stopping tool.

Treatment Plan and Clinical Considerations

Initial Assessment

When Marianne first came to see me several years earlier, I diagnosed her with an adjustment reaction disorder with anxious features. Her earlier symptoms related to an excessive stress response to financial and marital issues that she couldn't control. Once again she was responding with an excessive reaction to a situation over which she had little power. In this case, we see an example of the desire to fix or control, one of the pervasive yet destructive themes in relationships.

When I met with Marianne, it was clear that a quick intervention was all that was indicated at this time. She reported that her marriage was much more stable than it had been when she had been in treatment earlier with me. It seemed that other than this current issue with her adult daughter, she was in good shape. Remembering that she was an excellent hypnotic subject, I decided that one session devoted to counseling her on the limits of parenting an adult child combined with a couple of hypnotic sessions would likely suffice.

Treatment Goals

- Promote acceptance that she was unable to control an adult child.
- Interrupt impulse to confront daughter.
- Promote and maintain good relations with her daughter.
- Diminish fear and worried thoughts.

Tools Used with Marianne

Tool 16: Thought Stopping

Goals

- Interrupt intrusive thoughts.
- Develop positive expectancy to learn new skills.
- Utilize previously demonstrated successes in learning new skills.
- Master cognitive, visual, and kinesthetic tools to reinforce thought stopping.

Commentary

In the following script, I used the components of the Thought Stopping tool and individualized it by addressing the theme of interrupting Marianne's worried thoughts about her daughter and granddaughter. I also incorporated my knowledge of her interest and skill as a pianist, thereby incorporating Erickson's individualization strategy. Additional tools used in later sessions included Mindfulness with Detached Observation and Quick Impulse Control. See Chapter 6 for sample scripts.

Script

Take a moment, Marianne, to focus on your breath. You don't need to change your breath, simply notice it, and as you do, perhaps you can notice sensations that accompany your breath. With a gentle curiosity, you can notice the texture of your breath, the rhythm of your breath, even the temperature of the breath. And as you now take a deeper breath in and hold it for a moment, can you begin to experience a letting go of tension as you exhale? That's right. And it can be such a relief to let go, can it not? Letting go, letting go, of fears, letting go of expectations, letting go of judgments. That's right.

As you sit comfortably in the chair listening to my voice . . . letting your mind become very focused on the words that I say . . . thoughts may come and go . . . a rush of thoughts . . . a distracting thought . . . rapid thoughts . . . that is the nature of the mind as you begin to relax . . . but . . . as you go deeper into trance . . . increasingly focused on my voice . . . your attention narrows . . . and it becomes easier for you to focus on the central ideas which will enable you to gain greater control . . . control over your thoughts . . . You become able to choose the thoughts that are most important for you to focus on . . . and this is a learning process . . . and . . . .you've learned so many things before . . . and you remember when you learned to play the piano . . . how you began with your teacher showing you the basics . . . demonstrating . . . then having you practice . . . and as you practiced more and more . . . you became increasingly proficient . . . and your teacher added bits and pieces . . . musical pieces . . . moving from scales to tunes . . . putting together the pieces . . . piece by piece . . . learning . . . modeling . . . practicing . . . applying . . . until you could play the music on your own.

So it is with the process of learning . . . nearly any learning . . . and with this particular learning . . . you will have an opportunity to develop your ability to interrupt your worry . . . about your daughter . . . and your granddaughter . . . with very simple . . . but effective . . . basic tools . . . tools you can build on . . . to improve your relationship.

And it will be so nice . . . will it not . . . when you and your daughter can connect as adult to adult . . . and we've talked about how nearly every parent of an adult child wants so desperately to pass on their wisdom . . . to provide guidance and wisdom that they've accrued through their life learning . . . to protect their child from the inevitable knocks and bruises that are a part of gaining greater strength . . . gaining one's own life experience and one's own wisdom . . . the reason you have your wisdom . . . and not just from the teaching of your parents, but from your own discoveries . . . life lessons from setbacks, as well as successes . . . your own individual integration . . . toward which you could build your own sense of self-respect . . . sense of confidence . . . sense of who you are . . . and every mother wants her daughter similarly to feel respected . . . to develop self-respect . . . so we need to let go of the illusion that we can force the life directions that our adult children initiate or choose . . . and replace the illusions with sound knowledge that we can advise when asked to do so by them . . . but cannot control what they do with or without the advice . . . so that they can make their own decisions . . . decisions they can own as their own . . . decisions that affect the course of their lives . . . and the well being of their own children . . . and . . . hard as it can be . . . deep down . . . you know that's what you want . . . ultimately . . . even though it can be unsettling . . . even frightening . . . because you usually cannot see or control how things will work out . . . what directions your adult child's life will take.

So how to do it . . . Marianne . . . imagine that you're about to go visit your daughter and granddaughter, Laura and Emma . . . and . . . before you go . . . see yourself taking some time that will prepare you . . . and perhaps you're beginning to feel yourself become upset . . . because you will not only see your daughter and granddaughter . . . but will also see your daughter's boyfriend Jeremy . . . and as the worries and fears build . . . focus on your breathing . . . on taking deep . . . cleansing breaths . . . slow your system down . . . return to a self-reflective stance . . . where you can interrupt the thoughts . . . Picture yourself wanting to confront Laura about her poor decisions . . . Take a few moments to really feel that strong desire to confront her with what you so strongly believe to be in her best interest . . . feel the tension in your muscles . . . perhaps you feel your jaw clenching . . . the blood rushing to your head . . . or other reactions that are signs of your tension . . . and let those feelings really come up . . . those desires to protect your daughter and, even more important to you perhaps, to protect your granddaughter . . . and let that desire to confront . . . to influence . . . to control . . . come up full force . . . almost ready to burst . . . .

And when that feeling is really there, nod or let a finger come up . . . OK . . . good . . . and I wonder if you can be interested in just how quickly you can stop this impulse . . . with a very basic and effective tool . . . and you are going to learn three steps to control this impulse . . . One . . . bring your right arm up as if you're stopping traffic . . . See that stop sign . . . a red, octagonal stop sign . . . and say, "STOP IT!" . . . Say it louder . . . .bring your right arm up as if you're stopping traffic . . . see that stop sign . . . and say it again, "STOP IT!" . . . Good . . . well done. . . . And now . . . take a few deep breaths in and out and return to your safe place, saying to yourself, "I can control my thoughts and words" . . . "I am controlling my thoughts and words" . . . and when you next speak to Laura . . . or visit her and you feel that impulse to advise . . . it will be nice to know that you have this thought-stopping tool . . . that can immediately help you contain your impulse . . . And see yourself right now . . . at your daughter's house . . . lifting your arm or tapping your leg . . . and saying . . . perhaps subvocally, . . . "STOP IT!" . . . And see that stop sign again . . . and each time you practice the thought-stopping tool . . . you can be pleasantly surprised how the impulse to confront and advise will become weaker and weaker . . . and at the same time . . . a loving connection . . . based

on acceptance . . . and mutual respect . . . between you and your daughter
. . . can begin to bloom again.

Outcome

Marianne was seen for a third session, during which she reported that
she had successfully interrupted her worried thoughts and was able to
contain her impulses to give her daughter advice unless it was sought.
And if Laura did indeed seek her mother's guidance, Marianne had been
advised to give it softly, sharing her life experiences, including what
worked and what didn't, and what she did when things didn't work. She
had also been directed to phrase her comments carefully such as, "Have
you considered . . . ?" or "One of the things I've learned has been . . . "
For example, before therapy when Laura asked her mom if she thought
she should quit her teaching job, Marianne over-reacted with anger and
impatience. However, after our sessions, when Laura discussed the idea
of taking an exciting but high-pressured job in an advertising agency,
instead of over-reacting, her mother asked Laura to clarify her long-term
goals and then asked her how this move might help her meet those
objectives. This enabled Marianne to stay out of the power struggle and
allowed Laura to process the pros and cons and come to her own decision. When they had finished this particular conversation, Laura hugged
her Mom and thanked her for her good "advice." Additionally,
Marianne learned that if her guidance was met with resistance, even if it
had been solicited, she was to back off.

In the third and final session with Marianne, she was taught the
Quick Impulse Control tool (See Chapter 6, p. 86), as well as the
Mindfulness with Detached Observation tool. They were to be used
when she experienced sadness or fear regarding her daughter and granddaughter's well-being.

Laura scheduled an appointment with me soon after her mother and
I had completed three sessions. She greeted me with a radiant smile. "I
don't know what you said to my mother, but whatever you did, it was a
miracle! She's totally stopped interfering with my life. I can be around
her now without feeling all that ugly tension. I actually *enjoyed* her company this weekend when we all went off to the lake house together. She
was even nice to my boyfriend. Thank you so much."

Case Study 2: Application of the Toolbox with Adult Child/Parent Conflict (Deirdre and Her Mother)

Deirdre's Background

Deirdre, a 46-year-old woman, first came to see me subsequent to an acute and debilitating initial episode of panic, which was followed by an extended period of worry and anticipation of another attack. The majority of the severe symptoms subsided after about six months of treatment. When she contacted me again, at age 49, she was having trouble with her mother.

When we met for our first session, she immediately began to fill me in. "Dad died about a year ago. Since then my mother has moved into a nursing home, and her health's declined steadily. Rather rapidly, if you ask me. And now she's more demanding than ever. What's more, dad was always the one who could calm her down, you know, if she was in one of her huffs over my brother or if someone in her bridge club had gotten her angry."

In our previous work together, I had learned that Deirdre was one of two siblings. She and her older brother were both adopted when they were infants. Her father was quiet, often distant. In sharp contrast, her mother was highly demanding and narcissistic. Deirdre recalled that her mother demanded that she assume most of the household responsibilities when she was a child, and then criticized her for not meeting her expectations. Her mother complained that either the laundry was wrinkled or the dinner was overdone; Deirdre felt like she never could do it right. Deirdre's sense of self was further injured when she was compared to other girls who her mother viewed as smarter, prettier, or better academically.

By the time Deirdre was in junior high school, she was given the unrealistic assignment of trying to manage her older brother's oppositional behavior. She recalls her mother retreating to her bed with a headache and begging her to "Try to talk some sense into your brother. I can't take it anymore!" Deirdre's brother had become estranged from the family in adulthood. He had been diagnosed with a conduct disorder as an adolescent and had been imprisoned several times. Deirdre had always strived to be "the good one" in an effort to make up for her brother being so "bad."

Now that Deirdre's father was deceased and her mother was alone, living in an assisted-living facility, Deirdre was making daily visits to her mother. Again Deirdre was trying to compensate for another family member's absence, although this time it was her father's.

Not only did Deirdre feel that she wasn't meeting her mother's needs, but she became aware that she was no longer meeting her own. She had stopped exercising and had gone off her diet, which resulted in her putting on some unwanted weight. Furthermore, Deirdre's fear of not being able to adequately care for her mother emotionally, and now physically, was causing her a considerable amount of distress and worry.

"When I walk in and find her sleeping, I freeze. I stop breathing until I can see the rise and fall of her chest and know that she's just sleeping, and not . . . you know. But when she wakes up, it's just as bad. She'll want my help getting out of bed, because she can't manage it by herself. And I'm so afraid I'll let her slip, or fall, or if I'm helping her with her dinner that she'll start choking, and I won't be able to call a nurse in time. So I'll just sit there and not be able to help her, or worse, try to help and break one of her ribs, which could puncture a lung." At that moment Deirdre paused, took a breath, and stated, "You know, I've raised three infants, and I have never experienced this much fear, nothing more than the average parent, while I was caring for them. But I just can't seem to handle caring for my mom. And I'm starting to resent her for it, and now I've been dreading going to see my own mother and resenting myself for avoiding her and worrying about her all the time."

The more Deirdre spoke to me, the more it became clear that she had spent much time elaborating multiple catastrophic scenarios in her head. Such extensive, detailed ruminations are very common for people with anxiety disorders. In her case, however, her anxiety was compounded by the childhood injuries to her sense of self that she had sustained by the unrelenting criticism that she had received from her mother as a child. Her father's death had prompted her to slip into an old role of "the good one," trying, albeit ambivalently, to make up for yet another life circumstance she felt her mother didn't deserve.

Presenting Problems

Deirdre was scared that something catastrophic would happen on her watch with mother. She would get extremely anxious before seeing her. She was still afraid of not meeting her mother's never-ending demands and worried that if her mother choked in her presence and died, it would be her fault. Deirdre was still angry at her mother, yet she felt guilty about her feelings, which resulted in her wanting to avoid her mother as much as possible.

Treatment Plan and Clinical Considerations

Initial Assessment

Deirdre had made considerable progress combating her panic disorder. She not only had not had a severe episode in more than a year, she no longer lived in fear that the panic attacks would recur. Symptoms of anxiety persisted, however, as expressed in her ruminations about her responsibility toward her mother and her catastrophic thinking. When she anticipated visits with her mother, she would forget that she was competent in every other aspect of her life. As a result of the considerable injuries to her self-esteem, it was difficult for Deirdre to access the plentitude of personal strengths that were available to her.

Treatment Goals

- Connect to feeling of competency, even when she is scared.
- Connect to positive affect, even when she is angry.

Tools Used with Deirdre

Tool 25: Alternating Hands

Goals

- Know that there is always more than one feeling available.
- Experience the merging of negative and positive feelings.

Commentary

Even though the goal of introducing Deirdre to this tool was to help her get in touch with her competency, she may always feel some worry that she will "do it wrong," but with this tool she can access another part of her that feels safe and competent. I think it is unrealistic to attempt to completely eliminate a negative self-perception and its accompanying negative emotional state, particularly one that is as deeply rooted as Deirdre's. However, it is an attainable goal to help clients access another self-perception that they may be failing to acknowledge. In Deirdre's case, she had proved her competency and caretaking skills by success-fully raising her three exceptionally well-adjusted, high-achieving children and hav-ing a successful marriage.

Alternating Hands is one of the numerous tools used to elicit coexisting affective states. Other tools used in other sessions included Dialing Down Reactivity to dimin-ish her reactivity and Mindfulness and Releasing to demonstrate that she could be aware of feelings as they occurred yet be able to let go of them before they over-whelmed her.

Script

In your relaxed state . . . here and now . . . a relaxation that can be applied outside of here . . . you have an opportunity to learn a skill to cope effectively with the exces-sive suffering you experience before each encounter with your mother . . . And wouldn't it be nice . . . once and for all . . . to meet this responsibility . . . in a way that reflects the competent, intelligent woman you are . . . And with your permis-sion . . . I'm going to ask you to begin by picturing yourself anticipating a visit to your mother at the nursing home . . . see yourself getting things together to go . . . and allow the anticipatory anxiety that you have experienced so many times before . . . in preparation for these visits to emerge . . . Let the uncomfortable thoughts and feelings come up . . . feel the stress mounting in your body . . . perhaps notice your heart beating more rapidly . . . that dizzy feeling that comes to your head . . . a nau-seous feeling in your stomach . . . that's right . . . and tears may come. . . . It's safe right here with me to let them come . . . because they won't last very long . . . and imagine thinking that you don't want to do this today . . . maybe thinking of excuses to get out of going . . .

Raise a finger when you have that image and those feelings. (Pause.) Good . . . and now extend both of your arms out in front of you, bending slightly at the elbows . . . with your palms turned upward, gently cupping the air . . . that's right . . . that's good . . . focus your attention on one of your hands . . . and as you do . . . place all the feelings of inadequacy and incompetence in that hand . . . fears of making mistakes . . . and perhaps the anger you have felt that you could never quite measure up to your mother's expectations . . . Wrap the fingers of that hand around those painful feelings . . . and hold them . . . that's right. (Long pause.) Now focus on your other hand . . . and take a moment to get in touch with your competency . . . your competency as a parent . . . as a wife . . . running a busy house-hold . . . Take a moment to let those feelings of competency and self-assuredness emerge . . . Nod your head when you can feel it . . . maybe recalling a particular incident when you felt confident . . . and amplify that good feeling . . . that strong sense of self . . . That's right . . . can you feel it . . . really feel it? (Deirdre nods.) Good . . . and place all those feelings . . . those positive feelings . . . and wrap the fingers of that hand around the positive feelings . . . so that you're holding both now . . . the uncomfortable, negative feelings in the one hand . . . and the confident, positive feelings in the other hand . . . and . . . then . . . with your arms still extended . . . rub your right hand and your left hand together . . . blending those two opposing sets of feelings . . . accepting that they can coexist . . . and you can feel competent even when you are frightened . . . and perhaps you can be forgiving even at the same time that you are angry . . . and your realistic worries and regrets can become tolerable . . . modulated . . . the bitter part of life . . . balanced with the sweet . . . able to deal with the contradictions of life . . . the ebb and flow of feelings . . .

And with that understanding and whatever modifications your unconscious mind has added, I want you to let your hands come down gently toward your chest . . . gently resting them on the center of your chest . . . above your heart . . . and let the new learning . . . the feelings . . . the new skill seep into your heart and into your soul . . . into that safe, secure place you carry around inside of you . . . at the very core of who you are . . . That's right . . . feel it, soak in . . . thoroughly and completely . . . (Long pause.)

Outcome

Deirdre recently reported that she no longer has anticipatory anxiety before her visits to her mother. She stated that she has become increasingly comfortable in balancing self-care with a reasonable and responsible commitment to her mother. She also stated that she feels better about herself in general. It appears that the competent and mature part of herself has more psychological energy and is more easily accessed. "Now I think of all the things I am capable of handling as easily as I used to think of all the things I thought I couldn't deal with," Deirdre told me. "I feel better able to handle my life today."

Case Study 3: Application of the Toolbox with Adult Sibling Conflicts (Mike and His Siblings)

Background

Mike came to see me concerning a vast array of problems that arose after his father died. Shortly after Mike's father's death, his mother fell and broke her hip, leaving her unable to cook her meals and manage the large house where she still resided. Mike's three siblings, of whom Mike was the youngest, thought it would be best to move their mother into an assisted-living facility. When his mother heard of his siblings' decision, she phoned Mike. She did not want to lose both her husband and the home that they had shared for more than 30 years in just a few months. Mike's brothers and sisters, however, felt strongly that their mother could no longer function on her own and that they, not their mother, should be making the decisions regarding her care.

In response to his mother's needs, Mike had been going over to his mother's house early in the morning, preparing her meals, and even spending the night. After a month of his nearly round-the-clock care of his mother, Mike proposed to his siblings that he, his wife, and their daughter move from their apartment into Mike's mother's house. To him, this seemed like the most pragmatic living arrangement for the four individuals involved.

Soon after he announced the plan to his mother and his siblings, Mike began receiving phone calls from his three siblings. Much to his dismay, Mike's siblings accused him of having a hidden agenda: they suggested that he had resisted his mother's placement in assisted living so that he could live in her home with his family rent-free and earn favor with their mother that might win him a greater share of their inheritance—maybe even the house.

As Mike sat in my office explaining the situation, it became clear to me that an old family dynamic was being replayed. "They've always ganged up on me in the past, but it would be over smaller things, and mom would usually come to my defense. But this time . . . I've never felt so betrayed." I offered Mike a few possible explanations for his siblings' harsh accusation, saying that, in part, they may be driven by their own guilt at not wanting to take on the work that Mike was doing because they felt that they should be sharing in it. Another possibility was simple sibling rivalry because they felt that Mike had always been the "favorite."

Whatever the rationale for their behavior, Mike was deeply wounded, but rather than confront his older siblings, he chose to ruminate silently on his anger and hurt feelings. It had gotten to the point that he rarely got a full night of sleep and had constant "defensive" fantasies

233

in which he was being falsely accused and was trying to defend himself to his siblings. Although Mike felt unable to confront his siblings in person, he did so in his mind to the point of obsession.

Presenting Problems

Mike's reactivity and the accompanying stress reaction stemmed from several converging variables. He was still grieving the loss of his father, as well as experiencing feelings of loss related to his mother's increased fragility. In addition, he was obviously hurt by the treatment from his siblings.

Treatment Plan and Clinical Considerations

Initial Assessment

Mike tended to be a worrier by nature, first having sought treatment for symptoms of generalized anxiety disorder. He had difficulty tolerating his feelings and lacked effective self-soothing skills. Mike was used to reacting to stressors, both emotionally and physically, with fear and agitation rather than responding with effective coping skills and proactive behavior.

Treatment Goals

- Develop effective self-soothing skills.
- Diminish excessive worry.
- Handle emerging emotions without either suppressing them or becoming overwhelmed by them.
- Diminish stress by curtailing the excessive responsibilities he was assuming.
- Accept the reality that family burdens are rarely shared equally.

Tools Used with Mike

Tool 11: Mindfulness with Detached Observation

Goals

- Increase awareness of emotions.
- Eliminate self-criticism when emotions or negative thoughts emerge.
- Develop curious detachment.
- Practice self-soothing.

Commentary

The first tool that I used with Mike was the Mindfulness with Detached Observation tool. It was important that he become aware of the many feelings that his current life situation was eliciting. I wanted him to create a space for himself to honor the emerging feelings without self-recrimination. In later sessions, he was taught Postponement, Thought Stopping, Self-soothing Imagery, and Safe Place—Nature Scene, as well as Gratitude.

Script

You've been going through a rough time since your dad died, and I know you have been very concerned about your mother. And you've told me that you have such strong feelings toward your sister and brothers' criticism of you . . .

And Mike, you and I both know that emotions come and go . . . transient like a change in the weather . . . inevitably shifting . . . never constant, and I wonder if you would like to have an opportunity now to have a different way of attending to these changing feelings . . . experiencing the inevitable ebb and flow of emotions without being engulfed or overwhelmed? (Pause. Mike nods.) So, let's go to a place of peaceful detachment now . . . and you can look forward to experiencing emotions . . . to stand back and watch your feelings . . . as a kind of silent witness to your feelings . . . observing your emotions without reactivity or judgment . . .

Now . . . just take some time now to notice what it feels like to be calm . . . detached . . . just letting your mind become focused . . . as you watch the developing stillness in your mind . . . And that stillness will come . . . sooner or later . . . if you watch your mind . . . and watch your feelings. . . . Just attend . . . and I'm going to be quiet for a few moments to allow you to continue this process of mindfulness . . . this process of detached self-observation and calming . . . (Long pause.) Good.

And . . . now . . . I would like you to elicit a time when you were experiencing a feeling that was uncomfortable to you . . . I'm not sure if it will be sadness, fear, anger, or hurt that will come up for you, but I do know that since your father's death and the conflict with your sister and brothers, you have been experiencing a whole range of feelings . . . and when you can identify a particular uncomfortable feeling, nod again . . . (Mike nods.) Good . . . and now, I want you to amplify the feeling . . . just let those feelings come up . . . remember where you were . . . how you were triggered . . . and it is perfectly OK to let those feelings come up now in here . . . because they're going to go away in a few moments . . . and so, take all the time you need to remember a time when you were upset with your brothers and sisters . . . and you reacted . . . and, Mike, I want you to step back . . . simply observe the feeling . . . without judgment . . . without self-criticism or self-contempt for feeling this way . . . with acceptance . . . releasing judgment . . . like a detached observer . . . like a scientist observing an interesting phenomenon . . . just becoming aware and sensitive . . . and little by little . . . you get better at creating a space in which you can settle down . . . And now, re-elicit that upsetting exchange you identified before. Feel your reaction. Bring up details. (Mike grimaces.) Right, you can let the tension come up. Let yourself experience that time again . . . right now . . . you're doing very well. And now take a deep, calming breath . . . breathe through the uncomfortable emotion . . . and what do you notice now?

Mike begins to cry softly.

Mike: I really felt angry before, but now I just feel kind of sad.

    CD: And it is safe to feel the sadness . . . indeed, it is good to feel it, just let it come up. And I'm not sure what you'll notice next . . . when you'll be able to detach further . . . but I am sure as you practice mindfulness with detached observation . . . the uncomfortable feelings will inevitably soften and become less important . . . and I'm going to be quiet now while we create an opportunity for you to experience this healing on your own. (Pause for three minutes.) And what do you notice now?

Mike: I actually feel better, actually more relaxed than I've been in a while.

Outcome

Mike did move his family into his mother's home but not without due complaint and criticism from his siblings. Mike's siblings did not change; his reaction to their behavior did. He still avoided any direct confrontation with his siblings concerning their accusations and lack of support but was able to put to rest the incessant ruminations that plagued him. "I used to feel that if the world around me didn't change, I wasn't ever going to get any peace of mind," Mike told me toward the end of our work together. "Now I'm beginning to understand that serenity has little to do with what I considered *fairness* and everything to do with the emotions that I let in and the ones that I let go."

Case Study 4: Application of the Toolbox with Co-workers/Friendship Conflict (Christina)

Christina's Background

Christina initially came to see me to work on family of origin issues and their effect on her adult relationships with men. However, six months into her treatment with me, we began to shift the focus of our sessions to Christina's best friend and business partner, Renee, who had recently been diagnosed with cancer. Christina referred Renee to me, and I began working with Renee separately as she endured treatment for ovarian cancer. During this time, Christina assumed all the responsibilities of running their clothing and gift shop. There was an unspoken agreement that the profits from the shop would continue to be divided equally, even though Renee was not capable of working.

Renee was fortunate that the cancer was caught as soon as symptoms were present, and she immediately had surgery, which was successful. This was followed by an aggressive treatment of chemotherapy and radiation that went on for nearly a year. During that time, Renee was profoundly ill, depressed, and ridden with terror that she would not survive. According to Renee, Christina couldn't have been a more devoted friend. As often as she could, she accompanied her to treatment, listened to her late-night calls when Renee was overwhelmed with fear, and she told her friend not to worry about the business, that she would take over all of the responsibilities and that all she needed to do was get better.

During this year of Renee's cancer treatment, Christina was exhausted all the time, taking care of Renee, running the business on her own, and raising her two children as a single mother with little to no help from her ex-husband. But she believed the situation was time-limited and that it was the least she could do for her best friend.

A year after her diagnosis, Renee was given the good news that she was cancer free and that she could resume her normal activities. Renee did not, however, jump back into the business as Christina had expected. Instead, she took yoga classes, went to support groups, and focused on self-care. She frequently commented that "Cancer was the best thing that ever happened to me. It taught me how to take care of myself." Not surprisingly, Christina became quite resentful of Renee's seeming lack of gratitude.

Christina felt that Renee was taking advantage of her accommodating nature. She also resented the fact that she needed the profits of the business to survive financially whereas her friend had alimony; this also brought to mind that life had always been easier for Renee than it had been for her. While Christina had grown up as the caretaker of her siblings in an alcoholic home, Renee was an only child raised by parents who were indulgent yet inconsistently available.

Christina had been holding in this resentment for Renee for so long and was so angry that she could barely make eye contact with Renee when Renee did come into the shop. Christina was having difficulty sleeping and was waking up ruminating about her friend's thoughtlessness. She had chronic stomach pains that were diagnosed as a symptom of irritable bowel syndrome. Her gastroenterologist explained that the IBS was likely related to and clearly exacerbated by the chronic stress in her life. Further, she reported that she was deeply exhausted all of the time regardless of how much sleep she got.

The focus of my treatment for Christina became her resentment regarding unresolved issues in her and Renee's relationship. Renee also expressed concerns regarding Christina's seemingly inexplicable shift in attitude toward her. Renee said, "I don't know what's gotten into Christina. I don't know if it's her new boyfriend or what, but she is so cold and moody that I don't even want to be around her."

In therapy, Christina's instinct was to end the friendship and sell the business because she didn't see any hope for resolution. This was a pattern that had been repeated many times in Christina's life, starting with leaving her family at a young age due to her father's alcoholism, divorcing her first husband, and ending a series of unsatisfactory, codependent relationships. She was very resistant to confronting her friend and reported that the two times she had tried, Renee had agreed with her but hadn't changed her behavior.

Once again, as we saw in the case of Mike, Christina maintained an illusion of fairness, yearning that her work responsibilities be shared equitably with her partner. In her therapy sessions, Christina complained about her friend, expressing her judgment about Renee's irresponsibility and lack of thoughtfulness. In a plaintive tone, she said, "I might be crazy, but don't you think that she would remember how much time I spent with her when she was sick? I mean I'm not her, but I would think she'd really want to do her fair share at the store now that's she's better. Don't you think so?"

When asked if she wanted to leave the business, Christina reported that she felt an obligation to continue serving the customers who were regulars at the store. And she clearly was financially dependent on the income from the business to provide for her family.

Presenting Problems

Christina's relationship with Renee was a classic recapitulation of her role as a caretaker in her family of origin. Once again she found herself in a role that was too demanding for her to handle without sufficient support. Christina displayed the following characteristics typical of the classic codependent:

- difficulty being assertive
- unexpressed resentment
- habitual taking on of more than her fair share of burdens
- accumulation of anger leading to desire to leave relationships
- somatic symptoms that express prolonged stress
- accumulation of resentment leading to harsh judgments and contempt

Treatment Plan and Clinical Considerations

Initial Assessment

My initial impression of Christina was that she was overly stressed and physically and emotionally exhausted. She was sleep deprived and underweight and reported a host of other physical complaints. She also reported an unceasing sense that there wasn't enough time to handle all of her responsibilities and responded with a chronic feeling of time urgency.

Christina had an adjustment disorder with anxious features and a stress response that was manifesting somatically. She also displayed many of the classic features of codependency, resulting from childhood wounding in her alcoholic family.

Treatment Goals
- Diminish physical symptoms caused by chronic stress.
- Increase skill in identification of feelings.
- Increase assertiveness skills.
- Develop skills in asking for help.

Tools Used with Christina (Codependent)

Tool 14: Breathing in the Light (variation of Tool 3, Breathing—Attending and Deepening Breath)

Goals

- Know where her body holds tension when stressed.
- Deepen relaxed state by accessing a memory of comfort.
- Diminish irritable bowel symptoms.

Commentary

I was concerned about Christina's physical well-being, as she was experiencing gastrointestinal distress. Accordingly, the first tool I used with Christina was Breathing in the Light in order to address her chronic stress and its debilitating effects on her body. This tool incorporates a frequently used component of guided imagery to send light energy to the part of the system that is ailing, thus relieving symptoms. It engages the body's natural healing mechanisms.

In addition to Breathing in the Light, we also used the tools of Mindfulness, Imaginary Support Circle, and Behavioral Rehearsal in preparation for Christina having a conjoint session with Renee, the goal of which was to confront Renee with her resentments without causing damage to the friendship or the business.

I used the Mindfulness tool to help Christina become aware of her feelings without being overwhelmed by them. This enabled her to observe her feelings with respect but with some detachment. Then I had her draw on her imaginary support circle to gain support and strength to fortify her throughout her confrontation with Renee so that she wouldn't feel alone and unprotected, which is how she has felt most of her life when challenged to do things that are difficult for her. Finally, I led Christina through behavioral rehearsal to envision herself confronting Renee in an ideal way in the safe context of the office setting.

Script

CD: Christina, I'd like you to think of a time when you were really upset with Renee, a time when you really felt resentful toward her. Nod your head when you can access a particularly strong feeling of anger that triggered a strong reaction.

Christina: (She nods.) It was just last week, when there was a pre-holiday sale, and there were so many customers, and she left me alone in the store while she met a friend for a two-hour lunch. I was really upset and started having my stomach pains again.

CD: Now let those feelings come up. Nod your head when you feel that stress in your body . . . Scan your body to identify where you are experiencing your stress and put your hand there. (Christina puts her hand on her abdomen.) Now imagine a light in a soothing color emerge in front of you. The color doesn't matter; just allow the intuitive part of your mind to choose the right color for you. Now breathe in that colored light, and let it spread all around your abdomen, letting it spread all around your stomach, allowing that space in the center of your body to absorb the healing, soothing energy of the light . . . wondering perhaps just how easily it feels to take the light in . . . to receive the benefits of the light. And whether your conscious mind knows it or not yet . . . this imagery can relax your stomach, soothe your intestines, and even more . . . So that when you are feeling stressed from the toll your work and family and your relationship with Renee brings to you . . . you can look forward to creatively using the power of your imagination to soothe your body . . . to still your mind . . . which in turn will lighten your load, lighten your stress, and help you return to balance and health . . . just the right state of being to help you be resilient enough to handle . . . with equanimity . . . the challenges of your life. (Pause for 60 seconds.)

You can soothe yourself with this new tool whenever you notice the tension or stress in any part of your body. This simple tool will help you soften your muscular tension and soften your response, enabling you to very quickly regain control and balance.

(You can have the client elicit the triggering event again. If the client does not repeat the self-soothing somatic tool automatically, coach him or her through it in a wakeful state.)

Case Study 5: Application of the Toolbox with Co-worker/Friendship Conflict (Renee)

Renee's Background

Renee's relationship with her parents had shaped and reinforced the above-mentioned behaviors and expectations. Renee was the only child of two intermittently remote yet overindulgent parents. She experienced her mother as alternately self-absorbed in her own social activities and yet overly invested in her daughter's achievements. Renee's father was very focused on his work as the president of a company and frequently absent, but when he was present, he lavished his daughter with presents and compliments on her beauty. In his eyes, she could do no wrong, but he wasn't around enough to know when she was being troublesome.

Renee was not held accountable for the demanding behaviors she developed. Her parent's failure to set appropriate limits promoted her insensitivity to the needs of others. Renee also modeled much of her own behavior after her mother's self-absorbed personality style. Her mother's lack of attunement to her needs as a developing child set the stage for Renee's difficulties in her marriage and with her friends.

Presenting Problems

Although Renee did not have a full-blown narcissistic personality disorder, she clearly had several features of the overentitled individual that were delineated earlier in the chapter:

- diminished capacity to observe herself accurately
- reluctance to accept complaints
- assumption that others will suppress needs in order to serve her
- lack of reciprocity in close relationships

Treatment Plan and Clinical Considerations

Initial Assessment

Renee presented herself with self-assurance and charm. She was dressed exquisitely with carefully applied make-up, a sharp contrast to her worn and weary business partner who lacked the time and energy for such self-care. She thanked me profusely for the help I had given her when she was undergoing chemotherapy, making flattering statements about my skill as a therapist. When I refocused her attention onto the relationship with Christina, she appeared puzzled at first, expressing confusion as to why her friend had been so sullen and cold. Her obliviousness was in keeping with her underdeveloped sensitivity to others.

Treatment Goals
- Increase awareness of her impact on others.
- Increase openness to critical feedback.
- Eliminate selfishness.
- Diminish sense of entitlement and unreasonable expectations of others.
- Increase ability to take ownership of role in conflict.
- Access and increase empathy and compassion for self and others.
- Let go of short-term desires in the interest of long-term goals.
- Identify a more mature developmental state with adult nurturing abilities.
- Increase ability to understand her partner's perspective.

Tools Used with Renee (Narcissism)
Tool 28: Parts of Self

Goals
- Access and increase empathy and compassion for self and others.
- Let go of short-term desires in the interest of long-term goals.
- Identify a more mature developmental state with adult nurturing abilities.
- Increase ability to understand someone else's perspective.

Script
When you stop to think of it, we are all made up of contrasting parts, including those parts of us that are young, mature, self-absorbed, empathetic, possessive, giving, superficial, and substantive. You might think of many other contrasting parts of you that come to mind now. These parts reflect our life experiences . . . losses . . . successes . . . disappointments . . . injuries to our self-esteem . . . relationships with significant people in our lives . . .

We've been talking about your conflict with your friend and business partner Christina . . . which has been painful for you and for her . . . for some time . . . You and I both already know that it is more effective . . . in relationships . . . to interact from a more developed part of yourself . . . when the goal is for repair and reconnection . . . and the maintenance of a life-long friendship. It is understandable that when we're in conflict, we revert to the less mature part of ourselves . . . so that it is easy to be defensive and critical . . . and focused on one's own best interest . . . digging in one's heels . . . And what seems at the moment to be in our best interest . . . in the short term . . . contributes to us losing sight of the long-term goal . . . that true connections require . . . empathy . . . compassion . . . generosity . . . and the flexibility to view the world from another's eyes . . . And you have these skills. It is a matter of tapping them . . . tapping your inner resources. It certainly makes sense that when you are experiencing a conflict with Christina, you can access a mature, strong part of yourself that can not only comfort the younger, less developed part of yourself but can interact with Christina in a compassionate . . . understanding . . . empathetic way . . . This mature part of you is always there, even if you temporarily overlook it. So take a minute now to get in touch with that more evolved part of yourself and let a finger come up when you can feel that part of you coming into your awareness. (Pause.)

Now wait for words to come from the wisest, most evolved, strongest, or even most spiritual part of your being. Maybe images rather than words will come to mind, but really feeling your strength, maturity, and compassion. Look into the eyes of a younger, more helpless part of yourself, touch her hand, and reassure her. I'd like you to imagine encountering Christina . . . maybe at work . . . maybe meeting for lunch or dinner . . . perhaps for coffee outside of work . . . and imagine yourself interacting with her from the more mature part of self . . . that is most evolved . . . and strong . . . and compassionate. Imagine how good it feels, perhaps even spiritual . . . and allow the words to come that will reflect your best self . . .

And you can practice getting in touch with this part of yourself. Before you have your next encounter with Christina . . . you can take a few minutes . . . to get into a relaxed state . . . and once again access these developed parts of self . . . and you can look forward . . . to just how quickly . . . you can reconnect . . . almost effortlessly . . . to this more mature . . . developed part of you . . . reflecting the growth . . . being pleased with the growth that you have made . . . .

Now I want you to imagine an interaction with Christina . . . an interaction in which she says or does something that annoys or aggravates you. Develop that scene in your mind . . . experience it emotionally. That's right . . . let the emotions come . . . the desire to be critical . . . the feelings of being attacked . . . the desires to avoid or lash out . . . and then . . . picture yourself biting your tongue . . . catching the defensive, critical words before they leave your mouth . . . taking a few calming breaths . . . and then responding with the more empathetic . . . compassionate side of you . . . validating Christina's concerns . . . knowing that you can make your points later . . . if they are still important. That's right . . . that's good. . . .

Commentary

The Parts of Self tool allows a client to call on his or her more mature, nurturing self when he or she needs to regulate affect and reduce emotional reactivity. This wiser, more mature adult self can be a comfort to the frightened or overly reactive childlike part of the self. In addition to Parts of Self, I also used the tools of Age Regression to help her elicit memories of her earlier bonding with Christina and Impulse Control to help Renee stay at work when she didn't feel like it.

Conjoint Session with Christina and Renee (Narcissism and Codependence: Over- and Underentitlement)

After working with Christina and Renee individually, both clients achieved a number of their respective initial therapeutic objectives. Christina responded well to therapy, engaged eagerly in the process, and gained considerable insight regarding how the dynamics in her family had affected her interpersonal functioning. Her irritable bowel symptoms stopped almost completely. Through hypnosis and our good working relationship, she was able to feel supported and less vulnerable.

Using psychoeducation, hypnosis, modeling of validation and empathy, as well as confronting her directly, I was able to help Renee develop the ability to see situations from another's perspective. She became skilled in recognizing and interrupting her impulses to leave work in the middle of the day, a manifestation of her need for immediate gratification. Renee also became able to reconnect to an appreciation of her life-long friend Christina. The next step was to help Renee develop empathy for her friend. It appeared that it was now time to bring both women in for a joint session to try to salvage the relationship.

Although joint hypnotherapy sessions with friends, business partners, siblings, or adult children and their parents are not routinely done in clinical practice, I have found that conjoint sessions in these cases often result in dramatically positive outcomes. It is important to be aware that the clients might project partiality or favoritism onto the therapist, and one must be alert to this possible complication. There is of course a greater risk of this occurring if the relationship between the clients is characterized by rivalry or mistrust. A further complication can arise if you have had a longer therapeutic relationship with one of the clients. In the latter cases, I make a special effort to create a safe and welcoming environment. I make certain to validate each of their perspectives. These challenges withstanding, I find the extra effort sometimes required in these cases to be a worthy investment.

Tools Used with Christina and Renee

Tool 8: Self-soothing Imagery, Safe Place—Nature Scene

Goals

- Access empathy and compassion for their respective childhood injuries affecting their relationship.
- Soften defenses.
- Increase ability to validate each other's perspectives.
- Connect with underlying affection and caring for each other.

Commentary

In the relaxed state that the Self-soothing Imagery tool elicits, Christina and Renee were more easily able to let down their defenses, acknowledge their own limitations, and be open to each other's feedback. Both Renee and Christina had already established a safe place earlier on in their treatment, so I re-elicited this safe place in the conjoint meeting.

In the actual conjoint session, I started the session with deep breathing and imagery suggesting that they both go into their safe places and invite their girlhood selves into that safe place. I used the tool of Age Regression to elicit positive affect, reminding them of their close connection when they were girls. All of this served to soften the tension and encourage them to reconnect with their affection for each other.

After an induction that focused their attention and elicited a relaxation response, both women were asked to re-elicit a memory of the safe place that had been established earlier in treatment. Renee accessed her memory of being on the dock overlooking the lake at her family's cottage and was able to revivify the experience with all of her senses. Christina was able to recapture the memory of being in the backyard of her Grandmother's home. I suggested to Renee that she imagine her friend Christina at age seven and invite her to join her on the dock by the lake. Likewise, I suggested to Christina that she bring a representation of Renee as a young child into her own safe place. As it is always easier to soften one's heart to a child than to an adult, I hoped that this approach would help Christine and Renee feel empathy toward one another.

For Renee, once she was relaxed and receptive, my intention was to help her recognize from an adult perspective the wounding that her friend had experienced as a child overtaxed and stressed with demands that she had never had to deal with herself as a child. My goal was also to help her recognize that these wounds were being recapitulated within their relationship and more importantly that Renee had a role, albeit inadvertently, in re-eliciting these wounds and a responsibility to take ownership of that role.

My intent with Christina was to help her identify and appreciate the endearing qualities in Renee that are evident in all children. Further, I hoped that she could see the vulnerability in Renee that she experienced as a result of the deficits in her own childhood.

Script

And so with your body and mind more relaxed . . . you may be able to focus your entire attention . . . on developing an image of a pleasant, safe place . . . a safe haven that represents peace and security to you . . . perhaps to a wonderfully sheltering, soothing place in nature . . . or you can return to a safe place you've visited before . . . Renee, for you that may be that wonderful image of sitting on the dock . . . overlooking the lake . . . at your family's cottage . . . or, perhaps you would prefer to go somewhere else. Just let your mind drift . . . drift off to a warm and welcoming place . . . Let your intuition be your guide . . . and Christina . . . you can return to your safe place, as well . . . that place in your Grandmother's backyard . . . that you have elicited in previous sessions . . . or perhaps you may choose to develop another image . . . from your childhood . . . or a vacation . . . or a safe place you create in your imagination right now . . . a place that feels particularly soothing . . . and it really doesn't matter where you go . . . All that matters is that you allow yourself to float off . . . to your special place . . . and allow yourself to be enveloped in the cocoon of safety and security . . . that your safe place provides . . .

And each of you can drift off to your special, safe place now . . . and once you are at that safe place . . . let a finger . . . any finger . . . come up . . . (Both women raise a finger.) Good . . . that's right . . . look around . . . What do you see? . . . What images? . . . What colors? . . . Is the lighting dimmed or bright? . . . What smells do you notice? . . . What do you hear? . . . What's under your feet? . . . I'm not sure if you're walking . . . or sitting . . . or lying down . . . or just floating . . . Notice how it feels to be in that place . . . Just allow yourself to experience being in your safe, secure place . . . fully . . . with your whole body and mind . . . all your senses . . . and as you experience this place with all your senses . . . it becomes more real . . . and as you float there you can hold onto this feeling of comfort with all your senses . . . it can feel so good . . . can it not . . . so comfortable . . . that's right.

And I'm going to pause for a minute of clock time . . . (long pause for a minute). Now I'd like you to imagine, Christina . . . that you see Renee when she was a little girl . . . sometime before she was seven . . . or younger . . . And Renee . . . I'd like you to do the same thing . . . Imagine Christina as a young child . . . seven or younger . . . and . . . take a moment . . . to just imagine what that little girl was like . . . how she had been wounded . . . what she needed . . . but didn't get from her family . . . perhaps what she got too much of . . . or too little of . . . from her family . . . And you can encounter that child with compassion . . . and understanding . . . and acceptance . . . perhaps even imagine what you would like to have given that girl . . . if you had been there . . . and had been her parent . . . And now I'd like you to take that little girl's hand . . . and bring her to your safe place . . . invite her into your world . . . sharing this safe haven with her . . . And then, you can ask the little girl what she would like to do . . . Maybe she would like to go for a stroll . . . play a game . . . walk on the beach . . . Perhaps she would just like you to hold her . . . and talk softly . . . or be safely still together . . . and I don't know what she'll communicate to you . . . but I do know that . . . as you connect to her . . . with understanding . . . and empathy . . . that you can intuitively sense . . . just what this child needs . . . as you remain in your safe place . . .

Now . . . I want to say that this is an opportunity . . . an opportunity for you to really understand . . . how vulnerable . . . how frightened . . . that little girl is . . . and this is a moment in time . . . where you can genuinely understand . . . that her childhood wounds . . . are the basis of the defenses . . . that have impeded . . . your working relationship . . . and your friendship . . . as adults . . . (longer pause) and, my hope is that having had this experience of encountering and connecting and empathizing with the child . . . you can each soften your heart . . . to the adult woman . . . you are about to look at in a moment . . . and I'm going to be quiet for two minutes of clock time . . . in which you can prepare yourself . . . for coming back . . . and being with your friend and business partner . . . here and now . . . how you want to present to her . . . what you might want to say . . . the ways in which you want to respond to her . . . to truly listen . . . to empathize . . . to validate . . . So take two minutes now . . . to do just that . . . from your respective safe places . . . (pause for two minutes). And then, now . . . slowly open your your eyes . . . and look at each other . . . with soft eyes . . . Good. And now with your permission, I wonder if you would share your experiences with each other.

Outcome

After the conjoint session, Christina and Renee agreed to continue their business together for another two years, Renee having agreed to do her fair share of the work during that time. At that point, Renee would sell her share of the business to Christina at an affordable price. They began to socialize once again and resumed their relationship, respected and honored their differences and initiated dialogue when needed to resolve the inevitable impasses that arise in every relationship. In other words, they forgave each other.

Conclusion

Our relationships provide our greatest joys and our greatest challenges. The people we love disappoint us, frustrate us, irritate us, and challenge us to look at our shadow sides. Regardless of what presenting complaints our clients bring to us, therapy eventually focuses on their relationships. Whereas it is easy to join with them and validate the weaknesses they see in others, it is our job to help our clients take their own inventories and to let go of their desire to change others. This is not an easy process, but the mastery of affect regulation tools can assist in handling such relationships with equanimity.

CHAPTER 12

Roadblocks and Challenges

=========

My overall suggestion to help prevent roadblocks and/or meet them when they do arise is to teach a wide selection of the tools to each client and remain flexible in your approach. I think of this selection process as being like a box of Whitman's Samplers. If someone doesn't like a chocolate cream, he or she might prefer a caramel. If a client doesn't respond to a particular tool, switch to another so that he or she can experience success. Ask for feedback during the session with questions like, "How did it feel?" or "What did you notice?" Then incorporate the feedback when you customize subsequent interventions. In the next session, follow up with the client to assess whether or not the tools mitigated the over-reactivity. If a client reports success, then frequent practice of that tool is suggested.

Certain tools work better with certain personalities and temperaments. Recognizing individual differences in the way each client processes information is important, too. For example, it is important to note whether or not the client is primarily auditory, visual, or kinesthetic in the processing of incoming information and to shape interventions appropriately. Stephen Gilligan (1987) warns that a therapist's failure to provide feedback that is in accord with a dominant representational system often results in an unsuccessful outcome. For example, if the client is primarily visual, one might want to invoke visual imagery such as "Imagine a red, octagonal stop sign;" if the client is primarily auditory, then it might be best to use language that refers to auditory phenomena such as "And as you can hear my voice, you can begin to relax," or "You can hear the sound of the waves touching the shore." Developing sensitivity to preferred representational styles quite often lessens what appear to be resistant responses (Lankton, 1980).

Don't be discouraged. Finding the right fit between a client's personality and processing styles and the most effective tools is often a matter of time. For the most part, I have generally been able to find a tool that fits for each individual, although, like prescribing medication, sometimes it takes a bit of exploration and adaptation.

How to Handle Roadblocks and Challenges

There are some common roadblocks a therapist might encounter when teaching the tools. For example, I often work with clients who are noncompliant with practice sessions, who may have limited hypnotic capacity, or who demonstrate resistance to change. For clients who have such difficulties, here are some specific suggestions.

Noncompliance with Practice Sessions

The most significant challenge to a therapist's successful implementation of the Toolbox is getting the clients to practice. I have been able to find effective solutions with persistence and experimentation for nearly all of my clients *as long as they are willing to practice using the tools*. I have also addressed this common pitfall in Tier 4. Hypnotic visualization of practice sessions is necessary because, unfortunately, a verbal commitment to practice is not always honored.

I often hear the excuse "I didn't find the time to do my practice sessions much this week because I've been really busy" from clients with hectic lives. I respond to this with active listening by first paraphrasing the client's identified struggles with finding the time to institute the tools. This is followed by validation and empathy for their excuses, conveying to them that I do understand how hard it is to develop new habits. I might say something like, "It makes sense that it was hard to adhere to your practice time this week. Your kids had those school projects you needed to help them with, you had house guests this past weekend, and your boss is out of town. I can imagine that you probably felt overwhelmed and exhausted with everything on your plate this week. It makes sense that trying to add just one more thing to your day, even something that could be very *soothing and helpful to you*, could be a *temporary* challenge now." Phrasing the response in this way communicates to clients on two levels. First, it communicates that I accept the clients as they are, whether or not they have adhered to the practice regimen. Second, the inclusion of the words "soothing and helpful" provides an indirect suggestion that these interventions are indeed in their best interest. In addition, the word "temporary" plants a seed that the resistance to practice may be short-lived.

With some clients, direct confrontation regarding their resistance can be effective, particularly if it follows the empathetic joining described above. When I do confront clients I always try to communicate that I am acting with their best interests in mind. I stress that we are working together toward a reduction of their distressing symptoms and refrain from shaming them for any lack of compliance. With adults, just as with children, it is easier to hear direct confrontation if it is done in a context of caring. I have also found it helpful to educate my clients concerning the correlation between practice of the tools and successful treatment outcome. With some clients I take this approach a step further and confront them directly with the fact that they are spending considerable time and money for therapy, and it only makes sense to expedite the treatment. For example, to a client who had told me that she was a member of Weight Watchers, I said, "I know that you have been a Weight Watchers member for some time now. And you know that when you follow the diet *and* go to the meetings, you are more successful at weight loss. Of course, it's possible that you might lose weight just by showing up to the meetings, without strict adherence to the diet, because a part of you would be influenced by what you hear. But you get the best results, the best return on your investment, if you adhere to all parts of the program. And in that same way, I'm sure that coming here each week for your appointments, just showing up, you will get better and better at mastering your anxiety . . . but if you show up *and* use the tools when you are feeling your symptoms, and if you practice time-outs each day, think how much more quickly you'll progress."

As part of my direct confrontation with their noncompliance, I might also share the experiences of others who have used the tools. For example, I might say, "What I've noticed in working with other people is that there is a great variability in how much people practice. Some people practice the tools repeatedly . . . regularly . . . every opportunity they get . . . while others practice intermittently. Others may pull out their list of tools a year after therapy with me has ended. You have your own unique style of growing and changing . . . I don't know and maybe you don't know just when you'll figure how to fit in your practice times, but I do imagine there will come a time when taking care of yourself . . . honoring yourself enough to put some time in each day to practice . . . will become a very important priority to you."

Overall, a therapist needs to be creative, persistent, patient, and provide lots of encouragement and tireless support to increase compliance with practice. I call it the broken record approach to therapy. With clients who are well-meaning but resistant to practice, I have them take out their planners and write in specific times to incorporate the practice sessions. I convey to them that *I* care about their success by checking in on their assignments each session, even phoning between sessions when absolutely necessary. Again, I'd like to emphasize the importance of incorporating Tier 4 with *all* clients in *all* sessions.

Working with Those Who Have Low Hypnotizability
There are two schools of thought on the subject of hypnotizability. The Ericksonians would say that everyone has the capacity to learn hypnosis regardless of natural "talent." The other widely held perspective says that those who receive the most benefit from hypnosis are at least moderately hypnotizable (Brown & Fromm, 1986). What does it mean to be a good hypnotic subject? T. X. Barber and Sheryl Wilson identified ideal candidates for hypnosis as those with a "fantasy prone personality" who are imaginative and have rich fantasy experiences (Lynn & Rhue, 1991, p. 427). In my experience, those who are most responsive to a wide selection of the tools tend to be creative, intelligent people

with good imaginations who are capable of abstract thinking and are able to dissociate with ease, including children, actors, and artists, as well as clients who are survivors of trauma. In addition, Lynn and Rhue (1988) and Spiegel (1974) found that individuals who were responsive to hypnotic suggestion had a highly developed capacity for absorption. Those with less innate hypnotic capacity can benefit from some specific tools but overall need extra encouragement and support. For individuals who have low hypnotizability, there are multiple avenues to pursue. For example, the tools in the calming and focusing stage (Tier 2) of the work are easy for most anyone to master. Other tools that are concrete in nature, such as tightening and releasing a fist or cognitively identifying and interrupting destructive thoughts, may be more suitable selections for your less imaginative or less hypnotically responsive clients (see Chapter 6, Tool 18: Tight Fist and Tool 16: Thought Stopping).

Managing Resistance

Resistance can take a number of forms and can arise from a variety of underlying conditions. Sometimes it stems from clients' various personality styles or disorders, such as the narcissistic personality disorder or borderline personality disorder. In some cases, a history of early psychological injuries results in reluctance to trust the therapist or the therapeutic process. The therapist must be mindful of *transference*, wherein clients unconsciously ascribe qualities to their therapists that are similar to those of their parents, other caregivers, or persons of authority (Lynn, Kirsch, & Rhue, 1996). Brown and Fromm (1986) suggested that a sensitive hypnotherapist attempts to identify each client's unique patterns of transference.

In addition to transference, a client may also possess an underlying fear of change that results in a continual mode of self-sabotage. For example, one of my clients who was sexually abused as a child gained quite a bit of weight as a protective mechanism. Although she requested hypnosis to help her achieve weight loss, in fact, she then self-sabotaged the process by not practicing the tools. We traced this self-sabotage to her unconscious need to keep weight on because she believed it would deter untoward advances from men.

Another manifestation of resistance can come in the form of a client being hypervigilant and overly controlling the process. For example, a domineering client might not let you get a word in edgewise, thereby making it difficult to initiate a new tool, or the client may constantly ask what time it is. Hendrix interprets this need to control as a defense that emerges as an attempt to adapt to childhood injuries: "We use common defenses, including becoming overly controlling . . . as a way of trying to protect ourselves from further pain. We try to micromanage our environments as a way of keeping ourselves safe, and/or we hold tightly onto what's left of ourselves as a way of protecting against further encroachment" (2004, p. 105). Just as there are many forms and/or sources of resistance, there are also options as to how to best respond to it.

There are many differing theoretical perspectives within the hypnotherapeutic community concerning how to address resistance. Generally speaking, I follow a neo-Ericksonian approach to therapy and do not typically delve into uncovering the unconscious motivations and/or roadblocks to a client's resistance. However, there are times when these issues must be overtly addressed with the client in order to move forward. In these instances, I make use of a number of interventions from my colleagues in the field in order to determine the source of the resistance. I have drawn on the work of David Cheek and Leslie LeCron to attempt unconscious exploration with *ideomotor signaling*. Ideomotor signaling (a nonverbal way to communicate directly with the unconscious) frequently involves eliciting finger signals from the client to indicate yes, no, or "I don't want to answer." The therapist can ask the client various questions to uncover his or her resistance and in this way attempt to discover dynamics that may not be available to the client's conscious mind (Cheek & LeCron, 1968). Likewise, I have found hypnoanalytic approaches, such as hypnoprojection, that seek to discover the unconscious determinants of resistance to be helpful (Brown & Fromm, 1986; Hammond, 1998; Watkins, 1992).

After using these various approaches and reflecting upon what I already know about the client's history, if I determine that there is some underlying transference, I talk to the client when it actively interferes with the therapy process. For example, I might say something like, "It makes sense that you might be experiencing some resistance to this process because you had parents who were unreliable, unsafe sources of guidance. And would you be open to working today on that part of yourself that makes it hard to receive guidance from me?" In this instance, the Watchman tool (see Chapter 6, p. 101) is useful because it allows the person to have an observing, watchful self that will help him or her feel more in control of the therapist's directives. At this point, I might also use the Ego State or Parts of Self tool (see Chapter 6, p. 100) to facilitate a dialogue and resolution with those parts of the self that are experiencing resistance.

If I have identified that the source of a client's resistance is fear of change, I then break down the overall therapeutic goal into manageable steps to help reduce the potentially threatening nature of the treatment. For example, a client in a relationship might be afraid to develop and use assertiveness skills with an already strong-willed, controlling partner for fear that he or she might lose the little power that she draws upon through her passive-aggressive approaches. If the goal is to develop assertiveness skills, then I might ask the client to first practice this with someone who feels safer and more trustworthy such as a co-worker or trusted friend. Once the client has experienced some level of success, then I might encourage him or her to practice assertive responses once a day with the partner after having already practiced his or her own self-soothing and time out.

Finally, there are the resistant clients who either have a sense of entitlement and assume that it is my job to "fix" them, or the passive personalities who will put all responsibility for their problems and/or growth and healing on others, particularly those in authority positions. Passive clients need lots of hand-holding and present as being unable to do the practice on their own. Such clients often act on the erroneous belief that change will occur automatically merely as a function of showing up for therapy.

In both of these cases, I make sure that the client-therapist relationship is strong enough that the person will stay in therapy. Again, I do this by incorporating a lot of empathy and validation, as well as demonstrating my unconditional acceptance of the person. I never know exactly when the suggestions I make will take root, but I plant the seeds faithfully and water them with lots of patience and support. A fitting tool for both the passive as well as the overentitled client is the Parts of Self Tool (see Chapter 6, p. 100). I work with the client to identify and strengthen the parts of self that are more proactive, responsible, and self-efficacious.

Another possible tool for this type of client is the Imaginary Support tool, which I customize so that the client imagines resources to fortify and encourage action. For example, in a hypnotic state, I might suggest that the client invite into an imagined support circle caring friends, relatives, and/or teachers whom the client has identified as having a belief and investment in his or her ability to change and grow. It has been my experience that even the most isolated clients succeed in identifying at least one person to invite into their support circle. As therapy progresses, they may indeed identify more resources to invite into their circle.

Utilizing Resistance: Drawing from an Ericksonian Perspective

No discussion on resistance would be complete without referencing the enormous contributions of Milton Erickson who was a master at creatively using resistance as a resource that could be utilized for therapeutic change. Erickson not only respected resistance, he welcomed it. "If they bring in resistance, be grateful for that resistance. Heap it up in whatever fashion they want you to—really pile it up. . . . Whatever the patient brings to you in the office, you really ought to use" (Erickson & Rossi, 1981, p. 16). Erickson used resistance as a resource and honored it as part of the person's unique style of response. This perspective serves me well when I deal with clients whose resistance is particularly prominent and persistent. For example, I have one client whose anxiety manifests in part as an unusually high need to control situations. This is a man who is in severe, chronic pain as a result of a devastating car accident. He has indeed lost control of many areas of his life, including his occupation as a professor. There is a strong connection between the anxiety that he presents, his multiple losses, and his need to be in control. This need to control manifests as resistance when he frequently opens his eyes during hypnosis sessions and talks about issues that often seem, at least to me, to be tangential to the themes we are addressing. I remind myself that his personality style and his need to stay connected to me need not only to be respected but utilized. For example, when he interrupts the flow of the hypnotic process, I might respond with something like the following:

That's right, I really encourage you to open your eyes whenever you wish so we can talk. It's important that we stay connected. When you talk to me directly like this . . . while you maintain that relaxed state that you've been enjoying . . . you give me really important feedback and information so that you and I can work together most efficiently to move toward solutions that will be helpful to you . . . And now, can you turn your attention inside once again? (Client closes eyes.) That's right . . . closing your eyes again and perhaps discovering that you can return to a nice state of stillness and comfort . . . perhaps feeling even more connected to yourself, comfortably attending to yourself, even more deeply than you were a moment ago (pause) as I sit here with you attending to you, staying connected to you . . . as well.

Note that I respected his need to stay in control by reinforcing his desire to open his eyes and talk. Further, I validated his desire to stay connected to me while linking it with the suggestion of maintaining relaxation. Then, I reframed his comments as helpful feedback that could lead to positive therapeutic outcomes. Once I joined with his need to be in control, I encouraged him to redirect his attention inward. Finally, I suggested that he could trust that I would stay connected to him but emphasized that he could experience self-connection. This approach has worked well with this client. In time, he has become more comfortable with hypnosis and has used the tools successfully for pain management and reduction of anxiety.

It is always important to honor and work with whatever a client presents and not to push against the current by forcing the client to do something unnatural or uncomfortable for him. This is a very important part of the success of this approach. The client is always right! Whatever response the client presents needs to be framed as the right one. This decreases the possibility of engaging in a power struggle. Clients want to make sure that they are responding correctly. It is critical that you never make a client feel inadequate or shamed by sending the message that somehow they are doing it wrong.

Looking at Resistance from a Different Perspective

My colleague Sheryll Daniel, past president of the American Society of Clinical Hypnosis, stated that what is commonly called resistance is the clinician's inability to understand the client (Daniel & Weisberg, 2006). We need to own our respective part in a therapeutic relationship, just as we need to do so in our personal relationships. This brings to mind a comparison between a wise teacher and a weak one. A wise teacher will respond to the dilemma of meeting the needs of a student who is experiencing difficulty understanding a concept by saying to the student, "I guess I just haven't found the best way to explain this yet. Let me try again." This is a very different attitude than the teacher who gives the clear impression that there must be something wrong with the student if he doesn't learn a given concept right away. So, for example, what we might initially attribute to resistance on the part of the client may, in fact, be that we have not fully understood his or her learning style. The responsibility lies within us to do so.

It can be difficult to determine whether or not the source of the resistance is due to your own limited understanding and/or flexibility, or if, in fact, it stems from the client. I encourage you to seek out feedback from the client regarding what he or she is finding to be difficult or not helpful about the process. You can choose to receive this feedback as a gift and an opportunity to reexamine your understanding of their styles and unique ways of processing.

I encourage you to be curious about resistance, to wonder about it, and to be challenged to use it creatively in the therapeutic process. We need to commit to the persistent pursuit of knowledge regarding the client's current inner world along with his or her past. If resistance builds, the therapist must meet that resistance with unceasing curiosity. As Hendrix suggested in his work with couples, one needs to acquire "relational knowing," which involves moving from your "head into your heart" (2004, pp. 214–215). This kind of knowing comes from an attempt to envision the person's experience and connect empathetically to his or her reality.

Matching the Tools with Client Needs and Styles

Within the Toolbox, there are a variety of tools that could match with a number of cognitive or personality characteristics. For example, clients whose personalities are characterized by rigidity and suspicion may have difficulty trusting the process and fear being out of control. These clients find the Watchman tool to be reassuring because it incorporates an observing self that watches the process (see Chapter 6, p.

101). Tools that focus on self-talk are suitable for intellectually defended clients who find it difficult to allow their bodies to relax and to get out of their heads. Anxious clients almost always find relief with the tools that focus on mindfulness. Concrete thinkers who are less imaginative might respond to the tools that focus on kinesthetic interventions, such as the Tight Fist tool, or to highly structured interventions such as Thought Stopping or Self-statements. For depressed clients, the Age Progression tool can build positive expectancy and hope about the future regarding changes resulting from therapy. I frequently draw on Michael Yapko's emphasis on building positive expectancy, particularly with depressed clients (1988, 1992, 2001). Depressed clients should be encouraged to focus on internal resources, positive affect development tools, and age progression to a time when they will feel better.

Acceptance

There is a personal struggle regarding the resistance and noncompliance of my clients that I'm certain I share with other well-meaning clinicians, regardless of experience. Sometimes I wonder if I am more invested in the therapeutic outcome than some of my clients. Regardless of your skill as a clinician or the clinical potential of a given tool, individuals do not change until they are ready. Once again, I am reminded of the eye-opening encounter with my son, which I shared in the previous chapter, when he told me that it takes about a year for one of my ideas to become his. Even if your clients don't immediately incorporate your suggestions, remember that you have planted a seed for change that may eventually take root and blossom.

Epilogue

This book has focused on the client, specifically the over-reactive client. I would like to conclude the book by focusing on the therapist. In these final pages, I will reflect on some issues common to all healers and discuss the importance of developing and trusting one's own voice and style despite the inevitable self-doubt we all experience at times in our work. I'd also like to share some thoughts about the personal rewards that are an outgrowth of our professions and are linked to essential life satisfaction. I will conclude with encouragement to practice self-care.

Dealing with Self-Doubt

Being concerned about how we are perceived by clients is normal. And most of us feel self-conscious when trying out a new skill. Yet as we attend to our craft and continue to practice, the self-consciousness abates. And we must not forget that our relationships with our clients are infinitely more important than the cleverness of any given intervention or the ease with which it is delivered. Most of us have seen films that have great special effects yet nevertheless are disappointing. If we are not moved by the story line or feel no connection with the characters, it remains a weak film. Similarly, in healing relationships, the meaning in large part is about connection. It is your genuine interest in your clients and your felt and expressed caring and commitment to their empowerment that is of utmost importance. Just as we teach our clients mindfulness and acceptance of a given feeling, we must also be gently mindful of our own self-consciousness and self-doubt. This nonjudgmental mindfulness will inevitably help us feel more comfortable. Remember that even though you may be feeling some level of internal uncertainty, it is rarely evident to the client. Even as your confidence increases with practice, one of the most challenging aspects of the art of hypnosis remains discovering and trusting your own voice.

Trusting Your Own Voice

Although we are influenced by our teachers, we must also have the courage to be authentic and to listen to our own voice as we work. It is an ongoing process to discover one's own voice, style, and language. Havens and Walters (1989) adeptly captured this concept in the following excerpt:

> Although we have endeavored to provide hypnotherapy scripts that we have found to be useful with many different types of clients, it must be emphasized again that these scripts were designed to serve as templates or examples. To the extent that they are relevant to the needs and dynamics of any given individual, they may prove therapeutically useful. On the other hand, we encourage you to begin as soon as possible . . . to [develop] scripts [or your own tools] which are specifically selected to express the unique problems and personality of your client and your own unique style.
>
> Our initial injunction to . . . [students] to trust their own unconscious probably did not work very well because their unconscious minds had not yet had an opportunity to learn what was needed. Practice using the materials presented here, until you have developed a familiarity with the concepts and processes, then trust your unconscious. Its power of observation, comprehension and creativity may surprise you and your clients as well. (p. 190)

In other words, this process involves learning as much as possible from other people's work and then launching out on your own, not only gearing your interventions to clients' needs but also making certain that they resonate with your own personal style and voice.

The Satisfied Therapist

I recently attended a presentation given by Christopher Peterson who, along with Martin Seligman, has written extensively on positive psychology. Research has found that the most satisfied people experience "positive emotion, engagement, and meaning" in their lives (Seligman, Steen, Park, & Peterson, 2005, p. 410). These researchers stated that the following behaviors are among those that correlate with reports of happier, more satisfying lives:

- giving service to other
- performing acts of kindness
- doing extroverted things
- using your strengths
- creating flow

I was struck by how all of these behaviors are intrinsic to our work as therapists. This helps explain why we can feel fortunate to be in our line of work. In his lecture, Dr. Peterson also mentioned another correlate to happiness, which is gratitude. I remind myself on a daily basis that I am indeed privileged to hear my clients' stories and encounter the core vulnerabilities of the human condition. A daily decision to maintain an attitude of gratitude serves to soften the inevitable emotional drain, fatigue, and occasional frustration that we all experience in this fulfilling yet highly demanding work.

Self-Care for the Practitioner

For all therapists who earnestly try to care for others, I cannot overemphasize the importance of also caring for yourself. Louise Hay stated that the most important thing practitioners can do to help their clients is to "love themselves. When therapists really love who they are, it's easier for them to teach that love to their clients. When they don't, all the talk in the world, all the methods in the world, do not really get across" (1989, p. 23). Hay suggested that the first way to begin to love ourselves is to stop the self-criticism.

All too often we teach well, but we don't always practice what we teach. Inward attention is mandatory when we spend so much time with an external focus. Setting aside time each day for meditation or self-hypnosis is crucial to maintaining one's own equilibrium and for avoiding burn out.

David Spiegel stated that "Smart therapists know how to grow with their patients" (2001, pp. x–xi). I'd like to challenge you to grow at this very moment by taking a time out for yourself and practicing one of the tools. If you're anything like me, you're probably thinking "I don't have the time. I'll get around to it later." But in the words of singer/songwriter Tracy Chapman, "If not now, when?" Both you and your clients deserve the benefits yielded by setting aside time for yourself. I urge you to be open to the possibility of healing that can arise as you draw upon one or more of the tools that I've had the privilege of sharing with you in this book.

Resources for Clinicians and Clients

═══════════════

Resources for Clinicians

Hypnosis Training

The American Society of Clinical Hypnosis (ASCH)
140 North Bloomingdale Road
Bloomingdale, IL 60108
Web site: http://www.asch.net

The Society of Clinical and Experimental Hypnosis (SCEH)
Massachusetts School of Professional Psychology
221 Rivermoor Street
Boston, MA 02132
Web site: http://www.sceh.us

The Milton H. Erickson Foundation
3606 North 24th Street
Phoenix, AZ 85016
Web site: http://www.erickson-foundation.org

International Society of Hypnosis
Military Hospital University Medical Center
Utrecht Heidelberglaan 100
3584 CX Utrecht, The Netherlands
Web site: http://www.ish.driebit.com/page.php

Videotapes

Daitch, C. (2002). *Mingling the waters*. Farmington Hills, MI: Self-published.

This video demonstrates the mastery of the Juxtaposition of Two Feelings tool (Tool 22) with a client who is over-reactive in his marriage. Available at http://www.anxiety-treatment.com

Erickson, M. H. (2005). *Now, you wanted a trance demonstrated today.* Videotape and annotated transcript, Laguna Niguel, CA: The Southern California Society for Ericksonian Psychotherapy and Hypnosis. Available at http://www.scseph.org

Yapko, M. (2006). *Brief therapy inside out: Breaking the patterns of depression.* Redding, CT: Zeig, Tucker, & Theisen. Available at http://www.zeigtucker.com

Zeig, J. (1995). *Guiding associations*. Phoenix, AZ: Evolution. Available at http://www.ericksonfoundation.org

Books

Brown, D. P., & Fromm, E. (1986). *Hypnotherapy and hypnoanalysis*. London: Lawrence Erlbaum Associates.

Gottman, J. M., & Silver, N. (1999). *The seven principles for making marriage work*. New York: Three Rivers Press.

Hammond, D. (1990). *Handbook of hypnotic suggestions and metaphors*. New York: W. W. Norton.

(See pp. 40–41 for a list of commonly used hypnotic phrasing and language patterns.) See also the audio CD programs listed below for clients. They provide many examples of hypnotic phrasing and use of voice. *Theta Sailing II* is excellent background music to be played during hypnotic sessions.

Havens, R. A., & Walters, C. (1989). *Hypnotherapy scripts: A neo-Ericksonian approach to persuasive healing*. New York: Brunner/Mazel.

Hendrix, H. (1988). *Getting the love you want: A guide for couples.* New York: Harper.

Yapko, M. D. (1990). *Trancework: An introduction to the practice of clinical hypnosis.* (2nd ed.). New York: Brunner/Mazel.

Resources for Clients

Workbooks

Bourne, E. J. (1995). *The anxiety and phobia workbook* (2nd ed.). Oakland, CA: New Harbinger.

Davis, M., Eshelman, E. R., & McKay, M. (1982). *The relaxation and stress reduction workbook.* Oakland, CA: New Harbinger.

Hyman, B. M., & Pedrick, C. (1999). *The OCD workbook: Your guide to breaking free from obsessive-compulsive disorders.* Oakland, CA: New Harbinger.

CDs

I developed the following CD programs using many of the treatment protocols described in the book:

- *Dialing Down Anxiety*
- *Managing the Distress of Cancer and its Treatment* (formerly *Biovast with Dr. Hava Shaver*)
- *The Insomnia Solution*
- *Theta Sailing II*

These audio programs are not a substitute for professional treatment. They are designed to be an adjunct to the medical or psychotherapeutic treatment clients are receiving. The CDs also provide the practitioner with examples of hypnotic phrasing and delivery.

Dialing Down Anxiety
This audio program uses visualization, guided imagery, and proven stress and anxiety reduction techniques to address the over-reactivity that accompanies anxiety.

Managing the Distress of Cancer and its Treatment (formerly *Biovast with Dr. Hava Shaver*)

This audio program empowers cancer patients to relieve the emotional and physical distress of cancer and chemotherapy using techniques such as visualization, imagery, relaxation, and positive affirmation.

The Insomnia Solution

When used nightly, this audio program trains the listener's nervous system to elicit the appropriate level of relaxation to foster good sleeping habits.

Theta Sailing II

This musical CD is especially designed for clinicians who provide their clients with guided imagery, progressive relaxation, or hypnosis. It assists the client to quickly move into a state conducive to the development of therapist or self-directed experience. With repeated exposure in therapy sessions, the music becomes a cue for the client to re-elicit a state of relaxation. Clients who have had relaxation training or hypnosis accompanied by *Theta Sailing II* frequently request a copy of the music to play at home.

To order CDs or videotapes contact:

Carolyn L. Daitch, Ph.D.
28592 Orchard Lake Rd., #301
Farmington Hills, MI 48334
Web site: http://www.anxiety-treatment.com
Email address: carolyn.daitch@mac.com

References

American Psychiatric Association. (1994). *Diagnostic and statistical manual of mental disorders* (4th ed.). Washington, DC: Author.

Baker, E. (1981). A hypnotherapeutic approach to enhance object relatedness in psychotic patients. *International Journal of Clinical and Experimental Hypnosis, 124,* 136–147.

Bandler, R., & Grinder, J. (1975). *Patterns of the hypnotic techniques of Milton H. Erickson, M.D.* (Vol. 1). Cupertino, CA: Meta.

Barabasz, A., & Watkins, J. G. (2005). *Hypnotherapeutic techniques* (2nd ed.). New York: Brunner-Routledge.

Barber, T. X. (1999). A comprehensive three-dimensional theory of hypnosis. In I. Kirsch, A. Capafons, E. Cardena-Buelina, & S. Amigo (Eds.), *Clinical hypnosis and self-regulation: Cognitive-behavioral perspectives* (pp. 21–48). Washington, DC: American Psychological Association.

Barlow, D. (1988). *Anxiety and its disorders: The nature and treatment of anxiety and panic.* New York: Guilford.

Battino, R. (2000). *Guided imagery and other approaches to healing.* Williston, VT: Crown House.

Bear, M., Connors, B., & Paradiso, M. (2001). *Neuroscience: Exploring the brain.* Baltimore, MD: Lippincott Williams & Wilkins.

Beck, A. T. (1984). Cognitive approaches to stress. In R. L. Woolfolk & C. Lehrer (Eds.), *Principles and practice of stress management* (pp. 271–275). New York: Guilford.

Beck, A. T. (1990). *Beck anxiety inventory®* (BAI®). San Antonio, TX: Harcourt Assessment.

Beck, A. T., Emery, G., & Greenberg, R. L. (1985). *Anxiety disorders and phobias: A cognitive perspective.* New York: Basic.

Benson, H. (1975). *The relaxation response.* New York: Morrow.

Benson, H. (1983). The relaxation response: Its subjective and objective historical precedents and physiology. *Trends-in-Neurosciences, 6*(7), 281–284.

Berne, E. (1961). *Transactional analysis in psychotherapy.* New York: Grove Press.

Bourne, E. (1995). *The anxiety and phobia workbook.* Oakland, CA: New Harbinger.

Brown, D. P., & Fromm, E. (1986). *Hypnotherapy and hypnoanalysis.* London: Lawrence Erlbaum Associates.

Burns, D. D. (1981). *Feeling good.* New York: Signet.

Burns, D. D., & Spangler, D. L. (2000). Does psychotherapy homework lead to improvements in depression in cognitive-behavioral therapy or does improvement lead to increased homework compliance? *Journal of Consulting and Clinical Psychology, 68*(1), 46–56.

Cheek, D., & LeCron, L. (1968). *Clinical hypnotherapy.* New York: Grune & Stratton.

Coon, D. W., & Thompson, L. W. (2003). The relationship between homework compliance and treatment outcomes among older adult outpatients with mild-to-moderate depression. *American Journal of Geriatric Psychiatry, 11*, 53–61.

Crawford, H. J., & Barabasz, A. (1993). Phobias and fears: Facilitating their treatment with hypnosis. In J. Rhue, S. Lynn, & I. Kirsch (Eds.), *Clinical handbook of hypnosis* (pp. 311–337). Washington, DC: American Psychological Association.

Damasio, A. (1994). *Descartes' error: Emotion, reason, and the human brain.* New York: Penguin.

Daniel, S., & Weisberg, M. (2006, March). *Powerful healing: Catalyze your clinical effectiveness.* Presented at the annual meeting of the American Society of Clinical Hypnosis, Orlando, FL.

Davidson, R. J., & Goleman, D. J. (1977). The role of attention in meditation and hypnosis: A psychobiological perspective on transformations of consciousness. *International Journal of Clinical and Experimental Hypnosis, 25,* 291–308.

Davis, M., Eshelman, E. R., & McKay, M. (1982). *The relaxation and stress reduction workbook.* Oakland, CA: New Harbinger Publications.

Dolan, Y. (1985). *Path with a heart: Ericksonian utilization with chronic and resistant clients.* New York: Brunner/Mazel.

Dolan, Y. (1991). *Resolving sexual abuse: Solution-focused therapy and Ericksonian hypnosis for adult survivors.* New York: Norton.

Dolan, Y. (1992, May). *Resolving sexual abuse.* Paper presented at the meeting of the Milton H. Erickson Institute of Michigan, Southfield, MI.

Edgette, J. H., & Edgette, J. S. (1995). *The handbook of hypnotic phenomena in psychotherapy.* New York: Brunner/Mazel.

Ellis, A., & Harper, R. A. (1961). *A guide to rational living.* Englewood Cliffs, NJ: Prentice-Hall.

Erickson, M. H. (1954). Pseudo-orientation in time as a hypnotherapeutic procedure. *Journal of Clinical and Experimental Hypnosis, 2,* 261–283. In E. L. Rossi (Ed.), *The collected papers of Milton H. Erickson on hypnosis, Vol. IV: Innovative Hypnotherapy.* New York: Irvington, 1980.

Erickson, M. H. (1980). Naturalistic techniques of hypnotherapy. In E. Rossi (Ed.), *The collected papers of Milton H. Erickson on hypnosis. Volume I: The nature of hypnosis and suggestion* (pp. 177–205). New York: Irvington.

Erickson, M. H., & Rossi, E. (1975). Varieties of double bind. *The American Journal of Clinical Hypnosis, 17*(3), 143–157.

Erickson, M. H., & Rossi, E. (1979). *Hypnotherapy: An exploratory casebook.* New York: Irvington.

Erickson, M. H., & Rossi, E. (1981). *Experiencing hypnosis: Therapeutic approaches to altered states.* New York: Irvington.

Eysenck, H. J. (1967). *The biological basis of personality.* Springfield, IL: Thomas.

Foa, E., & Wilson, R. (2001). *Stop obsessing! How to overcome your obsessions and compulsions.* New York: Bantam.

Frederick, C. (2005). Selected topics in ego state therapy. *The International Journal of Clinical and Experimental Hypnosis, 53*(4), 348.

Frederick, C., & McNeal, S. (1993). Inner strength and other techniques for ego strengthening. *American Journal of Clinical Hypnosis, 35*(3), 170–178.

Frederick, C., & Phillips, M. (1992). The use of age progressions as interventions with acute psychosomatic conditions. *American Journal of Clinical Hypnosis, 35*, 89–98.

Fromm, E., & Nash, M. R. (Eds.). (1992). *Contemporary hypnosis research.* New York: Guilford.

Gafner, G., & Benson, S. (2003). *Hypnotic techniques: For standard psychotherapy and formal hypnosis.* New York: Norton.

Gawain, S. (1978). *Creative visualization: Use the power of your imagination to create what you want in your life.* Novato, CA: Nataraj.

Gilligan, S. G. (1987). *Therapeutic trances: The cooperation principle in Ericksonian hypnotherapy.* New York: Brunner/Mazel.

Gottman, J. M. (1994). *Why marriages succeed or fail.* New York: Simon & Schuster.

Gottman, J. M. (1998). *Marital therapy: A research-based approach.* Seattle: The Gottman Institute.

Gottman, J. M., & Silver, N. (1999). *The seven principles for making marriage work.* New York: Three Rivers.

Gray, J. A., & McNaughton, N. (1996). *The neuropsychology of anxiety: Reprise.* London: University of London.

Green, J. P., Barabasz, A., Barrett, D., & Montgomery, G. (2005). Forging ahead: The 2003 APA Division 30 Definition of Hypnosis. *Journal of Clinical and Experimental Hypnosis, 53*(2), 89.

Greenberg, P. E., Sisitsky, T., Kessler, R. C., Finkelstein, S. N., Berndt, E. R., Davidson, J. R. T., et al. (1999). The economic burden of anxiety disorders in the 1990s. *Journal of Clinical Psychiatry, 60*(7), 427.

Grinder, J., & Bandler, R. (1976). *The structure of magic II*. Palo Alto, CA: Science and Behavior Books.

Grinder, J., & Bandler, R. (1981). *Trance-formations*. Mohab, UT: Real People Press.

Haley, J. (1973). *Uncommon therapy: The psychiatric techniques of Milton H. Erickson, M.D.* New York: Norton.

Hammond, D. C. (Ed.). (1990). *Handbook of hypnotic suggestions and metaphors*. New York: Norton.

Hammond, D. C. (1998). Unconscious exploration with ideomotor signaling. In D. C. Hammond (Ed.), *Hypnotic induction and suggestion* (2nd ed., pp. 93–100). Chicago: American Society of Clinical Hypnosis.

Havens, R. A. (Ed.) (1989). *The wisdom of Milton H. Erickson: Hypnosis and hypnotherapy*. New York: Irvington.

Havens, R. A., & Walters, C. (1989). *Hypnotherapy scripts: A neo-Ericksonian approach to persuasive healing*. New York: Brunner/Mazel.

Hay, L. (1989). Healer, heal thyself. In R. Carlson & B. Shield (Eds.), *Healers on healing* (pp. 22–25). New York: G. P. Putnam's Sons.

Hendrix, H. (1988). *Getting the love you want: A guide for couples*. New York: Harper.

Hendrix, H. (1992). *Keeping the love you find*. New York: Atria.

Hendrix, H. (2004). *Receiving love: Transform your relationship by letting yourself be loved*. New York: Atria.

Hendrix, H., & LaKelly Hunt, H. (2005). *Getting the love you want: Couples workshop manual*. New York: Imago Relationships International.

Howard, P. (2000). *The owner's manual for the brain: Everyday applications from mind-brain research*. Atlanta, GA: Bard.

Humphreys, R. (2003, April). *Parasympathetic pathways to health*. Paper presented at the annual meeting of the American Society of Clinical Hypnosis, Alexandria, VA.

Humphreys, R. & Eagan, K. (2000, February). *The neurobiology of hypnosis: A comprehensive scientific foundation for clinical hypnosis.* Paper presented at the 42nd annual meeting of the American Society of Clinicial Hypnosis, Baltimore, MD.

Jacobson, E. (1938). *Progressive relaxation* (2nd ed.). Chicago: University of Chicago.

Jacobson, N. S., & Addis, M. E. (1993). Research on couple therapy: What do we know? Where are we going? *Journal of Consulting and Clinical Psychology, 61*(1), 85–93.

Kabat-Zinn, J. (1990). *Full catastrophy living: Using the wisdom of your body and mind to face stress, pain, and illness.* New York: Delacorte Press.

Kazantzis, N., & Lampropoulos, G. K. (2002). Reflecting on homework in psychotherapy: What can we conclude from research and experience? *Journal of Clinical Psychology, 58*(5), 577–85.

Khalsa, S. (2001). *K.I.S.S. guide to yoga.* London: Dorling Kindersley.

Kiecolt-Glaser, J. K., & Glaser, R. (1992). Psychoneuroimmunology: Can psychological interventions modulate immunity? Special Issue: Behavioral medicine: An update for the 1990s. *Journal of Consulting and Clinical Psychology, 60*(4), 569–575.

Kirsch, I., Montgomery, G., & Saperstein, G. (1995). Hypnosis as an adjunct to cognitive-behavioral psychotherapy: A meta-analysis. *Journal of Consulting and Clinical Psychology, 63,* 214–220.

Klippstein, H. (Ed.). (1991). *Ericksonian hypnotherapeutic group inductions.* New York: Brunner/Mazel.

Kroger, W. S. (1977). *Clinical and experimental hypnosis: In medicine, denistry, and psychology.* Philadelphia, PA: J. B. Lippincott.

Kutz, I., Borysenko, J. Z., & Benson, H. (1985). Meditation and psychotherapy: A rationale for the integration of dynamic psychotherapy, the relaxation response, and mindfulness meditation. *The American Journal of Psychiatry.*

Lankton, S. R. (1980). *Practical magic: A translation of basic neurolinguistic programming into clinical psychotherapy.* Cupertino, CA: Meta.

Lankton, S. R. (Ed.). (1985). *Ericksonian monographs number 1: Elements and dimensions of an Ericksonian approach.* New York: Brunner/Mazel.

Lankton, S. R., & Lankton, C. H. (1983). *The answer within: A clinical framework of Ericksonian hypnotherapy.* New York: Brunner/Mazel.

Lankton, S. R., & Lankton, C. H. (1989). *Tales of enchantment.* New York: Brunner/Mazel

LeDoux, J. (1996). *The emotional brain: The mysterious underpinnings of emotional life.* New York: Simon & Schuster.

Leonardo, E. D., & Hen, R. (2006). Genetics of affective and anxiety disorders. *Annual Review of Psychology, 57,* 117–37.

Linehan, M. M. (1993). *Cognitive-behavioral treatment of borderline personality disorder.* New York: Guilford.

Luthe, W. (Ed.). (1969). *Autogenic therapy.* New York: Grune & Stratton.

Lynn, S. J., & Kirsch, I. (2006). *Essentials of clinical hypnosis.* Washington, DC: American Psychological Association.

Lynn, S. J., Kirsch, I., Neufeld, J., & Rhue, J. W. (1996). Clinical hypnosis: Assessment, applications, and treatment considerations. In S. Lynn, I. Kirsch, & J. Rhue (Eds.), *Casebook of clinical hypnosis* (pp. 3–30). Washington, DC: American Psychological Association.

Lynn, S. J., Kirsch, I., & Rhue, J. W. (Eds.). (1996). *Casebook of clinical hypnosis.* Washington, DC: American Psychological Association.

Lynn, S. J., & Rhue, J. W. (1991). *Theories of hypnosis: Current models and perspectives.* New York: Guilford Press.

Meichenbaum, D. (1977). *Cognitive-behavior modification: An integrative approach.* New York: Plenum.

Middeldorp, C. M., Cath, D. C., Van Dyck, & Bloomsa (2005). The co-morbidity of anxiety and depression in the perspective of genetic epidemiology: A review of twin and family studies. *Psychological Medicine, 35,* 611–624.

Moss, D., McGrady, A. V., Davies, T. C., & Wickramasekera, I. (Eds.) (2003). *Handbook of mind-body medicine for primary care.* Thousand Oaks, CA: Sage Publications.

Naperstek, B. (1994). *Staying well with guided imagery.* New York: Warner.

National Institute of Mental Health. *Facts about anxiety disorders.* Bethesda, MD: National Institute of Mental Health, National Institutes of Health, U.S. Department of Health and Human Services; NIH publication No. OM-99 4152. Retrieved April 9, 2004 from: http://www.nimh.nih.gov/publicat/adfacts.cfm#readNow

O'Hanlon, W. H. (1987). *Taproots: Underlying principles of Milton Erickson's therapy and hypnosis.* New York: Norton.

Otto, M. W., & Deckersbach, T. (1998). Cognitive-behavioral therapy for panic disorder: Theory, strategies, and outcome. In J. F. Rosenbaum & M. H. Pollack, (Eds.), *Panic disorder and its treatment* (p. 15). New York: Marcel Dekker.

Payson, E. D. (2002). *The Wizard of Oz and other narcissists.* Royal Oak, MI: Julian Day.

Pert, C. B. (1997). *Molecules of emotion: Why you feel the way you feel.* New York: Simon & Schuster.

Pert, C. B. (1999). *Molecules of emotion: The science behind mind-body medicine.* New York: Touchstone.

Phillips, M. (2000). *Finding the energy to heal: How EMDR, hypnosis, TFT, imagery, and body-focused therapy can help restore mind-body health.* New York: Norton.

Restak, R. (1994). *The modular brain: How new discoveries in neuroscience are answering age-old questions about memory, free will, consciousness, and personal identity.* New York: Scribner.

Rimm, D. C., & Masters, J. C. (1974). *Behavior therapy: Techniques and empirical findings.* New York: Academic.

Rossi, E. L. (Ed.) (1980). *Collected papers of Milton H. Erickson* (Vols. 1–4). New York: Irvington.

Rossi, E. L. (1993). *The psychobiology of mind-body healing: New concepts of therapeutic hypnosis* (Rev. ed). New York: Norton.

Rossi, E. L. (2002). *The psychobiology of gene expression.* New York: Norton.

Rossi, E. L., & Cheek, D. B. (1988). *Mind-body healing: Ideodynamic healing in hypnosis.* New York: Norton.

Rossi, E. L., & Nimmons, D. (1991). *The 20-minute break: Reduce stress, maximize performance, and improve health and emotional well-being using the new science of ultradian rhythms.* New York: St. Martin.

Rossman, M. L. (2000). *Guided imagery for self-healing.* Novato, CA: H. J. Kramer/New World Library.

Sapolsky, R. M. (1994). *Why zebras don't get ulcers: A guide to stress, stress-related diseases, and coping.* New York: Freeman.

Sargent, J. D., Green, E. E., & Walters, E. D. (1972). The use of Autogenic feedback training in a pilot study of migraine and tension headaches. *The Journal of Head and Face Pain, 12,* 120–124.

Schoenberger, N. E. (1996). Cognitive-behavioral hypnotherapy for phobic anxiety. In S. J. Lynn, I. Kirsch, & J. W. Rhue (Eds.), *Casebook of clinical hypnosis* (pp. 33–49). Washington, DC: American Psychological Association.

Schoenberger, N. E. (2000). Research on hypnosis as an adjunct to cognitive-behavioral psychotherapy. *International Journal of Clinical and Experimental Hypnosis, 48,* 154–169.

Schore, A. (2003). *Affect dysregulation and disorders of the self.* New York: Norton.

Schore, A. (2006, April) *Recent advances in neuroscience, attachment theory, and traumatology: Implications for psychotherapists.* Paper presented at the meeting of the Southeast Michigan Trauma and Dissociation Study Group, Beverly Hills, MI.

Schwartz, R. (1995). *Internal family systems therapy.* New York: Guilford.

Seligman, M. E., Steen, T. A., Park, N., & Peterson, C. (2005). Positive psychology progress: Empirical validation of interventions. *American Psychologist, 60*(5), 410–421.

Selye, H. (1978). *The stress of life* (Rev. ed.). New York: McGraw-Hill.

Sheehan, D. V. (1986). *The anxiety disease.* New York: Bantam.

Siegel, D. J. (1999). *The developing mind: How relationships and the brain interact to shape who we are.* New York: Guilford.

Spiegel, D. (1974). The grade 5 syndrome: The highly hypnotizable person. *International Journal of Clinical and Experimental Hypnosis, 22,* 303–319.

Spiegel, D. (2001). Foreword. In S. Kahn & E. Fromm (Eds.), *Changes in the therapist* (pp. x–xi). Mahwah, NJ: Lawrence Erlbaum.

Spiegel, H., & Spiegel, D. (1978). *Trance and treatment: Clinical uses of hypnosis.* New York: Basic.

Spielberger, C. D. (1969). *The state-trait anxiety inventory.* Palo Alto, CA: Consulting Psychologists Press.

Spielberger, C. D. (1972). *Anxiety: Current trends in theory and research.* New York: Academic.

Stein, C. (1963). The clenched fist technique as a hypnotic procedure. *American Journal of Clinical Hypnosis, 6,* 113–119.

Stone, H., & Stone, S. (1989). *Embracing ourselves: The voice dialogue training manual.* San Rafael, CA: New World Library.

Thompson, J. G. (1988). *The psychobiology of emotions.* New York: Plenum.

Thompson, K. (1995, March). *The magic of hypnosis: Psychosemantics.* Paper presented at the annual meeting of the American Society of Clinical Hypnosis, San Diego, CA.

Tolle, E. (1999). *The power of now.* Novato, CA: New World Library.

Torem, M. S. (1992). Back from the future: A powerful age-progression technique. *American Journal of Clinical Hypnosis, 35,* 81–88.

Watkins, H. H. (1993). Ego-state therapy: An overview. *American Journal of Clinical Hypnosis, 35*(4), 232–240.

Watkins, J. G. (1987). *Hypnotherapeutic techniques.* New York: Irvington.

Watkins, J. G. (1992). *Hypnoanalytic techniques: Clinical hypnosis* (Vol. 2). New York: Irvington.

Weitzenhoffer, A. M. (2000). *The practice of hypnotism.* New York: John Wiley & Sons.

Wester II., W. (1987). *Clinical hypnosis: A case management approach.* Cincinnati, OH: Behavioral Science Center, Inc.

Williamson, M. (1996). *A return to love.* New York: HarperCollins.

Wolpe, J. (1958). *Psychotherapy by reciprocal inhibition.* Palo Alto, CA: Stanford University.

Woolfolk, R. L., & Lehrer, P. M. (Eds.). (1984). *Principles and practice of stress management.* New York: Guilford.

Yapko, M. D. (1988). *When living hurts: Directives for treating depression.* New York: Brunner/Mazel.

Yapko, M. D. (1992). *Hypnosis and the treatment of depression: Strategies for change.* New York: Brunner/Mazel.

Yapko, M. D. (2001). *Treating depression with hypnosis: Integrating cognitive-behavioral and strategic approaches.* Philadelphia: Brunner-Routledge.

Yapko, M. D. (2003). *Trancework: An introduction to the practice of clinical hypnosis.* (3rd ed.). New York: Brunner/Routledge.

Zeig, J. K (Ed.). (1980a). *Experiencing Erickson: An introduction to the man and his work.* New York: Brunner/Mazel.

Zeig, J. K. (Ed., with commentary). (1980b). *A teaching seminar with Milton H. Erickson.* New York: Brunner/Mazel.

Index

abandonment, 168, 172, 173, 220
Ablon, S. L., xii
abreaction, 170
acceptance, 261
active listening, 15, 58, 191, 195, 201, 213, 252
addiction/addictive behaviors, 26
adrenaline, 39, 43, 169 (*see also* hyperarousal)
affect (regulation)
    bridge technique, xiii
    coexisting/disparate, 48, 78, 79–80, 93,
        94–95, 96–97, 231 (*see also* dual per-
        spective)
    dyadic regulation of, xi
    dysregulation, *see* affect dysregulation
    juxtaposing, 93, 152, 190–91 (*see also* Tool
        22)
    negative, *see* affect dysregulation
    neuroscience study of, xii
    neutralization of, xi
    positive, *see* positive affect
    psychophysiology of, 31–32
    regulatory skills, xiii, xiii–xiv (*see also* affect
        regulation toolbox)
    "sandwich," 96 (*see also* Tool 24)
    stage models for development of, xii
    see also emotion
affect dysregulation
    controlling, 72, 94–95, 226
    diminishing/softening, 82, 83–84, 85, 95–96,
        133–34

interrupting, 14, 69, 70, 82, 112–13, 162,
    206, 211, 212
intensifying/eliciting, 197, 206–7, 226, 236,
    240–41
manifestations of, 16
underlying all psychiatric disorders, 17
warning signs of, 65, 131, 195
see also emotion; flooding; hyperarousal;
    hypervigilance
affect regulation toolbox
    as adjunct to psychotherapy, 47–48, 188–89
    with adult sibling conflict, case example of,
        232–36
    for anxiety disorders, 121–22
    with children and adolescents, 217
    with couples, 185, 190–92
    with co-workers/friendship conflict, case
        example of, 236–241, 242–45
    customizing, 54–55
    genesis of, 2–4
    introducing to new or established clients,
        50–52
    linking skills, 69
    matching with client needs and styles, 260–61
    overview of, 10–11, 28–29
    with parent/adult child, case examples of,
        221–27, 228–232
    preparation for using, 56–59
    teach a wide selection of, 251
    see also individual disorders/issues